Studies in Women Writers in English

VOLUME–VI

Edited by

MOHIT K. RAY
RAMA KUNDU

ATLANTIC
PUBLISHERS & DISTRIBUTORS (P) LTD

Published by

ATLANTIC

PUBLISHERS & DISTRIBUTORS (P) LTD

B-2, Vishal Enclave, Opp. Rajouri Garden,
New Delhi-110027
Phones : 25413460, 25429987, 25466842

Sales Office
7/22, Ansari Road, Darya Ganj,
New Delhi-110002
Phones : 23273880, 23275880, 23280451
Fax : 91-11-23285873
web : www.atlanticbooks.com
e-mail : info@atlanticbooks.com

ISBN 81-269-0816-5 (Vol. VI)
ISBN 81-269-0338-4 (Set)

Printed in India
at Nice Printing Press, Delhi

Preface

The new series—*Studies in Women Writers in English*—is a grateful acknowledgment of the contribution and public recognition of the emerging voice of women in the arena of literature during the last few centuries, and especially in the latter half of the twentieth century. Women writers across the globe have made their distinctive mark, with their own perception of life—be it feminine, or feminist or female.

The critique of work by women writers introduced in the present volume, the sixth in the series, bears evidence to the growing critical attention towards authors writing outside the mainstream, in America, Canada, and especially in India, who can be seen sharing similar awareness and feelings regarding the woman's angst and aspirations.

The sixteen essays included in the present volume cover a wide spectrum. The women writers discussed herein include two from Britain, i.e. the canonized Jane Austen and the contemporary Doris Lessing; one from America, i.e. Toni Morrison, the Nobel Laureate for literature in 1993; two renowned authors from Canada, i.e. Margaret Atwood and Susan Swan, and a bunch of Indian avant-garde writers of our own times—ranging from masters like Shashi Deshpande to young innovators from Arundhati Roy and Jhumpa Lahiri to Cauvery Madhavan and K.R. Usha.

After all is said and done about the importance of innovations, experimentations, symbolism and all such interesting departures from the traditional storytelling, the charm of Jane Austen's conventional yet exquisite 'ivory work' still holds its sway over a vast majority of readers both inside and outside the academy. Bhaskar Roy Barman's comprehensive overview of Austen's oeuvre allows us a glimpse into the secret of this charm.

Liza Das examines another mainstream woman writer who is apparently poles asunder from Jane Austen in her perception and treatment. Ms. Das in her scholarly paper attempts to illustrate Lessing's critical interrogation of English cultural politics with particular reference to the constructs of sexuality, madness and communism.

Mallikarjun Patil discusses *Sula,* an early novel of Toni Morrison, from a feminist perspective.

Raja Sekhar Patteti makes an in-depth analysis of two poems of Margaret Atwood with focus on Atwood's use of 'mini-narrative' as a literary strategy interrogating the relevance of the 'grand narratives' of women's exploitation and victimization.

Pedro Carmona Rodríguez's interesting and scholarly essay on the two well-known Canadian writers—Margaret Atwood and Susan Swan—highlights the narrative strategies used in their novels in order to connect the issues of sex and gender to the discourses of nation and community; she shows how eventually the female body is turned into a metonymic frontier in the treatment of these authors.

The awareness that the female body can be a site for exploitation as well as rebellion, a script for violation as well as defiance, has also entered the realm of Indian women writing; Jaydeep Rishi's fine analysis of Arundhati Roy's landmark novel *The God of Small Things* adequately brings out the point.

Arundhati's novel, already nearly a decade old, still continues to fascinate readers, and young scholars continue to address

Roy's work from various angles. R.S. Jain looks at the novel from the feminist angle, whereas Nandini Sahu draws our attention to the nostalgic note.

Nandini Sahu also includes another younger author in this study—Jhumpa Lahiri, whereas Manisha Sharma's essay is exclusively on Jhumpa Lahiri's novel, *The Namesake,* with special reference to its image pattern which effectively serves to project India for the consumption of an alien world.

Shubha Tiwari, on the other hand, foregrounds the Indians' perception of the alien world at the turn of the century as it is projected in Cauvery Madhavan's *The Uncoupling,* a delightful novel about the pleasantly unsettling experience of 'the voyage out' which can be usefully compared to Mark Twain's *Innocents Abroad.*

In her article on K.R. Usha's *The Chosen,* however, Shubha Tiwari registers her sensitive response to the personal spiritual voyage of an Indian girl through the common travails and trials attending her situation, from which Nagaratna, Usha's heroine, emerges triumphant and serene, if not unscathed.

R.K. Mishra makes a general study of the portrayal of this inner life of the Indian woman in the writings of our women authors. Mishra's wide spectrum includes a wide range of authors as different and varied as anything, from Toru Dutt—Krupabai—Sorabji to Swarna Kumari Ghoshal—Kamala Markandaya, and Anita Desai—Rama Mehta—Shashi Deshpande to Kamala Das—Arundhati Roy—Manju Kapur, *et al.,* while he also tangentially relates them to the mainstream canon by tracing points of correspondence and contrast with some of their major British counterparts.

The last four essays together make one comprehensive unit as these examine a single author, Shashi Deshpande, from different critical positions. The notions of 'silence' and 'voice', which had been central to feminist discourse all along, have been subjected to ceaseless revaluation and re-interpretation in recent women's writings; as constructs they have acquired new connotations and gathered new dimensions of meanings in the process.

Urvashi Sinha and Gur Pyari Jandial have registered their sensitive response to Shashi Deshpande's novels with particular reference to the author's treatment of silence and articulation, whereas Santwana Haldar makes a close study of Deshpande's novel, *That Long Silence* in the light of 'patterns of feminism'.

Asha Sharma analyses Deshpande's *A Matter of Time,* whereas V.R. Badiger addresses Deshpande's recent work, *Moving On,* as a culminating point in which her previous themes get merged into one dominant preoccupation with death and the 'unbearable problem of living'.

Since most of the authors discussed in these articles are prescribed in the English syllabus in the universities of India, both the teachers and the students will find them extremely useful, and the general readers who are interested in literature in English and/or women writers will also find them intellectually stimulating.

We thank all the contributors to this volume for their learned papers which have enriched the anthology.

Our heartfelt thanks go to Dr. K.R. Gupta, Chairman, Atlantic Publishers and Distributors (P) Ltd., New Delhi, for the confidence evinced in us and also for seeing the book through the press.

Mohit K. Ray
Rama Kundu
Editors

Contents

The Art of Jane Austen

1

BHASKAR ROY BARMAN

In a criticism of a literary work written particularly by a female author, the writer of the criticism tends to characterize the author in question as a woman author or novelist. Every literary historian earmarks in his history a particular section exclusively for women writers, for they are regarded much inferior to men. Genius is bi-sexual. We regard, as always we do, sex in terms of physical differentiation. The ultimate analysis of sex shows it as nothing but a psychical problem and lends so great an interest to the contributions made by women, Jane Austen among them, to literature and they, women writers, certainly contributed their mites to enriching literature. The analysis says of woman as not undeveloped man but diverse: her outlook, essentially differs from that of a man and her work, to accord with her outlook, complements and supplements his. Partly owing to the exigencies of their historical development and partly because of their psychological contributions, women have proved, with certain reservations, literary artists of secondary order, and inferior to men as poets, philosophers and historians. But when it comes to writing fiction, they can certainly claim equality and rival men on their own special masculine ground. It should be said of them at the same time that thanks to their feminity they bestow upon their prose certain qualities such as are absent from the prose by men.

We should remember, while discussing or reviewing a particular work, sexual differences are not, nay, should not be bound by physical determinations. Every man—doesn't he?—possesses something feminine in him and every woman something masculine; and where these two elements get mingled proportionately, a work of classical penchant is produced, isn't it? The writers, be they men or women, whenever they have blended masculine and feminine qualities in their works, they have presented to the literature the greatest masterpieces. As I have said earlier, genius is bi-sexual, always it is.

Where the masculine qualities comprehend a broad grasp of general principles, a logical constructive power as well as a faculty for dealing largely and sanely with the big issues of life, the feminine qualities nourish themselves on subtlety rather than vigour of perception, on an intuitive insight into the delicate complexities of character and on an intensity and tenacity of passion.

Henry Fielding and Jane Austen best illustrated the masculine and feminine methods respectively of approaching the social life of the late eighteenth century. Painters of manners, both Fielding and Austen, concerned as they were in the difference between town and country and satirical in treatment, eschewed sentiments as far as possible and successfully portrayed a picture of time? and they complemented each other, for their differences are rather sexual than purely literary—the one, bold and dashing, painted in strong and vivid colour and the other, delicate and subtle, avoided violent contrasts and dealt rather in nuances.

Jane Austen has a good share of masculine qualities and we should discuss her novels in this light. Her art as a novelist is commensurate with her delineation of the social situations from a masculine point of view.

Born in 1775 and died in 1817, Austen was rightly acclaimed as the greatest of all the novelists of manners of the eighteenth century, particularly because she did raise the whole genre to a new level of art. Armed with an exhibitionist apparatus, with the theory of the comic epic expostulated by Fielding and with a moral purpose akin to the purpose advocated by Richardson, and aware at the same time that she was doing more than merely essaying some novels in an established social mode, and helped as well by her quietly penetrating vision of a man as a social animal and by her awareness of the tensions between spontaneity and convention and between the claims of personal morality and those of social and economic propriety, Jane Austen produced, egged on by her polished and controlled wit and her steady moral apprehension of the nature of human relationships, some of the greatest novels in England.

Ironically enough, the contemporary reviews of her novels were pedestrian and the later nineteenth century criticism was unenlivened by disputes or by infectious enthusiasm, nor were those moments of insight which occur when one great mind is engaged by another, as when Johnson writes about Pope, Blake about Milton or Coleridge about Shakespeare. Austen's novels have never commanded such level of attention, such a degree of imaginative empathy. But her novels revealed to the nineteenth-century reading public that fiction was capable of unsuspected power, that it was to be taken seriously as a form of literature and that criticism of the novel could seriously be an intellectual activity.

Jane Austen had begun writing at an early age, but the readership of her novel was confined to the circle of friends and relatives. With the experience of a youngster, she produced a history of England and enriched it with her exuberant wit and burlesque. She also wrote short stories which, vibrant with ebullient humour, manifested a fine sense of caricature, as they pasquinaded the literary fashion of the day. Live as she did amidst English country society of neither the highest nor the lowest status, her life taught her about the social pretension and ambition, on balls and on visits and speculations about marriage and giving in marriage and particularly on the hopes and fears of general people of moderate means; in fact it helped her to peep into a world which she in her novels embellished with her delicate and highly finished art and turned into a microcosm of life in its social aspect.

She garnered raw materials for her novels from the daily routine of visits, shopping, sewing, gossip and other trivial matters meticulously recorded in her letters. The world depicted in her novels is essentially an eighteenth-century world in its habits, tastes and appearance. Jane Austen wrote just before the Industrial Revolution changed for the worse so much of the face of England, and the clean stillness of her country towns, the unspoiled beauty of her countryside with its well-kept estates and cheerful farms, provided a perfect background to her firmly etched pictures of social life. There is a luminous clarity about her style as well as about the scenes portrayed. She portrayed, or we would rather say, she succeeded to a great extent in portraying in her novels the last generation of Englishmen and Englishwomen who could face life as they face a minuet with cheerfulness, decorum and with determination to go through the appropriate motions with grace, elegance, even though she was not aware of this. This is neither romanticism nor sentimentalism, but reveals a remarkable insight into the relation between social convention and individual temperament.

It has often been said apropos of Jane Austen that the Napoleonic wars which were going on throughout her writing career left no impact upon her; she rested contented with dashing off a hazy sketch of soldiers dallying with girls. This certainly testifies to the calm accuracy with which Jane Austen saw her subject. It should be remembered in this context that at the time when Jane Austen was writing her novels, wars were fought by small professional armies and the impact of the fighting on the daily life of the people living in small countryside was negligible: it would have been unrealistic and artistically inappropriate as well on the part of Jane Austen to have attempted to expand her horizon to include discussion of world affairs which would be certainly out of tune with the situations she delineated in her novels. She kept her pen in control and restricted her scope deliberately at par with her microscopic intention to create a world in perfectly proportioned detail and an accurate model for the total social world of which this was only a small part.

It is quite difficult to ascertain the chronology of Jane Austen's works; this difficulty arises from the fact that her novels were revised considerable times after they were written with a view to publication. It is almost impossible to tell at this moment how much rewriting was involved in revision. *Pride and Prejudice* published in 1813 was a recession of her early draft 'First Impressions' written around 1797. When the publisher had rejected 'First Impression' Austen resumed reworking her still earlier work 'Elinor and Marianne' and it took on the new title *Sense and Sensibility*; it was the first of her works to be published. It appeared in 1811, to be followed by *Pride and Prejudice*. *Northern Abbey*, published posthumously, was written in 1797 and 1798. It is thus the first written of all her published novels apart from juvenile works and fragments not published until long after her death.

As he was not confident of commercial success of the novel, Thomas Egerton, publisher of *Sense and Sensibility*, produced it at the expenses of the author. The first edition of the novel estimated at about 1000 copies, published in November 1811, was sold out, to mock the publisher's fear, by July 1813. Enthused and encouraged by this minor success, Egerton published *Pride and Prejudice* in January 1813, in an addition of 1,500 to see it sold out, too. This testifies to the popularity of Jane Austen as a novelist. We need not chronologically go further just to tell about her popularity.

In order to understand about Jane Austen's art, we must bring into focus another novelist popularly known as Miss Burney. The literary careers of Miss Burney and Jane Austen and that of the poet, Crabbe which had started in the period stretching from 1770 to 1800 continued well into the decisive years of the Romantic Era. But their work, only when judged by its essential features, shows the stamp of the years preceding this age. But the reaction of these writers to the characteristic traits of the new literature evident long before 1800 verges on hostility, their artistic impulses swinging back to motives, themes and forms which have entitled them to adhere to the essence of the classical tradition and their temperaments carrying about, to the very end, the mark of their early choice. Their outlook corresponds to that of the close of the eighteenth century.

These traits stand manifested in the work of Jane Austen, further developed and much refined by her stronger personality and keener sense of delicacy in art.

At the time Jane Austen's two novels *Sense and Sensibility* and *Pride and Prejudice* were published fiction-reviewing was groping for dignity; in the light of the standard that obtained then the two novels were well reviewed and the reviewers entertained no doubt as to the superiority of these two works. Allowing for the limitation of their notices in scope, they commented upon some subtle points such as any modern critic would make the high comedy of the second chapter of *Sense and Sensibility*, the liveliness of characterization and the vigour of the writing in *Pride and Prejudice*, the unnatural abruptness of the change in Dancy, from indifference to ardour. In fact on a more classical note, Jane Austen was commended for her having combined amusement with ethical teaching, a very important point much emphasized in *Sense and Sensibility*.

Sense and Sensibility is, at least on the surface, directed against a fashionable taste, an enthusiasm for picturesque beauty and a self-indulgent cultivation of feeling. The female protagonist, Marianne her name, falls passionately and sentimentally in love with a young man later to be jilted by him. Her love fructifies in a marriage with a man much older than her and she had regarded previously in any other light than that of a lover. As a contrast to her, her sister, Elinor possesses a rare quality of controlling her feelings throughout with more decorum and a deeper sense of privacy of personal emotion and this quality shadows her through a variety of difficulties on her way to the man she loves and, thus, she acts as a foil to her younger sister. The irony still remains restricted to its object and the characterization to the needs of the plot and the ironic intentions, the plot itself being rather awkwardly contrived. But the novel lacks the crystal precision of style, the beautiful poising of sentences and paragraphs and the skilful marshalling of dialogue that enrich her later novels. Though the character of Elinor and that of her lover, Edward Ferrars are somewhat wooden and though Mrs Ferrars poses an obstacle to the course of true love, Marianne is drawn, to make up for the flaws in characterization, with a fine mixture of affectionate sympathy and gentle mockery. Mrs Jennings is beautifully portrayed as an archetype of vulgarity and her good nature in course of time asserts itself and overshadows her vulgarity.

Now the time has arrived for us to peep into the family of Dashwood to understand about the characters we have just discussed in relation to the family and the society they live in. Besides, we shall get introduced to other members of the family who have still now remained in the shadow.

The family of Dashwood consists of a mother and three daughters and we are introduced to them only on the death of Mr Dashwood. The residence of Mr Dashwood was at National Park, Sussex. Mr Dashwood had not inherited his estate long enough to save anything for his three daughters and what remained devolved upon his only son by a former marriage. On his deathbed Mr Dashwood enjoins upon his first son, Mr J. Dashwood, already married to a woman of fortune, to look after the interest of his stepmother and three sisters and elicits his promise to do all in his power to make them happy. The young man appears to us as a respectable character who conducts himself with propriety in discharge of his ordinary duties. He does not lack the intention to make them happy, but has to postpone execution of his intention till the arrival of his wife who is but a narrow-minded and selfish woman and has a barrel over him. Mrs Dashwood and her daughters never get a chance to reap the fruit of his good intention.

Mrs Dashwood is somewhat fickle-minded. This fickle-mindedness often threatens to hurl her into an awkward situation, but her eldest daughter who has a strong understanding and cool judgement, as we already know, saves her from falling headlong into such situation.

In course of time Mrs Dashwood and her daughters retreat into Devonshire and stay in a house owned by Sir John Middleton. Sir John, a relation of hers, is presented as a good-humoured gentleman and a keen sportsman, to boot, quite conversant in horse flesh and with the nature of dogs and well-skilled, as well, in management of the dog kennel. Though not easy to grapple with, he often takes it upon himself to provide different kinds of amusement and arrange pleasure parties for young people. His lady, though a handsome stupid woman, piques herself upon the elegance of her person, her table and domestic arrangements. In the friendly attentions of the family and the society they meet at Barton Park, the seat of Sir John, Mrs Dashwood and her daughters regain their cheerfulness and Marianne bumps into Mr Willoughby who answers to her idea of perfection.

We find two sisters placed before us, similarly circumstanced in point of education and accomplishments, exposed to similar trials; but whereas one, thanks to her prudence and clear judgement, overcomes all obstacles with fortitude, the other gets flung into an abyss of sorrow owing to her impetuosity which overshadows her judgment. An intimate knowledge of life and that of the female characters are exemplified in the various personages and incidents which are introduced, but nothing can equal the portraiture of the character of the elder brother who, despite his promise to his dying father that he would see to the comforts of his stepmother and three sisters, first resolves to give his sisters a thousand pounds apiece, then on the suggestion and advice of his amiable wife, persuades himself that it will suffice for him to send them a little fish and game occasionally and in doing so he will fulfil the promise he gave to his father and his obligation to his step-mother and sisters. Next in importance as concerns portraiture is Marianne, who falls immediately and violently in love with a male coquet, without listening to the judicious expostulations of his sensible sister, Elinor.

As we have seen by intruding into the privacy of the Dashwood family, Mr Dashwood, that is, John Dashwood, whose unmalicious egotism precipitates the action of the novel, presents a perfect picture of not-ill-disposed youngman. The relations of these characters with each other, and with other characters that occasionally appear in the novel are manipulated with wit and dexterity.

There are few novelists in English who can achieve so much meaning with simple descriptive sentences: with a few brief strokes Jane Austen can give the reader the sense of a solidly based social world, a world in which the adjustment of personal relationships is the most interesting and significant of the problems that confront the characters, a world in which individuals, however sensitive or retrospective, belong in the first instance to a community pattern, whose smallest important unit is the family and the largest no point larger than the circle of relatives, friends and acquaintances within and around which the individual moves. There is no point in criticizing Jane Austen for the limitation she imposes on herself, because the world she has portrayed in the novel is of course the world in which most middle-class people live. Hers is an art of delicacy, and precision and shrewd insight; she takes it upon herself to probe those aspects of human emotion and behaviour which are most clearly associated with the social and economic framework that looms so large in most people's lives. If Marianne possesses a sensibility in excess of what is imposed upon her by the kind of society she lives in and of what is justified by the facts of human nature manifested in that world, Austen arranges for life to teach her, as a teacher does. In fact all of Jane Austen's heroines are tutored by the lives they live, as is Marianne. The firmness with which she goes through that education is a tribute to the unsentimental realism at the core of her art. She is firm, but not tragic nor melodramatic. In the delineation of the characters like Marianne and Elinor, she presents herself as an affectionately ironic observer of the relations between society and individual personality who expects no more from human nature than what it has to offer, and who thoroughly enjoys it even when she is most ironical at its expense.

Willoughby, the youngman who jilts Marianne, bears more than a mere resemblance in name to Wickham of *Pride and Prejudice*: both are beguiling scoundrels and exemplify a constant menace in the social world in which Jane Austen's heroines live. It is advisable, as well, for gentle but unmoneyed young ladies who depend upon their good looks to secure for themselves congenial marriage that can only guarantee economic and social security, to always beware of equally unmoneyed gallants who have nothing to offer but their gallantry. Mere gallantry symbolizes in Jane Austen's novels cowardice, selfishness and general lack of moral principle.

In *Pride and Prejudice*, by far the most popular novel, the precision and vivacity of style carry the reader through it with ease and spirit; the sparkling life about the characters and the rain-washed freshness about the scenery combine to make this the gayest of Jane Austen's novels in spite of the deeper overtones which manifest themselves the moment Charlotte Lucas agrees to marry the egregious Mr Collins or when Lydia is discovered to have eloped with Wickham with no prospect of marriage. Equally remarkable are the speed and the skill with which the author moves into the story.

The story has no great variety, though. Jane Austen introduces us to the whole family and every member of the family excites interest and draws the attention of the reader.

Mr Bennet who heads the family is portrayed as a man possessing sarcastic humour and combining a good deal of caprice and reserve in his demeanour. He owns an estate of about two thousand a year and lives in Longbourne, in Herdfordshire, a pleasant walk from the market town of Meryton. Captivated by the handsome face and the appearance of good temper, he had married a daughter of a country attorney. In course of time he discovers that he was duped by the facial beauty and the good temper on the surface into marrying a woman of mean understanding, little information, and uncertain temper.

The consequence of his discovery that he had been beguiled by her facial beauty is a disappointment. He retreated into a country life and devotes himself to studying books, to compensate for his disappointment. Thus his five daughters stand deprived of patriarchal duties.

With the help of their silly mother, the five daughters are looking out for husbands. Jane, the oldest one, a beautiful girl, possesses great feeling, good sense, equanimity, cheerfulness and elegance of manner; Elizabeth, the second combines quickness of perception and strength of mind with a playful vivacity which reminds us of the vivacity of her father; Mary, a female pedant, affects great wisdom that often smacks of stupidity, and is, as says Mr Bennett, "a lady of great reflection, who reads great books and makes extract"; Kitty is well-spirited and fretful; but Miss Lydia, the youngest daughter, "is a stout, well-grown girl of fifteen, with a fine complexion and good-humoured countenance; a favourite with her mother, whose affection had brought her into public at an early age. She had high animal spirits, and a sort of self-consequence."

Miss Lydia is mad after the officers who are quartered at Meryton and the attentions they bestow upon her turn her into a most decided flirt.

Elizabeth towers above all her sisters in drawing the attention of the reader by displaying archness and sweetness of manner which contributed to rendering her a most attractive object in the family. She is in fact the Beatrice of the tale and falls in love on much the same principle of contrariety. On being informed that Netherfield Park adjacent to the Longbourn estate is let to a young single gentleman of good fortune, the family finds itself put on the high fidgets and Mrs Bennet, thinking the intelligence augurs well, determines to bestow one of her daughters in marriage upon that young gentleman of good fortune and persuades her husband to visit the young man without delay.

Mrs Bennet is delighted to find that Mr Bingley, the young man, is charming and handsome and is fond of dancing, 'which was a certain step towards falling in love.' Mr Bingley picks on Jane, to the great delight of Mrs Bennet, as his dancemate, but his friend, Mr Darcy, a man of high birth and great fortune, prevents him making his proposals of marriage. Mr Bingley heeds his friend's advice and leaves Netherfield, letting Jane wear the willow.

In spite of having greatest reserve and hauteur and a prodigious quantity of family pride, Mr Darcy can't help being captivated with the lively and sensible Elizabeth. With a view to humbling his pride and hauteur, Elizabeth delights in playing the Beatrice upon him; but, when she finds his manners unbending, she starts disliking him. This dislike heightens into hate when he learns that he was himself instrumental in separating Mr Bingley from her sister. She is also prejudiced against him on account of his cruel conduct to a young man who happens to have been left to his protection. But to her great surprise that gentleman himself comes over to her and declares that he loves her. But Elizabeth, remembering how he had Mr Bingley separated from Jane, refused him forthright.

Next day comes a letter from Mr Darcy in which he explains his conduct and this explanation exculpates him from the charges levelled against him and makes Elizabeth repent of her percipiency in believing the rumours about him.

From this moment Elizabeth bids adieu to her prejudice and dislike and takes to loving Darcy. The main interest of the reader is riveted on the character of Elizabeth and how the eclaircissement is brought about between Elizabeth and Darcy by the author. Elizabeth's sense of conduct is revealed as of a superior order to those of common heroines of novels. Thanks to her independence of character which she keeps within the proper line of decorum and her well-timed sprightliness, she succeeds in teaching the man of family-pride—Darcy is to know himself and beware of how far he can go.

As readers we also learn a lesson from the elopement of Lydia, as the novel pinpoints the danger on the part of young girls of flirting with the officers who may be quartered near or around where they live. Jane Austen has made lively portraiture of other characters imbued with her experiences in the society she lived in.

Mr Collins is a kind of grotesque who takes his place in the stately ballet of social life with fantastic gaucherie. His proposal to Elizabeth spotlights another side of the marriage-seeking business, the economic stability to be won at too great a cost. When Elizabeth's friend Charlotte accepts Mr Collins, we are for the first time made aware of some of the ugly realities of the stately social ballet: it is a dance on a sunlit grass, but some of the dancers are at least earnest and if they do not secure their permanent partners before the end of the day they will be left alone for ever on the dark and deserted lawn, or forced to find refuge in the pathless woods which surround the trimly kept grass plot. Rather than be left alone with no prospect of social or economic security in an age when few means of earning an independent livelihood were open to the daughters of gentlemen, Charlotte Lucas who, as an intelligent girl enjoys the friendship of such a discriminating person as Elizabeth marries the grotesque Mr Collins. As she, being an intelligent girl, knows herself it is her last chance, she takes it deliberately, weighing her future husband's intolerable character against the security and social position he offers. We have no difficulty to feel how painful the choice was and Charlotte has chosen the lesser of two evils.

Elizabeth's visit to the Collinses after their marriage bestows upon Jane Austen the opportunity of elucidating the aspect of marriage and showing how calmly and deliberately Charlotte makes a liveable way of life out of her situation—a scene Jane Austen uses to show her underlying compassionate awareness of the ordinariness of ordinary life that shows off as well as enriches her sharp irony. With skilful structural economy, she makes use of the same episode to reintroduce Darcy in connexion with Mr Collins' patroness, Lady Catherine de Bourgh. This introduction—if offers Mr Darcy an opportunity to propose to Elizabeth and be refused—marks the turning point in the relationship of these two, for the refusal is followed by Mr Darcy's letter of explanation about Wickham so that from that point Mr Darcy is in the ascendance and Wickham's stock is steadily falling. It also illustrates how Mr Darcy moves away from pride to a genuine awareness of values that has lain outside his class-bound scheme of things and how Elizabeth moves away from her undue dependence on her own judgement and a greater concession to social view.

Let us move on to Jane Austen's next novel, *Mansfield Park* published around 1814, which contains more light and shade. Fanny Price, the heroine, lacks the vivaciousness and wit of Elizabeth Bennet, but is kind and humble. Brought up a poor relation among her rich cousins, she has developed passivity and the circumstances themselves have reduced her to passivity and thus Fanny has turned out to be the most passive of all Jane Austen's heroines. The wit in the novel appears in the end to be entirely on the side of the evil in contrast to the wit which befriends virtue in *Pride and Prejudice* so far as the principal characters are concerned. In fact, the wit of *Mansfield Park* lies in the texture of the narrative rather than in the texture of the dialogue of hero and heroine. It should be noted in this context that though Fanny is passive in terms of plot in that all decisive actions are taken by others and her fate seems to depend upon what others do, she is the most active in terms of the moral pattern of the novel. In spite of passivity, timidity, shyness and lack of social brilliance, she sustains strong opinions, attitudes which prompt her in her refusal to marry the charming Henry Crawford who has captivated everyone else in the novel. The way she maintains this refusal notwithstanding well-meant pressure from those she holds in high esteem speaks of a negative action, but her adherence to it is a decisive action in the working out of the whole pattern of the novel. True virtue, as in this novel, is tolerant and gentle in behaviour, but firm in moral decision. The main characteristic of *Mansfield Park* is sympathy, not the ironic wit.

Mansfield Park utilizes a simple Cinderella theme and bestows upon it a new dimension by using the subtlety and complexity of its execution. Sir Thomas and Lady Bertram, Fanny's uncle and aunt, do not ill-treat her and we can't blame her cousins for assuming that she is socially inferior to them, for this assumption does not contribute to her real suffering. She has the reason to be irritated at the petty spitefulness of her Aunt Norris who personifies mean-spirited selfishness, but this irritation does not enhance her suffering and, besides, the understanding affection of her cousin, Edmund, more than makes up for this irritation. Sir Thomas, a good man though he is, lacks sympathetic imagination and gives vent, to cover up this deficiency, to pomposity of manner. He presents himself to us as a bore and, as we progress through the novel, as a rather pathetic character who simulates the dignity of the head of a dignified family and this simulation makes him ridiculous and seem out of touch with reality. But admirable is the behaviour he displays when he, on his hurried return from Antigua, finds his family engaged in amateur theatricals and we can't help marveling at the firmness and justness of his behaviour. In Sir Thomas's absence when his children and niece are left home under the supervision of the vain self-importance of Mrs Norris and the languid unimaginativeness of Bertram, the whole moral atmosphere degenerates and the degeneracy owes itself to a great extent to the influence of Henry and Mary Crawford who are staying at the parsonage and to that of Tom Bertram's light-headed friend Mr Yates. Henry makes love to both the Bertram daughters, but finally his love concentrates on Mary who herself is engaged to the rich and dull Mr Rushworth. They choose to perform a play which is itself sentimental and melodramatic about a wronged woman and her noble illegitimate son and this provides them with an opportunity to indulge in various kinds of love-making under the plea of rehearsing, even though they all know that Sir Thomas would disapprove of the rehearsing if he were home. The planning of the performance of the play brings out the worst in all characters: Julia is in grumps because her elder sister is Mr Crawford's favourite; Maria, though already engaged, triumphs in her affair with Mr Crawford; and even the good and strong-minded Edmund finds himself swayed away by his passion for Mary Crawford so much so that he acquiesces and in fact participate in the plan which he at first protested at. It is only Fanny who sees the truth steadily throughout the whole proceedings and keeps aloof from them and observes them from a distance. She does not budge an inch from her view of the impropriety of the amateur theatricals and sticks to this view. Towards the end of the novel Henry's running off with the now-married Maria reveals his true character and justifies her refusal to marry a man about whom everybody had persuaded her that she should love.

Emma, published around 1816, is as a novel more acceptable to those who take *Pride and Prejudice* as the type of Jane Austen fiction. In the first appearance, the novel was the legitimate child of the romance. Though the manners and general turn of the composition were altered just to suit the modern times, Jane Austen allowed herself to be fettered by many characteristics peculiar to the original style of romantic fiction, traceable in the conduct of the narrative and the tone of sentiment attributed to the fictitious personages. Miss Emma Woodhouse is the daughter of a gentleman of wealth and consequence, residing at his seat in the immediate vicinity of a village called Highbury. The father, a good-natured, silly, valetudinary, leaves the management of his household over to Emma and lets his time be occupied by his summer and winter walk, apothecary, his gruel and his whist table. Many other interesting characters crowd in the milieu of the novel. There is a smiling and courteous vicar who nurtures the hope of winning the hand of Emma, Mrs Bates, the wife of a former rector, past everything but tea and whist, her daughter, Miss Bates, a good-natured, vulgar and foolish old girl; have Mr Wetson, a gentleman of a frank disposition and moderate fortune who lives nearby and his wife, an amiable and accomplished person who had been Emma's governess and is devotedly attached to her. Miss Emma Woodhouse towers over other characters and walks forth, superior to all her companions in wit, beauty, fortune and accomplishments and is doted upon by her father and the Mestons and admired and almost worshipped by the more humble companions of the whist table. Miss Emma Woodhouse, anticipating the taste of a later period of life on one hand and preferring, as befits a good sovereign, the weal of her subjects of Highbury to her own private interest on the other, takes it upon herself to make matches for her friends, caring a fig for her own marriage, thus setting herself apart from the run of young ladies seeking a desirable connexion in marriage. We are informed she had been eminently successful in the case of Mr and Mrs Weston; and when the novel commences she is exerting her influence in favour of Miss Harriet Smith, a boarding-school girl without family or fortune, very good-humoured, very pretty, very silly, and, what suited Miss Woodhouse's purpose best, very much disposed to be married.

In the machinations, Emma is frequently interrupted, not only by the cautions of her father who cherished a particular objection to anybody committing the rash act of matrimony, but also by the sturdy reproof of Mr Knightley, the elder brother of her sister's husband, a country gentleman in the vicinity of thirty-five in age who had known Emma from the cradle, the only person who ventured to find fault with her. In spite, however, of his censure and warning, Emma plans on marrying Harriet Smith to the vicar; and though she achieves success to a great extent in alluring Harriet Smith's thoughts off an honest farmer who had made her a very suitable offer and flattering her into loving Mr Elton, Emma commits a serious mistake in understanding the nature of the encouragement held out to him and attributes the favour which he found in her eyes to a lurking affection on her part. This prompts him to a big-headed declaration of his sentiments; upon receiving a repulse he looks everywhere and enriches the Highbury society by uniting himself to a dashing young woman, rich as well as ill-bred.

While Emma occupies herself in forging wedlock-fetters for others, her friends likewise occupy themselves in forging a wedlock-fetter for her in favour of a son of Mr Weston by a former marriage who bears the name, lives under the patronage, and is to inherit the fortune of a rich uncle. Unfortunately, Mr Frank Churchill, his name, had already settled his affections on Miss Jane Fairfax, a young lady of reduced fortune; but since he keeps the affair concealed, Emma nurtures a thought of being in love with him, when he appears on the scene. It does not take her much time to discover her mistake; she desires, instead, to bestow him upon her deserted friend Harriet Smith who has already fallen desperately in love with Mr Knightley. But the whole village is agog with rumour that Churchill and Emma are attached to each other. In fact, all these entanglements bring on only a train of mistakes and embarrassing situations, dialogues at balls and pleasure parties, in which Jane Austen displays her peculiar powers of humour and knowledge of human life and she very dexterously extricates the plot. The death of the aunt of Frank Churchill leaves his uncle unfettered to her baleful influence so much so that he consents to his nephew marrying Jane Fairfax and this marriage flings Mr Knightley and Emma into the consciousness that they had been in love with each other all along. Mr Woodhouse's objections to the marriage of his daughter is reduced to a naught by the fears of house-breakers, and the comfort he hopes to derive from having a stout son-in-law resident in the family; and the facile affections of Harriet Smith are transferred to her former suitor, the former farmer, who had managed to obtain a favourable opportunity to renew his address. Such is the simple plan of a story.

The author's knowledge of the world and the peculiar tact with which she presents characters remind us something of the merits of the Flemish school of painting. The subjects are not often elegant, nor are they grand; but they are finished up to nature and with such a precision as delights the reader.

We have got acquainted with the plot of the story and let us recapitulate the story to get to the art of Jane Austen in delineating the characters. It necessitates delving deep into the plot.

Frank Churchill whom Emma picks on to give in marriage to Harriet Smith is attractive to Emma herself and we can perceive an interesting tension between her admiration of his vitality and wit and her half-realized love for Mr Knightley. Mr Knightley, some seventeen years older than Emma, is a wealthy landowner, grave, generous, kind to his tenants and intolerant of deceit and cruelty and has none of the superficial gaiety of Frank Churchill, while Emma is planning on marriage between Frank and Harriet, Knightley imagines that she is herself falling in love with Frank. The situation is further enriched and embellished with ironies by the introduction of Jane Fairfax who acts as a foil to Emma. Fairfax, though genteelly poor—she is a splinter daughter of a clergyman and stays with her aunt—is equally talented and more talented at music. Emma conjectures Miss Fairfax in secret love with one Mr Dixon who lives away in Ireland and her conjecture proves true. She indulges in hinting and speculating about Miss Fairfax's relation with Mr Dixon and even goes to the extent of joking on her score with Frank. This joke smacks of her jealousy. The truth is that the relation between Fairfax and Mr Dixon Emma has conjured up and so often joked about with Frank has no basis in fact, and all the time Jane Fairfax and Frank Churchill were secretly engaged and this realization flings Emma into an awkward position. At every point Emma's wit and knowingness have thrown her into a pit of humiliation/ saved by Mr Knightley standing by to give gentle and affectionate reproof. It is the relief of discovering that Emma did never love Frank (to belie everyone's expectation) that precipitates his declaration. Brilliant is the contrivance of the whole plot and the exploration of different kinds of selfishness unfolded through action, aided by sharply ironic character sketches of such characters as the Etons and Miss Bates, gives the novel real depth below the surface brilliance. The character of Emma's father, whose concern for other people is a mask for a profound selfishness, opens and closes the book; it is a masterly picture of combined gentleness and querulousness which flourished on the assumption that what is bad for him should be prohibited to others and, thus, symbolizes the ambiguities of selfishnesses, which is one of the themes of the novel.

Interrogating Culture: Sexuality, Madness and Marxism in the London Novels of Doris Lessing

2

LIZA DAS

Given both the reality and the potential of cultural forms to dominate and legitimate cultural axioms and forces, women writers' inquiry into the workings of cultural politics in society assumes considerable importance in feminist studies. According to critics like Janet Batsleer, there seems to be a propensity in "the ruling culture of Englishness—white, male, and (whatever its electoral habits)," for "depoliticizing culture [...] (and) deculturalizing politics" (Batsleer et al. 9, 6). And it is the 'subjugated' components of English culture—Irish, Scots, Welsh and Black peoples, and women—who are aware of the inextricability of these two terms. This knowledge derives from their experience of cultural politics in everyday life. In a broad sense, the term 'cultural politics' is analogous to Kate Millett's concept of sexual politics, though the latter is only one aspect of the former. The dominant or ruling force of culture, together with the cultural norms and forms it produces, establishes power/politics over other components of culture, in the same way as patriarchy exerts power over women. This chapter attempts to illustrate the critical interrogation of culture in the London novels—novels with London as a backdrop—of Doris Lessing. Her encounter with English cultural politics is manifest in her critique of three cultural 'constructs' (in the Foucauldian sense): sexuality, madness and communism.

In the 1950s and 1960s, post-war English culture was trying to create a "fetishized femininity" (Coote and

Campbell 3) by wooing women with the new consumer economy and by attempting to establish a sort of Neo-Victorianism that demanded women's unquestioning attention to domestic and familial realms. This demand stemmed from a cultural insecurity in men who feared a resurgence of the post-First World War cultural power of women. Once again, English culture asserted that women's faculties were meant for a Ruskinian "sweet ordering" (Ruskin 107), and not for economically lucrative work. Women who did not work and who capitulated to the feminine ideal were glorified as "real" women (Coote and Campbell 4). Culturally, then, the period was a "sexually contumacious" one (Lessing, *GN* 9). The sex antagonism or sex war portrayed in the novels of Doris Lessing was thus an indication of women's encounter with cultural politics. Sex, however, is only one of the many concerns in Lessing's novels. And, in *The Golden Notebook* (1962)—recognized as her finest work—it is certainly not the overriding theme. In fact, Lessing was dismayed at the way the novel was received as a treatise on sex antagonism or as a banner of a "latter-day feminism" (Howe 7). With money and a room of her own, the post-war woman writer's obsession is not so much with sexual politics as with the cultural politics of her time. Marion Vlastos Libby's assertion that, in *The Golden Notebook,* sexuality is "the prime impetus for the protagonist's struggle to establish meaning, dignity and pleasure in her existence" (Libby 107) is a rather reductive reading of the novel. *The Golden Notebook* rallies against prevailing cultural forms, beliefs and forces, and becomes a multipronged attack on English culture. It is an analysis of modern chaos, but is presented, significantly, from a gendered viewpoint. Lessing explains: "I wrote from inside a woman's viewpoint, naturally, since I am one [...]. I articulated [the problem of chaos] from a female point of view" (Howe 8-9). Thus the novel has a woman writer as its protagonist who is a kind of fictional *doppelganger* for Lessing. The choice of a woman writer as protagonist is an apt one because it is the woman-as-writer who is a powerful observer and critic of cultural politics. Anna Wulf, the woman writer portrayed in this *Kunstlerroman,* cannot write—has a writer's block—despite her secure financial position and comfortable material life. She and her friend, Molly, are divorcees, and their relationship is, in feminist terms, a kind of Boston marriage. They lead "free lives, that is, lives like men" (*GN* 59). Yet Anna knows that culture does not consider them free: "[t]hey still define us in terms of relationships with men [...]" (26). Lessing brings out the irony of their freedom in the opening sentence of the novel: "[t]he two women were *alone* in the London flat" (25, emphasis added). However, Anna's idea of freedom goes beyond sexual and financial freedom. A single woman, she already has sexual freedom, and, with a room and money of her own, she is financially free. Yet, despite this enviable situation—given the context of the 1950s—she cannot write. In the post-war chaotic situation she feels an "awful moral exhaustion" (59) that does not allow her to write a novel like her earlier *The Frontiers of War*, on the proceeds of which she depends for a living. In a world fraught with chaos, violence and fragmentation, where the centre cannot hold, she fails to find the appropriate form and words to write a new novel. Her freedom as a writer is thus inextricably bound to, and even depends on, the condition of her culture. Unlike Caroline Helstone in *Shirley* who felt that "women have so few things to think about" (Brontë, *Shirley* 229), Anna thinks about and assumes responsibility for the whole world. The kind of novel Anna does wish to write is one "powered with an intellectual or moral passion strong enough to create order, to create a new way of looking at life" (*GN* 76), a book with "the quality of philosophy" (75). In other words, she wishes to write the kind of novel of social realism of the nineteenth century. But the most un-nineteenth century situation of post-war culture, a condition in which "everything's cracking up" (25), cannot provide her the milieu and language for writing the kind of novels written in the nineteenth century. Anna, therefore, decides to break up her writing into separate fragments in an attempt to encounter formlessness with compartmentalization. She keeps four notebooks instead of one to record her fragmented and disparate experiences. In the

'Black Notebook' Anna writes about the problem of art; in the 'Red Notebook' she records her experiences with the British Communist Party, the 'Yellow Notebook' contains a novel, "The Shadow of the Third," and the 'Blue Notebook' she keeps as a diary. *The Golden Notebook* is comprised of these four notebooks kept by Anna, together with sections of a conventional novel, *Free Women*, about Anna. Later, after Anna has understood and worked out the problem of chaos, she is able to write her '*The Golden Notebook*.' The four notebooks and the Golden Notebook, as well the novel *The Golden Notebook* itself, form Anna/Lessing's critique of culture and cultural forms.

In the 'Black Notebook', pondering over the problem of art, Anna finds that most of the novels being written in the post-war period are not art but mere "outpost[s] of journalism" exploring exotic locales and lesser known social groups and countries. Mirroring the fragmentation of culture, novelists cannot write novels with the quality of philosophy. The novel, therefore, has been reduced to a "novel-report" (75) in order to satisfy the readers' facile curiosity. This tendency is the literary reflection of the extreme parochialism of English culture. In an essay written in 1957, Lessing castigates English culture, and writers like Colin Wilson and John Osborne, for this parochialism:

> [England] is a country so profoundly parochial that people like myself coming in from outside, never cease to marvel [...]. To discuss politics in Britain with most people means that in five minutes one is astounded to find that the talk is of whether old Freddie or Tory is going to be sent over to govern New South Wales [...]. Thinking internationally means choosing a particular shade of half-envious, half-patronizing emotion to feel about the United States; or collecting money from Hungary, or taking little holidays in Europe, or liking French or Italian films. ("SPV" 24)

Such parochialism mars the writing of Wilson and Osborne and others of the Angry Young Men group, making the authors unable to write a novel with a holistic vision (Lessing,

"SPV" 25-26). Lessing's Anna despairs because she cannot bring herself to write the conventional, well-made, parochial novel. And the only kind of novel she wants to write seems anachronistic in the present world. Torn between two literary forms, one available and the other ideal, she decides to write "simply, the truth" (*GN* 77). But the truth cannot be written out in a single notebook for then she would be leaving out parts of it. Anna explains to Molly's son, Tommy, that writing the truth in a single notebook would amount to chaos: "it would be [...] a scramble [...] a mess" (240), as she could not leave out the ordinary things, her everyday experiences which were probably the real things and more important than dramatic thoughts like committing suicide (246). Lessing's Anna is like Dorothy Richardson's Miriam in *Pilgrimage* who resents the "dreadful enclosure" of conventional novels and knows that "the torment of all novels is what is left out" (Richardson 239). Like Virginia Woolf, Anna Wulf does not view life as a series of gig lamps symmetrically arranged (Woolf 189), but as a chaotic conglomeration of disparate experiences.

The English novel is not the only cultural form criticized by Lessing in *The Golden Notebook*. The pettiness of English culture is also reflected by the media, particularly the television, and by the critical reviewers. To Anna "the literary world [...]. [is] prissy, maiden auntish [...] classbound," and its commercial side is "blatant" (*GN* 151). A number of film and television agents approach her as they wish to make feature films and television plays on "The Frontiers of War". Anna is amused and dismayed at the way they manipulate the text and transform it according to their commercial needs. "The Frontiers of War" was based on the colour bar in Africa and its subject matter had come directly from Anna's observation of colonial culture during her days at Mashopi. This fact is, however, nonchalantly brushed aside by the agents who conveniently see it as a simple love story. Tongue-in-cheek, Anna writes a maudlin parody of the novel to suit the new title suggested by the film agents: "Forbidden Love." The television agents are full of other suggestions: one is of the opinion that it should be made into a comedy, another wants to turn it into a musical, while a third wants to rework it as an adventure story. But such simplifications would only mutilate the novel and Anna refuses to agree to their demands. The parochialism of the agents is further revealed when most of them suggest that the locale be changed from the African to an English one. Anna's friend, the "equine Englishm[a]n", Harry, interprets her novel as "the tragedy of the whites" in Africa (388), as a novel symbolizing "the true superior spiritual status of the white man [...] dragged down into the animal mud of Africa" (389). Communist reviewers praise the novel for its exotic locale—"[m]ajestic and untamed is Africa!" (392)—but criticize it because they see it as negative and desperate. It becomes clear that the writer's block that Anna suffers from stems partly from the parochialism of existing cultural forms in England.

In a desperate bid to ward off fragmentation, to cling to some act of faith, Anna considers joining the British Communist Party. This she does despite the knowledge that her critical mind would invariably question some of the Party's assumptions and beliefs. Anna muses: "[...] I won't be able to say anything I believe to be true to any comrade I know [...]" (151). However, disgusted with the literary world and half-envious of Molly's committed enthusiasm, Anna joins the Party. But the British Communist Party is just another cultural institution and the lies and contradictions within it compel her to give up her membership. The 'Red Notebook' records Anna's tryst with communism and becomes, in effect, a scathing attack on the hypocrisies of the Party. Communism fails to provide Anna, the writer, the answer to the correct balance between the individual and the collective. According to her, since it places all importance on the collective, it necessarily negates the importance of personal emotion in writing. Reading the literature of the communist countries, Anna discovers that all articles and short stories cater to the myth of communism. "[m]ost of the writing is flat, tame, optimistic, and on a curiously jolly note, even when dealing with war and suffering" (311). This kind of impersonality in art, she considers, is false and banal. While delivering a lecture on community art, Anna stammers and then realizes that she was delivering a lie. She, unlike the Party activist, Rose Latimer, cannot declare unconditional commitment to "the salt of the earth" people (317). Despite its avowed aim of removing the sufferings of the downtrodden, communism is cruelly impersonal. The Party is only another cultural institution of the "ruling culture of Englishness [...] [that] depoliticiz[es] culture and deculturaliz[es] politics" (Batsleer et al. 6) for it does not adequately connect culture and politics with the everyday life of all people. For instance, Rose Latimer defends working-class men who ill-treat or neglect their wives, and extols them as "wonderful marvellous people" who could never do wrong (*GN* 317). Like Anton in *A Ripple from the Storm,* most of the members of the British Communist Party pay lip service to communism and are fiercely ambitious. They are blindly committed to the icons of communism. A badly written pamphlet by Stalin is defended as a bad translation and, though the members are well aware of Stalin's ruthless policies, they still have a "tone of simple, friendly respect for him" (273). After Khrushchev's 1958 revelations of Stalin's atrocities, many members admit to being disillusioned and some renounce their communist faith to become ruthless capitalists. Lynn Sukenick seems to believe that Lessing rallies against sensibility and emotion in her writings. However, through Anna, Lessing reiterates her belief that literature stems from emotion. When Molly tells Anna that she knows Anna does not write "little novels about the emotions", Anna retorts:

> That remark you've just made is an echo from Communist Party criticism [...]. If Marxism means anything, it means that a little novel about the emotions should reflect "what's real" since the emotions are a function and a product of society [...]. (*GN* 57)

Lessing's understanding of Marxism differs from the parochialism of the British Communist Party, and is more humanist and philosophical. Anna is echoing Lessing's statement in "The Small Personal Voice":

> [...] The jolly, jaunty, curiously unemotional novel about the collective farm, the factory, the five-year plan [...] is reminiscent of nothing so much as a little boy whistling in the dark. The simple demand for simple statements of fact produces art so dull and false that one reads it yawning and returns to Tolstoy. ("SPV" 19)

But Lessing is as much impatient with and critical of "the monstrously isolated, monstrously narcissistic" ivory-tower artist (*GN* 12), as she is with the communist novel. As a woman writer she cannot relinquish her personal, emotional responses to culture. What she seeks is to strike a judicious balance between the personal and the impersonal, to see them as inexorably linked to each other:

> The way to deal with the problem of 'subjectivity' [...] is to see [the individual] as a microcosm and in this way to break through the personal, the subjective, making the personal general, as indeed life always does, transforming private experience [...] into something much larger [...]. (913)

It is in the light of the above statement that the two other notebooks—the 'Yellow' and the 'Blue'—ought to be read. In the 'Blue Notebook' Anna records the development of her relationship with Michael. In order to analyze this relationship, she creates fictional doubles for herself and her lover in the 'Yellow Notebook'. She writes a novel, "The Shadow of the Third", in which the lovers Ella and Paul represent Anna and Michael. This endistancing device Anna uses not only to observe her relationship with Michael, but also to tell herself that her experiences in love are similar to other women's. By writing about Ella and Paul, she builds a safety-device which later helps her to cope with the breaking up of her relationship with Michael. Moreover, the breaking up of the relationship of Ella and Paul, and of Anna and Michael, are not seen as private happenings; they are symptomatic of, and a result of, the general breakdown or fragmentation of post-war culture. If the 'Black' and the 'Red' notebooks record Anna's disillusionment with literature and politics respectively, the 'Yellow' and the 'Blue' illustrate her disillusionment with romantic love. In Ella she projects her romantic-idealist self. Though divorced, Ella is not 'free' because she still defines herself in terms of relationships with men. But the old order of security in love has vanished and Ella realizes that "women's emotions are all still fitted for a kind of society that no longer exists" (*GN* 283). Her emotional dependence on Paul only makes her naive:

> Paul gave birth to Ella, the naive Ella. He destroyed in her the knowing, doubting, sophisticated Ella and again and again he put her intelligence to sleep, and with her smiling connivance, so that she floated darkly on her love for him [...]. (197)

Paul's inability to submit himself totally to Ella stems partly from his acute awareness of the chaotic condition of the world. A psychiatrist and welfare worker, he is a doctor "who sees his patients as symptoms of a world sickness" (197). He has taken upon himself the task of a modern Sisyphus pushing the boulder of truth up the mountain of culture's "stupidity" (196). Paul, like Osborne's Jimmy Porter, also fears the 'power' of women. He tells Ella fantastic things that stem from his fear of women: "[y]ou can apply ice to a woman's ovaries [...]. She can have a child. Men are no longer necessary to humanity" (198). Ella, on the other hand, resents the fact that men have the ability to separate sex and emotion. A conversation between Ella and her friend, Julia, brings out this resentment.

> "Free," says Julia, "Free! what's the use of us being free if they aren't. I swear to god, that every one of them, even the best of them, have the old idea of good women and bad women."
>
> "And what about us? Free, we say? Yet the truth is they get erections when they're with a woman they don't care a damn about, but we don't have an orgasm unless we love him. What's free about that?" (404)

Learning from Ella, Anna resolves not to resent men's sexual amorality:

> [...] I want to be done with it all, finish with the men *vs* women business, all the complaints and the reproaches and the betrayals. Besides, it's dishonest. We've chosen to live a certain way, knowing the penalties, or if we didn't we know now, so why whine and complain [...]. (62)

By analyzing Ella, Anna realizes that romantic idealism is an anachronism, and, thereby, she becomes 'free' by accepting the limitations of love. Patricia Spacks rightly notes that Molly and Anna see men's sexual amorality as "an index of moral inferiority", of men's "emotional superficiality and exploitativeness" which they, as women, can never endorse or embrace (Spacks 569).

In a final attempt to bring some semblance of order out of chaos, Anna undergoes psychoanalytic treatment under a Jungian psychoanalyst, Mrs Marks. But, like literature, communism, and love, such clinical treatment is also plagued by a false order. Mrs Marks, too, does not relate Anna's fragmentation to the larger cultural situation. Anna and Molly nickname her "Mother Sugar" for her tendency to 'sugar-coat' reality. "Traditional, rooted, conservative [...] [and] amoral" (*GN* 26), Mrs Marks interprets Anna's dreams in terms of archetypes and labels of human 'types'. But it is this very pigeon-holing that Anna decides to avoid. She refuses to negate or obliterate the myriad facets of her personality, her experiences as a mother, a lover, a writer and a woman. She realizes that "the raw unfinished quality in [her] life was precisely what was valuable in it [...]" (*GN* 217). However, this clinging to 'rawness' is not possible within the cultural definition of normality. Anna voluntarily undergoes the experience of madness in order to feel this rawness that is 'real', and because she has the intuitive feeling that the experience of madness would eventually lead to something new:

> What is happening is something new in my life. I think many people have a sense of shape, of unfolding, in

> their lives [...] this new person is important to me [...] she, is the beginning of something I must live through. (421)

Anna is mad only in terms of a culture that attests to a false order. In feminist terms, as Adrienne Rich observes, madness occurs when "women are in touch with [their] best instincts" (Rich, "Conversations" 117). In Lessing, however, this madness is not only women's prerogative. Often, sensitive men, like Anna's lover, the American Saul Green, also undergo mental breakdown. Yet there is a crucial difference between the madness of Paul and that of Anna. Saul slips into one role after another too easily, almost irresponsibly, and he indulges in his madness, not really wanting to learn something from it. Anna's madness is a means to an end: it helps her counter breakdown with breakdown. As her writer's block dissolves, she purchases a golden notebook and resolves to write with a newfound vision of unity beyond chaos.

Though critics have commented on the structure of *The Golden Notebook* (*e.g.*, Schweickart, Mulkeen), few have seen the "extremely carefully constructed" structure (Howe 7) as a woman writer's attempt to avoid writing a conventional novel, which leaves out the *trauma* of the act of creative writing. Schweickart reads *The Golden Notebook* as a (proto)-Derridean text, while Mulkeen focuses on its 'grid' structure. But the structure of *The Golden Notebook* is so designed as to avoid the deletion of ideas and thoughts that had gone into its writing. Lessing and Anna, like Dorothy Richardson and Miriam, avoid writing "men's books" which go "[b]ang, bang, bang [...] like an L.C.C. tram [...] unable to make [one] forget them, the authors, for a moment" (Richardson 239). Lessing finds the novels of male writers like Camus, Sartre, Genet and Beckett, "despairing statements of emotional anarchy" (Lessing, "SPV" 19). In order to avoid such egotism and anarchy she breaks up *The Golden Notebook* into structures through which the subject matter, by itself, would break out. The formal structure helps ward off emotional anarchy. Another woman writer observes: "[formalism] [...] like asbestos gloves [...] allowed me to handle materials I couldn't have picked up bare-handed" (Rich, "When We Dead" 94-95). The novelist, Antonia Byatt, too, informs that she had kept two notebooks to write novels of ideas (qtd. in Musil 200). Improvising the early twentieth-century stream-of-consciousness technique, Lessing uses a "cinematic technique" (Carey 24) to focus on the multifarious experiences of the sensitive woman.

In *The Four-Gated City* (1969), Lessing's acute observation and subversion of cultural politics is made through three aspects of the novel: the radical defense of a subjugated component of culture—the apparently mad people, the sharp criticism of London, and the prophecy of a new, highly-evolved civilization replacing decadent Western civilization. Martha has left Zambesia and has migrated to London. In sharp contrast to the endearing African landscape, the London environment repels her from the very beginning. She is employed as a secretary by Mark Coldridge, a writer, and she moves in to the posh Coldridge household near Bloomsbury. Mark's wife, Lynda, who has been diagnosed as a schizophrenic, lives in a mental asylum. Martha observes London and Londoners with the critical eye of an outsider. *The Four-Gated City* records Martha's wide criticisms of London culture and of the city's griminess. This critique is to a considerable extent a gendered one. Many have read *The Four-Gated City* as a representation or documentation of the London of the 1950s. Pickering observes that, in British literature, *The Four-Gated City* is the best "documentation" of the culture of Britain in the 1950s and 1960s (Pickering 72). A closer look at the novel reveals that it goes beyond 'documenting' culture to become a counter-cultural treatise undermining the very culture it apparently documents. Lessing believes, with R.D. Laing, that madness is a positive state/stage of the mind and a way to recuperating from the modern predicament of chaos. In Lessing one discerns not a radical assertion of the self but a wider exploration of the self and its potential to fully grapple with cultural forms. Through hysteria, the self reaches a "new place", it "break[s] into something new" (*FGC* 82) which, in its normal state, it cannot comprehend. It is significant that the two persons who undergo this breaking into new awareness are two women—

Martha and Lynda. Lynda Coldridge, for whose husband, Mark, Martha works as a secretary, and to whose son she is a governess, is variously diagnosed by psychiatrists as "depressed [...] manic-depressive [...] paranoiac [...] schizophrenic [...] neurotic psychotic" (206), and is kept in a mental asylum. Even before she has met Lynda, Martha feels a strange affinity towards her. Because Lynda "could not stand being Mark's wife, and Francis's mother, she came too close to Martha" (125). Martha herself has rejected the culture-allotted roles of wife and mother. Like Lynda, she is free of these roles. Martha has developed from a young adolescent into what she herself calls "a soft dark receptive intelligence" (47), capable of being a number of persons at a time, of being split personalities:

> Somewhere in one's mind was a wavelength, a band where music jigged and niggled, with or without words: it was simply a question of tuning in and listening. (48)

Martha becomes aware that this state of being "giggly, silly, overreceptive" is a positive phase in mental health, a "rehearsal" for sanity (82). In order to cope with a fragmented world, one could not go back to a false order; one had to breakthrough chaos by allowing oneself to 'heal' through chaotic experiences, through tuning into various parts of the mind. Martha becomes increasingly aware of this through Lynda when the latter comes to stay in the Coldridge household. Lynda tells Martha that she is one of those persons "[n]ot [fit] for ordinary life" (133), one who has chosen not to give into cultural role-playing, one who safeguards what she 'knows': her "bit of freedom, a little space [...]" (134). She has adopted the role of an outsider, an observer of culture. This curiosity about culture is what keeps Lynda from killing herself: "[...] I decided to stay alive and see what happens next. It is interesting" (187). Lynda's freedom is what Adrienne Rich has called "the freedom of the wholly mad":

> The freedom of the wholly mad
> to smear and play with her madness
> write with her fingers dipped in it.
>
> (Rich, "Phenomenology" 68)

Doubly subjugated—as a woman and as 'mad' person—Lynda is labelled a "nothing-but" (*FGC* 237), a useless part of culture.

The basement in the house where Lynda is staying with another schizophrenic—her friend Dorothy—becomes a ghetto, a place of refuge for these cultural misfits. Martha initially avoids the basement but cannot help being attracted to its inmates when her understanding of Lynda grows. The basement becomes a base-camp of female solidarity where Lynda and Dorothy becomes a "defensive unit", bound together "in a world-hating friendship" (189). The house becomes increasingly chaotic while the basement grows into a place of possibilities:

> [Martha] thought how strange it was [...] a few weeks ago it was in the basement that people [...] talked of death, of suicide, of killing. Now, with no outside circumstance changed, the basement was alive again, and futures were possible and talked about [...]. Death had moved up to Martha's room in the second floor. (212-13)

Martha has moved beyond Virginia Woolf's classic idea of freedom for women—money and a room of one's own—into a broader realm of freedom: the mind. The mind becomes the fullest, the most promising site of freedom for women like Martha and Lynda. Martha becomes aware that other women she knew—Patty Samuels, Mavis Wood, Rosa Mellendip, and Mrs Gerald Smith—were also breaking up and were being labelled neurotic. In *The Four-Gated City*, Doris Lessing subverts Charlotte Bronte's portrayal of the archetypal madwoman in the attic in *Jane Eyre*. In both these novels there is the classic love-triangle of the man, his mad wife, and his beloved/lover. But Lessing symbolically rescues Bronte's Bertha Mason in her portrayal of Lynda. Instead of the isolated mad wife in the attic, *The Four-Gated City* has a sensitive woman in the basement to whom the female protagonist is increasingly drawn, in whom she looks for mental succour. Lynda's psychiatrist, Dr Lamb, is a variant of Mrs Marks of *The Golden Notebook*. Like Mrs Marks, Dr Lamb's aim is to label persons according to psychiatric types. In a session with Dr Lamb, Martha realizes that the psychiatrist was trying hard to pigeon-hole her into the category of "manic depressive with schizoid tendencies":

> With great skill, playing her like a fish, he brought her again and again to points where she would be angry. Watching, she avoided, fought, backed away, because more than anything else she dreaded the exhaustion that would follow. Then she cracked as she was bound to [...]. (*FGC* 250)

If English culture is dull, banal, unable to 'connect', the city of London is a physical reflection and symbol of this banality and colourlessness. Arriving in London from Zambesia, Martha Quest is in culture-shock. Everything about the city of London was tasteless and dull: its houses, shops and the goods in them, its celebrated river Thames, its citizens and the dresses they wore, were ugly and repelling. The first two paragraphs of *The Four-Gated City* fully evoke this griminess through the detailed description of the London restaurant, "Joe's Fish and Chips":

> In front of Martha was *grimed* glass, its lower part covered with *grimed* muslin. The open door showed an oblong of *browny-grey* air swimming with globules of wet. The shop fronts opposite were no particular colour. The lettering on the shops, once black, brown, gold, white, was now shades of *dull brown.* The lettering on the upper part of the glass of this room [...] was flaking like *stale* chocolate.
>
> She sat by a rectangle of pinkish oilcloth where sugar had spilled, and on to it, orange tea, making a *gritty smear* [...]. Her cup was thick *whitey-grey,* cracked. The teaspoon was a whitish plastic [...] the elastic brittleness natural to it had gone into an erosion of hair lines, so that it was like a kind of sponge. (11, emphases added)

Later, observing the city, Martha wonders: "What kind of a race is this that chooses, inevitably and invariably, [...] the ugly, the graceless?" (42-43). Walking down the streets of London, Martha is repelled by the Londoners. Their existence is a somnambulistic one in which they are not aware of themselves, not to talk of other people. They are isolated, "locked in an invisible cage [...] inside a net of wants and needs that made it impossible for them to think of anything else" (529). Indifferent to the ugliness of their city, they are complacent, unable to comprehend their decadence. Only Lynda and Martha have realized that England is hurtling towards ruin. In a prophetic dream, Lynda sees English landscapes covered with a frozen dew and she cries out: "England has been poisoned, it looks like a poisoned mouse lying dead in a corner" (589). In one of her 'hysterical' phases, Martha realizes that Londoners, whom the world envied, were one of the most unenviable peoples of the world. They were "drugged with anxiety or day-dreaming [...] absorbed in fantasy [...] distorted by anger, or worry, or greed [...]" (530). In *The Golden Notebook,* the women characters are also repelled by London. To Molly, Londoners are "bloody dull" (*GN* 61); to Ella the very prospect of leaving the house to walk on the streets is a frightening thought:

> [...] the city frightened her. To move, mile after mile, through the weight of ugliness that is London in its faceless peripheral wastes made her angry; then the anger ebbed out, leaving fear [...]. Ahead of her the street of grey mean little houses crawled endlessly [...]. For miles in all directions, this ugliness, this meanness. (168)

To Ella, too, England is a "poisonous" country (178) over which she wants to run a giant bulldozer and then to bring the people back into "fine new cities, each one an architect's dream" (179).

In *The Four-Gated City,* the British Isles are destroyed by a catastrophe, probably by a unclear accident. Martha Quest survives along with a group of people on an island off the coast of Scotland. In a letter to Francis Coldridge who has moved to Nairobi, Martha describes her life in this new world. It is a place with "a rare fine air [...] a crystalline gleam" (*FGC* 658), and the children whom she helps raise are sensitive, "superlatively ordinary" (660), for they 'hear' and 'see' things the adults cannot. They are a new generation with parapsychological capabilities akin to what Martha and Lynda had experienced. They are most unlike the Londoners who "could not communicate across the dark that separated them" (92). They are the future builders and inhabitants of the ideal city of Martha's dreams. The "Children of Violence" series becomes a *Bildungsroman* with a difference: a *bildung* of the human mind, of its myriad possibilities. As Catherine Stimpson rightly observes, the series becomes "an urgent, urging cultural achievement, a composition meant as explanation and guide" (Stimpson 198) for post-war culture.

In *The Memoirs of a Survivor* (1974), London is shown as a gradually degenerating city. Unlike in *The Four-Gated City,* London is not destroyed by a sudden catastrophe; its citizens are shown going through a regression towards a primitive stage of civilization. Set in the future, the novel documents the spiritual and material degeneration of Londoners. The female protagonist, who is a 'survivor', narrates the events that had led to the falling-apart of the city and its social systems. Money had been replaced by barter, all essential systems like gas and electricity were cut off, people had moved from an agricultural to a nomadic way of life, and London was being threatened by tribes of cannibals from the underground. *The Good Terrorist* (1985) describes the emergence of a rather naive group of London terrorists who are led more by emotion than by any objective grasp of their social situation. Ben, the Lovatts' fifth child in the novel, *The Fifth Child* (1988), is Lessing's prophecy of times to come. An allegorical novel, it criticizes modern liberal humanism as embodied in Ben's parents, Harriet and David Lovatt. Settled in a large Victorian house in the outskirts of London, they naively believe that they can lead a Victorian life complete with a number of children. Their complacency is devastated by the birth of their fifth child—a monster-child—who throws his parents' life out of gear. Ben is a mutant unable to adjust to the culture of his time. A regressive version of the mutant child, Joseph, in *The Four-Gated City,* Ben does not possess paranormal powers. Instead, he is like a "little troll or a hobgoblin" (*The Fifth Child* 63) who kills pet animals. His companions are punks and unemployed youths of London—misfits created by the modern world. Much like Mary Shelley's Frankenstein monster,

Ben is a metaphor for modern Western civilization. He is Yeats' rough beast finally born. While the other novels of Lessing concentrate on particular cultural forces and forms, *The Fifth Child* serves as a fitting blow to the essence of Western civilization.

Unlike *The Golden Notebook* and *The Four-Gated City, The Summer Before the Dark* (1973) is a conventional novel about a conventional English woman. Its protagonist, Kate Brown, is not a writer like Anna Wulf, nor a visionary like Martha Quest. Lessing's choice of the theme of an ordinary woman's encounter with culture is a deliberate one. In an interview with Joyce Carol Oates, conducted in October 1973, while Lessing was still writing this novel, she revealed that the source of *The Summer Before the Dark* was her keen interest and curiosity about the ordinary, conventional woman, about "the phenomenon of a woman [...] totally defined by her marriage" (Oates 877). Kate Brown is the wife of a successful jet-set neurologist and lives in Blackheath in south London with her husband and four children. She is a housewife totally devoted to her family, a "healthy, serviceable woman" (*SBD* 13) whose life has been characterized by "passivity, adaptability to others" (23). She bears the painful knowledge of her husband's casual relationships with other women, and of her children's growing indifference towards her. Kate's situation is a textbook case of the housewife's predicament as described in Ann Oakley's *The Sociology of Housework* (1974). Like the lives of the forty British housewives interviewed by Oakley in 1971, Kate's existence is fraught with dissatisfaction, monotony, loneliness and an inferiority complex (Oakley 182-83). That Kate Brown represents these women, that she is intended to be a "mid-twentieth century Everywoman" (Jong 501), is testified by Lessing's frequent reference to her in the third person. The novel is full of sentences beginning with the phrase, the opening sentence of the novel could well serve to introduce any housewife: "[a]woman stood on her back step, arms folded, waiting" (*SBD* 7). Variations on the above sentence appear nine times in the brief first chapter entitled "At Home", each sentence opening a new paragraph. The identification of Kate with all women is made explicit in one of these key sentences: "[a] woman, as she might have done any time during the past several hundred years, stood under a tree, holding a crowded tray" (12). The novel, however, is no journalistic 'novel-report, on the life of a housewife. It explores and records Kate's widening consciousness as she steps out of her roles of housewife and mother, on her growing awareness of the gap between her outer and inner selves. When Kate accepts a temporary job for the summer as translator for the organization, Global Food, she embarks on a process of deculturalization from her prescribed roles. The Browns' house is to be rented out for the summer as all its members, except Kate, are to be out of the city from June till September. Kate, who has become used, in the past twenty-five years, to identifying herself with her house, is apprehensive of leaving it:

> [...] she, this kingpin, was to be at a loose end from June to late September. With not so much as a room of her own. A very curious feeling that was, as if a warm covering had been stripped off her, as if she were an animal being flayed. (24)

This deculturalization is initially painful but Kate begins to adjust to it. As she immerses herself in her job, she experiences a relaxation she had never had in the past. Kate gradually hopes for a different future. Her transformation is an apt illustration of Oakley's belief that the "deconditioned housewife is a potential revolutionary" (Oakley 197). Kate, who had always suppressed her desire of paying attention to her personal appearance, now busies herself new clothes and dyes her hair a very dark red. She dresses up as a young woman does, "suddenly conscious of her powers of generalized attraction [...] floating in the air of general appreciation and approval [...]" (*SBD* 40). She no longer desires to be the kingpin, the pivot of the family. The small, neat, impersonal room allotted to her by the organization she works for is more endearing to her as it is appropriate for her new personality. A recurring dream symbolizes Kate's nurturance of this new self. She dreams of a seal stranded on a cold hillside and she knows that she has to reach it to the sea. As her need for individuality grows, Kate makes more effort to carry the heavy seal to its destination. A typhoid scare in London leads to a change of venue of the Global Food conference and Kate finds herself in Istambul. Away from London, she finds time and space to reflect on her past. She analyzes her married life and ponders on its injustice to herself:

> Injustice, the pain of it, had been waiting for her all these last years. But she had *not* allowed herself to feel it, or not for long. She had instead carefully tended the image of the marriage [...] she had not allowed herself to get much closer to what she had been feeling than the humorous grimace. (56, original emphasis)

Kate's is a predicament common to most women like her. Her mind has been like that of the archetypal middle-aged woman as portrayed in Rich's "Snapshots of a Daughter-in-Law": her mind had "molder[ed] like wedding cake/ heavy with useless experience" (Rich, "Snapshots" 12). When the conference is over, Kate does not return to London but goes on a holiday to Spain with a young man, Jeffery, she has met during the conference. Though Kate is aware of the limitations of this sexual relationship, it does help her come to terms with a long-buried self. She realizes that she has been a "sponge" (*SBD* 93) all along, an old nurse (95), a wounded bird or "an animal teased by her children" (99). She also feels grossly cheated of her sexuality:

> All those years were now seeming like a betrayal of what she really was. While her body, her needs, her emotions—all of herself—had been turning like a sunflower after one man, all that time she had been holding in her hands something else, the something precious, offering it in vain to her husband [...] it had never been taken, had not been noticed. (126)

Kate's inner voyage into self-realization is, however, not an easy one. Like the typical Lessing protagonist she experiences mental illness. Her appearance gradually degenerates until she becomes pale and haggard and she is easily labelled insane by onlookers. Returning to London from Spain, Kate checks into a hotel where she is repeatedly sick. The dream about the seal recurs again. The animal's present condition—it has slipped into a coma—reflects her precarious mental and physical health. But, unlike Susan Rawlings, the protagonist of Lessing's short story, "To Room Nineteen", who rents a hotel room because she too is starved of existential space, Kate does not gas herself. She leaves the expensive hotel and rents a basement flat to spend the rest of the summer. In the room in the flat, Kate confronts her sexuality, not with a man, but in the full freedom of solitude and anonymity, "alone and outside a cocoon of comfort and protection" (168). She allows herself to masturbate, using it as a "safety valve" (168), and cries in relief. Walking down the streets of London she just about manages to stop from exposing herself to a group of roadside loafers to demand sexual attention. This incident finally destroys the sedate Angle in the House in Kate Brown, turning her into a sort of Demon in the Flat. Kate's madness is not a nihilistic breaking down. Like in Anna, Martha and Lynda, its inevitable corollary is self-knowledge, a full exploration of the mind stretched to its very limit. Kate becomes aware of the workings of cultural politics on women like her. She observes her flat mate, the young Maureen, and can visualize the latter's future with the rich man she has agreed to marry for social and financial security:

> One could easily imagine them together, in their large house in Wiltshire or somewhere, deep in plentiful horses, children and dogs, everything according to the pattern, including the humorous comments on it. (240)

In the last dream about the seal, Kate sees herself sliding it into the waters of the sea and, simultaneously, she realizes that she had finally completed her journey towards understanding herself. As the summer ends, Kate prepares to join her family. In a symbolic gesture of defiance to reculturalization, she refuses to dye or dress her hair, tying it straight back, with the grey band "showing like a statement of intent" (237). It is surprising that Lorelei Cederstrom misses the point of this crucial symbolic gesture and sees Kate Brown as an "absurd Nora closing the door of introspection in order to re-enter the drawing room wearing a new hair style" (Cederstrom 145).

What Cederstrom perhaps wished was to see Kate attain the complex wholeness of an Anna Wulf or a Martha Quest. But Kate Brown is meant to be Everywoman, a representative of ordinary women who do not being to the intellectual cadre of the likes of Anna or Martha. It is a credit to Lessing that she has deliberately chosen to explore and account for the ways in which the ordinary housewife may be a victim of cultural politics and yet have the potential to encounter cultural norms and forces.

Lessing's interrogation of culture is thus inextricably bound to the individual's relation to culture. She goes way beyond the traditional idea of the term 'politics' and discovers that the mind is the most potent site and source of political action. Women like Anna, Martha, Lynda, and Kate are not humans *manqué* (Markow 88), nor are they bogged down by "an oppressive lassitude" (90). Politics is for Lessing and her women characters an assertion of their individuality. As Marilyn Webb rightly observes, "[Lessing's] politics [...] suggest that individual strengths, arising from deep understanding of the self, will tell what should be done" (Webb 15) to comprehend the complex relationship between women, culture, politics, and everyday life.

WORKS CITED

Batsleer, Janet, *et al.*, Eds. *Rewriting English: Cultural Politics of Gender and Class.* New York: Metheun, 1985.

Bronte, Charlotte. *Jane Eyre.* 1847. *Introd.* Storm Jameson. London and Sydney: Pan, 1967.

——. *Shirley.* 1849. Eds. Herbert Rosengarten and Margaret Smith. *Introd.* Margaret Smith. Oxford and New York: Oxford UP, 1981.

Carey, John L. "Art and Reality in *The Golden Notebook.*" Pratt and Dembo. 20-39.

Cederstrom, Lorelei. "Doris Lessing's Use of Satire in *The Summer Before the Dark.*" *Modern Fiction Studies* 26 (Spring 1980): 131-45.

Coote, Anna and Beatrix Campbell. *Sweet Freedom: The Struggle for Women's Liberation.* Oxford: Basil Blackwell, 1987.

Fletcher, John. "Sex, Class, Politics, and Religion." *Dictionary of Literary Biography* Vol. 15 Pt. 2. Detroit. Gale Research Company, 1985. 627-34.

Howe, Florence. "A Conversation with Doris Lessing." Pratt and Dembo. 1-19.

Jong, Erica. "Everywoman Out of Love?" *Partisan Review* XL. 3 (1973): 500-03.

Laing, R.D. *The Politics of Experience* and *The Bird of Paradise.* 1967. Harmondsworth: Penguin, 1981.

Lessing, Doris. *The Fifth Child.* New York: Knopf, 1988.

——. *The Four-Gated City.* 1969. London: Paladin-Grafton, 1990. [Referred to in parentheses as *FGC*].

——. *The Golden Notebook.* 1962. London: Paladin-Grafton, 1990 [Referred to in parentheses as *GN*].

——. *The Good Terrorist.* London: Jonathan Cape, 1985.

——. *The Memoirs of a Survivor.* 1974. London: Pan, 1976.

——. *A Ripple from the Storm.* 1958. London: Paladin-Grafton, 1990.

——. "The Small Personal Voice." *Declaration.* Ed. Tom Maschler. London: MacGibbon & Kee, 1957. [Referred to in parentheses as "SPV"].

——. *The Summer Before the Dark.* London: Jonathan Cape, 1973 [Referred to in parentheses as *SBD*].

—— . "To Room Nineteen", *To Room Nineteen: Collected Stories I.* Rpt. in *The Doris Lessing Reader.* London: Paladin-Grafton, 1991. 25-55.

Libby, Marion Vlastos. "Sex and the New Women in *The Golden Notebook.*" *Iowa Review* 5.4 (Fall 1974): 106-20.

Markow, Alice Bradley. "The Pathology of Feminine Failure in the Fiction of Doris Lessing." *Critique* XVI. I (1974): 88-100.

Millett, Kate. *Sexual Politics.* New York: Equinox, 1971.

Mulkeen, Anna M. "Twentieth-Century Realism: The 'Grid' Structure of *The Golden Notebook.*" *Studies in the Novel* 4.2 (Summer 1972): 262-74.

Musil, Caryn Tighe. "A.S. Byatt." *Dictionary of Literary Biography.* Vol. 14. Detroit: Gale Research Company, 1983. 194-205.

Oakley, Ann. *The Sociology of Housework.* 1974. Oxford: Basil Blackwell, 1988.

Oates, Joyce Carol. "A Visit with Doris Lessing." *Southern Review* IX. 4 (Oct. 1973): 873-82.

Osborne, John. *Look Back in Anger*. 1957. London: Faber and Faber, 1960. Rep. 1983.

Pickering, Joan. *Understanding Doris Lessing*. Columbia, South Carolina: U of South Carolina P, 1990.

Pratt, Annis, and L.S. Dembo, Eds. *Doris Lessing: Critical Studies*. Madison: Wisconsin P, 1974.

Rich, Adrienne. *Adrienne Rich's Poetry*. Eds. Barbara Charlesworth Gelpi and Albert Gelpi. New York and London: Norton, 1975.

——. "The Phenomenology of Anger." *Diving into the Wreck*. 1973. Rpt. in Rich, *Poetry* 68-72.

——. "Snapshots of a Daughter-in-Law." *Snapshots of a Daughter-in-Law*. 1963. Rpt. in Rich, *Poetry* 12-16.

——. "Three Conversations." Rich, *Poetry* 105-22.

——. "When We Dead Awaken: Writing as Re-Vision." *College English* XXXIV (Oct. 1972). Rpt. in Rich, *Poetry* 90-98.

Richardson, Dorothy. *Pilgrimage* IV. London: Virago, 1979.

Ruskin, John. "Of Queen's Gardens." *Sesame and Lilies*. 1865. London. Allen, 1933. 87-143.

Schweickart, Patricinio P. "Reading a Wordless Statement: The Structure of Doris Lessing's *The Golden Notebook*." *Modern Fiction Studies* 31.2 (Summer 1985): 263-79.

Spacks, Patricia Meyer, "Free Women." *Hudson Review* XXIV. 14 (Winter 1971-72): 559-73.

Stimpson, Catherine R. "Doris Lessing and the Parables of Growth." *The Voyage In: Fictions of Female Development*. Eds. Elizabeth Abel, Marianne Hirsch, and Elizabeth Langland. Hanover and London: UP of New England, 1983. 186-205.

Sukenick, Lynn. "Feeling and Reason in Doris Lessing's Fiction." Pratt and Dembo. 98-118.

Tuttle, Lisa. *Encyclopaedia of Feminism*. New York and Oxford. Facts on File, 1986.

Webb, Marilyn. "Feminism and Doris Lessing: Becoming the Men We Wanted to Marry" *Village Voice* XVIII. 14 Jan. 1973: 1.

Woolf, Virginia. "Modern Fiction." *The Common Reader: First Series*. London: Hogarth, 1962. 184-95.

Toni Morrison's *Sula* as a Feminist Novel

3

MALLIKARJUN PATIL

Toni Morrison is a great American novelist. She is a black writer. More than that, she is a feminist. Toni Morrison was born in Lorain, Ohio. She now divides her time between Rockland County, New York, and Princeton, New Jersey. She is Robert S. Goheen Professor, Council of Humanities, at Princeton University. She is the author of seven novels so far: *The Bluest Eye, Sula, Song of Solomon,* which won her the 1978 National Book Critics' Circle Award for fiction, *Tar Baby, Beloved*, which won her the 1998 Pulitzer Prize for fiction, *Jazz* and most recently *Paradise.* Toni Morrison was awarded the Nobel Prize for Literature in 1993.

Toni Morrison's novel *Tar Baby* is a beautiful novel, quite moving. The theme is that: "Into a while millionaire's Caribbean mansion come: Jadine, a graduate of the Sorbonne, art historian—an American on the run, uneducated, violent, contemptuous—an American black from small-town Florida. He is a threat to her freedom: she is a threat to his identity. . ."

The theme of Toni Morrison's *Beloved* is: "It is the mid-1800's. At sweet Home in Kentucky, an era is ending as slavery comes under attack from the abolitionists. The worlds of Halle and Paul D. are to be destroyed in a cataclysm of torment and agony. The world of Sethe, however, is to turn from one of love to one of violence and death—the death of Sethe's baby daughter Beloved, whose name is the single world on the tombstone, who died at her mother's hands, and who will return to claim retribution."

Paradise is based around eight chapters, each bearing a woman's name, each adding a different point of view to the narrative. It is set in Ruby, a fictitious black town founded by Proud, racially pure men who emerged from the fight against slavery only to find there was yet another hierarchy—this time based on gradations of skin colour—to keep them down. Yet the myth of Ruby's own racial genealogy, its piety and self-righteousness is fragile, and the women who skirt the town's boundaries, preferring to take refuge in their own company threaten to blow it apart." The novel explores the culture and religion of black race.

Toni Morrison's *Song of Solomon* is a complex, wonderfully alive and imaginative narrative. The novel is about a single family with its hundred years history.

The novel *Sula* is about the mother-daughter matriarchal relations. Sula has three pairs of women going hand in hand with one or the other. *Sula* explores women's feminine psyche.

The story opens with a description of the town called Medallion with its particular hamlet called Bottom. The little suburb is known as Bottom not for it is a down area, but it is a hilltop area inhabited by blacks. Of course, there is a valley to the town of Medallion in the state of Ohio. The suburb is known for its lively activities, which include music and banjos dance. Morrison writes of it as follows, "A shucking, knee-slapping, wet-eyed laughter that could even describe and explain how they came to be where they were." Bottom is rather a hilly area. The blacks that worked with their rich, land-owning white brethren get their shares of land on the hill though such lands are less fertile. Yet they are helpless against all kinds of injustice meted out to them in the world. Oh! People are always alive to the village activities such as Shadrack's deathly matter and Sula's wayward life.

In the second chapter just named '1919' Morrison gives an elaborate description of Shadrack, a Bottom man who participated in the World War I in France and got back home wounded. At the outset we find him in the hospital where a nurse takes care of him. Afterwards he is released and he goes to his house. He is called 'Private'. He is wild, heady and violent. He has his own cell in the Bottom. Once he is prisoned for his alcoholism. He institutes National Suicide Day for the people of Medallion. This is rather strange and funny though it is apt for the suffering blacks.

'1920' elaborates about Helene also called as Helen. She is a matriarch. She has married one seaman Wiley Wright. Helene is heady, and violent. She has egoistic nature. She has, after nine years of marriage, a daughter called Nel. Yet, 'All in all her life was a satisfactory one.'

One day Helene wants to see her grandmother at New Orleans. So both the mother and daughter take a train. Soon they face a worrying ticket collector. The white man insults her by not allowing her to go to restroom. In her enquiry Helene finds some black people in the coach, not taking any sympathy for her. So she likes to hate them. Later she finds another black woman with four children boarding the train at Tuscaloosa. The train stops at Ellisville, Hattisburg, Pontchaitrain, Slidell and finally at New Orleans.

Cecile Sabat, the grandmother of Helene had her house in New Orleans. When Helene and her daughter Nel reach they find the death of Cecile Sabat. One man, Henri Martin welcomes them. Of course, Helene's mother Rochelle speaks of the family matters. She speaks Creole. Soon Helene and Nel get back to Medallion. Nel thinks of her trip seriously. She thinks she should not go out again. But such a hard feeling does not stay with her for long. Her feeling of 'me' is strong. She remembers Sula with whom she studied at Garfield Primary. Sula's home, unlike Nel's, is a kind of public house where many things—both funny and serious—happened.

Toni Morrison writes of Sula's family graphically. The chapter '1921' is all about this. Sula's grandmother Eva Peace is a singularly woman. She married a man called BoyBoy, a tough womanizing Negro. She got three children—Hannah, Pearl and Plum (Ralph). The last one being a weakly son. Unfortunately, BoyBoy fell in the company of women and alcoholics. He did not care for the family. One day he went off to work with a carpenter in some distant place. Eva managed her house with much difficulty. Her neighbors particularly, the Suggs helped her. Eve later built a big house with many rooms and she rented several of them for money. Her house is in the Carpenter's Road in Bottom, Medallion. Once BoyBoy visits her and she does not know how to behave with him. Of course, he comes there with his mistress. Morrison speaks of black women's passion for children and their helping nature. Eva goes on sheltering many people, particularly children. She likes males specially. She likes to chat and pass her time with them. She has a passion for company. Later she shelters a boy called Tar Baby, a semi-white black man. This fellow is a heavy drinker. Meanwhile, Eva loses her one leg and works with a crutch. It is said she lost the leg deliberately and claimed insurance. People are amused of this though they never speak to her of the same.

Pearl, Eva's second daughter, marries at fourteen and moves to Flint, Michigan. Hannah, Eva's eldest daughter, is another peculiar woman in the Peace family. She is married to one Mr Rekus. Shortly she loses her husband and she, with her three-year-old daughter Sula, moves back to her mother's house in Medallion.

Morrison writes of Hannah's bad life. She writes, "Hannah simply refused to live without the attentions of a man, and after Rekus's death had a steady sequence of lovers, mostly the husbands of her friends and neighbors. Her flirting was sweet, low and guileless. Without ever a pat of the hair, a rush to change clothes or a quick application of paint, with no gesture whatsoever, she rippled with sex." She indulges in lovemaking. That way she is a debauch. Yet such things are allowed in American society.

Meanwhile, Plum who participates in the First World War returns in 1920. Like Tar Baby he is a heavy drinker. His mother is fed up of his laziness. So she bums him one day. In the chapter '1922' we find Nel and Sula befriending each other. They meet mischief making white boys, some of them Irish immigrants. Morrison says, "They were solitary little girls whose loneliness was so propound, it intoxicated them and sent them stumbling into Technicoloured visions that always included a presence, a someone, who, quite like the dreamer, shared the delight of the dream." At this time both the girls are twelve years old. They wander at the Bottom for mischief. They go to a river and find a small boy called 'Chicken Little'. They talk to it and notice that it dies soon due to drowning. Later Sula is accused for the boy's death. They all attend its funeral ceremony. In the next chapter '1923' we find Hannah asking Eva whether she loved her. The former tells yes. She tells situations where she loved her daughter. Later, for some vague reason, Hannah passes away. It is said she burns herself. It seems she was paralyzed.

In the chapter '1927' Morrison describes Helene's merriment at her daughter Nel's wedding. Nel's husband is one Mr Jude Greene who works as a waiter at the Hotel Medallion. Details about progress of the town are stated. The emotions of the newly-weds are commented upon here and there. So Part I of the novel ends with Nel's marriage.

The story of Nel and Sula continues in Part II. The first chapter of Part II is called '1937'. The people of Bottom or of Medallion are simple folks. They believe that death was as certain as birth. Sula's life does not matter much. She does not like to marry. She even picks up some bad air with her grandmother Eva. However, both the young women—Nel and Sula—live closely. Sula speaks of blacks' life when she comments upon Jude Green at Nel's house one day:

> I mean, I don't know what the fuss is about. I mean, everything in the world loves you. White men love you. They spend so much time worrying about your penis they forget their own. The only thing they want to do is cut off a nigger's privates. And if that ain't love and respect I don't know what is. And white women? They chase you all to every corner of the earth, feel for you under every bed. I knew a white woman wouldn't leave the house after 6 o'clock for fear one of you would snatch her. Now ain't that love? They think rape some one; they see you, and they don't get the rape they looking for, they scream it anyway just so the search won't be in vain. Colored women worry themselves into bad health.... (104)

The chapter '1939' has something interesting to show us. Nel and Sula separate from each other. This is because of the reason the 'young and beautiful' Sula falls in love with Nel's husband Jude Brown.

Apart from this Sula loves several others, or she sleeps with several others. Morrison writes, "They (people) said that Sula slept with white men...Every one of them imagined the scene, each according to his own predilections—Sula underneath some white man—and it filled them with choking disgust. There was nothing lower she could do, nothing filthier" (114).

Later events related to Sula include the mentioning of the life of Teapot (Betty), Mr Finley's death, Dessie's talk of Sula's trafficking with Shadrack one day and the like.

The Medallions' women gossip about Sula almost everyday. They even took care of their husbands scared of their going to Sula. They think of Eva's arrogance, Hannah's self-indulgence and Sula's having both—arrogance and indulgence. Morrison says Sula made an experiment with life. It is said, "The first experience taught her there was no other that you count on; the second that there was no self to count on either. She had no center, no speck around which to grow. In the midst of a pleasant conversation with some one she might say, 'Why do you chew with your mouth open?' not because the answer interested her but because she wanted to see the person's face change rapidly. She was completely free of ambition, with no affection for money, property or things, no greed, no desire to command attention or compliments—no ego. For that reason she felt no compulsion to verify herself—be consistent with herself." Sula liked the comedy of sex rather. She liked the variety of it.

One day Sula befriends a fine man called Ajax. He meets her everyday. He gives her gifts of all kinds. Morrison writes of Sula with Ajax for long. Sula begins to discover what possession is. Meanwhile, Sula makes trips to different places like Detroit. One day when she returns to Bottom after some illness, Nel goes to her. She gets her some medicine. Both speak of their misery. Nel complains that Sula betrayed her. Nel's grief may be seen in the following passage:

"But..." Nel held her stomach in. "But what about me? What about me? Why didn't you think about me? Didn't I count? I never hurt you. What did you take him for if you didn't love him and why didn't you think about me?" And then, "I was good to you, Sula, why don't that matter?"

The illness drags Sula to Death one may say. Sula's death is counted here:

> While in this state of weary anticipation, she noticed that she was not breathing, that her heart had stopped completely. A crease of fear touched her breast, for any second there was sure to be a violent explosion in her brain, a gasping for breath. Then she realized, or rather she sensed, that there was not going to be any pain. She did not need oxygen. She was dead.

Sula felt her face smiling. "Well, I'll be damned," she thought, "It didn't even hurt. Wait'll I tell Nel."

The author comments, "The death of Sula Peace was the best news folks up in the Bottom had had since the promise of work at the tunnel." All people did not mourn Sula's death, for she had lived an evil life. Not many people, even the blacks did go to Beechnut Cemetery. In fact, some white people buried her. Eva, whom Sula had put in Sunny dale, an old-age home, too did not mourn her granddaughter's death.

Afterwards the life-conditions in Bottom and in Medallion change. They improve, one may say. The next generation people are quite different from Sula's generation. One day Nel pays a visit to Eva Peace at Sunnydale. But their conversation runs a rough weather. Eva accuses Nel of the death of Little Chicken. Nel denies it. She just cries at the end:

> "All the same, all that time, I thought I was missing Jude." And the loss pressed down on her chest and came up into her throat. "We were girls together," she said as though explaining something. "O Lord, Sula," she cried, "girl, girl, girlgirlgirl."

"It was a fine cry—loud and long—but it had no bottom and it had no top, just circles and circles of sorrow."

Sula is a fine novel about Afro-American experience. The novel is about Sula's quest for selfhood. The element of protest is the hallmark of the novel. Sula emerges as a rebel. She is a female hero. She is a masculine character. Morrison depicts Sula as a feminist ideologue ahead of her time. Mickelson observes, "She is a rebel—one who exceeds boundaries, creates excitement, tries to break free of encroachment of external cultural forces, and challenges destiny."

REFERENCE

All the textual references are from Toni Morrison's *Sula,* Vintage, London, 1973.

Mini Narratives: A Reading of Margaret Atwood's "A Woman's Issue" and "The Animals in that Country"

4

RAJA SEKHAR PATTETI

Apart from the existence of the diversity of solitudes in the Canadian socio-literary scenario, women's voice is represented with universal authenticity in the writings of Margaret Atwood. Margaret Atwood's *Survival* (A Thematic Guide to Canadian Literature), 1972, was the first exhaustive and extensive treatise on Canadian literature. This work has aptly subscribed the theme of survival which has become pertinent in relation to Canadian sovereignty and cultural survival. Most of the works of Atwood, namely *The Edible Woman* (1970), *Surfacing* (1972), *The Journals of Susanna Moodie* (1970), *Power Politics* (1973) and even the recent *Blind Assassin* (2001) are preoccupied with feminist concerns. All the narrators in her works consciously address issues such as sexual rights, procreative rights, social and vocational rights. Most of her collections of poetry has addressed the problems of power politics at every level of existence. Her collections of poetry *The Circle Game* (1966), *The Animals in that Country* (1968), *You are Happy* (1974), *Two Headed Poems* (1978) kept the readers' consciousness alert and evolved a poetic process. The proposition here is to decipher the two representative poems of Atwood, "A Woman's Issue" and "The Animals in that Country", from the postmodern perspective of mini narrativity.

Margaret Atwood's "A Woman's Issue" remains as the poem of high voltage subjective subversion that any writer with feminist concern could dare to venture. The poem is the product of female physiology that woman celebrate in their writings. The poem evokes emotion (a complicated poetic process) than allowing the reader to express emotion. The life of the women becomes a museum, where the experiences and atrocities perpetrated are exhibited like pieces of art. Exhibit A is of the woman in spiked device: 'A woman in the spiked device that locks around the waist and between the legs, with holes in it like a tea strainer.' Woman is considered like a material net 'strainer'. Exhibit B is the picture of woman who is jammed up with wooden peg. She becomes an ineligible object for being raped: 'The woman in black with a net window to see through and a four inch wooden peg jammed up between her leg. So she can't be raped is exhibit B.' In exhibit C Atwood exposes the sterility that persists in the lives of the people and of the land. Children are considered a drain or a worry. Husbands remain hostile and incommunicative. One can find similar examples in the character of Minn in Miriam Engles' *The Honeymoon Festival* and Stacey in Margaret Laurence's *The Fire Dwellers*. In such a barren atmosphere the children are sterilized. In Margaret Laurence's *A Jest of God*, Rachel thinks she is pregnant but manages to squeeze only a tumour: 'dragged into the Bush by the midwives and made to sing while they scrape the flesh from between her legs, then tie her thighs till she scabs over and is called healed.' For each childbirth the woman is cut open. This makes men to dislike women. Some women who lose their lives in this process are buried unwept: 'The ones that die are carefully buried.' The next exhibit portrays the condition of women caught in the evil practice of prostitution. This profession engulfs the lives of many women and the causes for the pervasiveness of the profession remain obscure: 'She looks at the ceiling, listens to the door open and close. A bell keeps ringing. Nobody knows how she got here.'

Another obvious reference is Rapunzel syndrome that becomes a general pattern of living for normal woman. Atwood in *Survival* describes this syndrome: "In the Rapunzel syndrome there are four elements: Rapunzel the main character, the wicked witch who has imprisoned her (her mother or her husband, father or grandfather, the tower she is imprisoned in) the attitudes of society symbolized usually by her house and children which society says she must not abandon; and the Rescuer, a handsome prince of little substantiality who provides momentary escape" (209). Here, the rescuer is of no solution.

Atwood brings in another comparison between the Canadian landscape and the women's body. Canadian land remains no man's land, enemy territory. It is owned, fenced, occupied but never surely. An easy parallel meaning is established with the central character in *Bodily Harm* who confronts the stark realities. Here, the protagonist flees from constricting consumer society and develops a broken relationship with another alien territory. Marian in *Edible Woman* who confronts predatory and sexiest society could also be perceived from this perspective.

Atwood ends the poem by questioning the sagacity of the word 'Love': 'This is no museum, who invented the word love?' Atwood exposes the sadistic deceptions implicit in the myth of romantic love. Love with predatory and Cannibalistic connotations is abhorred. Here, Atwood parodies the traditional romantic forms of love.

The whole poem is rendered in different diction. Atwood perceives the normative language as male oriented and subscribes to the notion of French feminist theorists who posited for the existence of an 'ecriture feminine' (the term is that of French theorist Helene Cixous, from her essay 'The Laugh of the Medusa'). 'Ecriture Feminine' provides a space for a free play of meanings within the framework of loosened grammatical structures. Here, for the appropriate rendering of experiences related to 'social castration' Atwood adopts 'ecriture feminine'. On the whole the poem proves Atwood as perennial freedom fighter in an archaic realm of perpetual opposition.

Atwood's another remarkable poem "The Animals in that Country" reflects the Canadian situation to the complete extent. It is pertinent to observe that Canada was found on fur trade and it remains a hunting ground for Americans to quench their recreational fancies. The animals in the poem are the Canadians and 'that country' metaphorically stands for Canada. In Canadian literature the animal stories hold their inevitable social significance. Atwood in *Survival* is of the opinion that English animal stories are about 'social relations', Americans ones are about people killing animals and Canadians ones are about animals being killed. The rhetoric of Atwood exposes the fact that the animal stories are written by people. Indian animal stories are written by whites and they project white man's desire and fear. In this poem metamorphosis becomes a recurrent symbol and the uncomfortability of contemporary men and women with their bodies is observed as the reason for metamorphosisation.

The poem is based on anti-thesis between 'ceremonial', 'elegant', and 'heraldic'. The animals have the faces of animals. 'The ceremonial cats possessing the streets' indicates the cats becoming the household pets. The animals giving up their beastly nature and acquiring human attributes is seen in contrast to the humans playing the role of huntsmen. The humans adopt different mannerisms of using heavy coloured threads woven together to produce a scenario to attract the animals: 'the fox run politely to earth, the huntsmen standing around him, fixed in their tapestry of manners.' The death of hunted animals is embroidered with blood and given an elegant and heraldic colour. This atmosphere of hunting enables everyone to observe that animal as victim is a persistent and recurrent image. The concern of the Canadians with slaughtered and doomed animals spreads beyond the range of animal stories. In Alden Nowlan's *The Bull Moose* and Irving Layton's *The Bull Calf* animals are sacrificed and the sacrifices redeem none. Atwood is of the opinion that Canadians becoming hunters lies in their stance toward nature. In contrast, the animals assimilate human behaviour and emotions when they are hunted mercilessly, the last gaze of the hunted animals convey the haunting sign that they are really human: 'When he rolled on the sand, Sword in his heart, the teeth in his blue mouth were human—he is really man.' Atwood while being highly critical of the attitudes of Americans in taming the nature, places the Canadians in ironic framework.

Canadian literature provides abundant examples of animal victim tradition. These works symbolize the national psyche of the Canadians. Fred Bodsworth's *The Last of the Curlew* deals with rare species. It records the agony of the male curlew when female curlew is shot. Farley Mowatt's *Never Cry Wolf* is study of Arctic wolves that emerge as finest human beings. Graeme Gibson's *Five Legs* deals with mutant water buffalo with five legs. In this work, the deformity of the animals is seen with sympathetic perception. In resonance with the animal victim perception Atwood considers the death of some animals is not elegant as 'the animals have the faces of animals' and considers the life destroying sources as personal and internal.

From the postmodern sensibility these two poems contemporarily theorize the very meaning of Canadian history. These poems are mini narratives. Lyotard's definition of incredulity towards meta narratives becomes pertinent in this analysis. Atwood creates literary strategies and techniques for the survival in the diasporic Canadian situation. As the grand narratives of women's exploitation and victimisation are no longer tenable, Atwood's subscription to mini narratives could be seen as one of the literary strategies. Atwood deconstructs the unified sensibility of women's victimisation and reposes trust in mini narratives as they are provisional, contingent, temporary and relative. This could also be perceived as post-modern attack on the authority of the text. This method of dislodging the authority of text becomes authorial disempowerment. This process of disempowerment in mini narration adopts understatement prosaic voice. The blurring of the demarcation between literary genres like prose and poetry becomes an obvious postmodern element that one sees particularly in Atwood's poetry. These two poems run like prose pieces fulfilling the postmodern sensibility to the brink. On the whole, it is Atwood's elliptical style (leaving out the words or word when the meaning is understood) which proves that writing is a means of exploration and not a means of communication.

WORKS CITED

Gibson, Graeme. *Communion*. London: Anansi, 1970.

Polk, James "Lives of the Hunted: The Canadian Animal Story and the National Identity." *Canadian Literature*. Summer, 1972.

Atwood, Margaret. *Surfacing*. Toronto: McCleland and Stewart, 1979.

Atwood, Margaret. *Survival*. London: Anansi, 1972.

Atwood, Margaret. *The Edible Woman*. London: Putnam, 1958.

5

Limiting the Body, Embodying the Limit: Sexuality, Homogeneity, and Difference in the Imagined Communities of Two Canadian Women's Novels

PEDRO CARMONA RODRÍGUEZ

"They were only men, and in that paradaisal drifting they invented their mythologies of the flesh" (94), explains one of the narrators in Robert Kroetsch's *Badlands* (1982 [1975]) when referring to the itinerary of the novel's male characters in their search for the primary foundations of life in the Canadian plains of Alberta. *Badlands* is a text that, in spite of heavily relying on a male *mythology of the flesh,* posits an explicit critique of the male design of a microcosmic society whose metaphorical borders are maintained on issues of gender and sexuality. That communal politics of desire and the compulsory reproduction on which the community's survival depends leads women to occupy a role that greatly dispossesses them of their own bodies. "Possibilities for community in *Badlands* are closely tied to women and their houses," Frank Davey states, "[...] Anna Yellowbird's tipi, with the well-worn trail that connects it with Dawe's camp, suggests a sexual community, a group constituted by the common link of her body" (247).

Kroetsch's men reify women as Timothy Findley's do in *Not Wanted on the Voyage* (1996 [1984]), a text inscribed in the biblical episode of the flood and spatially enclosed within Noah's Ark. The novel dramatises the extinction and rebirth of a human community, and, consequently, it is ingrained in a social genesis somehow different from that *of Badlands*. Significantly, in Findley's fiction that rebirth also opens with the assertion of men's rights on the female body when Noah and Shem rape Emma, Japeth's wife, with the unicorn's horn. The growth and proliferation of the microcosmic society that the Ark hosts would be in jeopardy unless Emma accepts her role as reproducer and rejects Hannah's sensual touch. Emma's former refusal materialises in the closure of her vagina to Japeth, and when Noah understands the problem, he willingly solves the conflict by *opening the way* to his son: "We have solved all your problems [...]. She is able to take you, now. It was not your fault, before—but hers. This was necessary [...]"[1] (265).

In similar forms, therefore, these otherwise different and distant novels make the gendered and sexual side of the discourse of nation and community an intertext of their fictions, and thus, they participate in and enhance the prominent path that such a dimension acquired in the final quarter of the twentieth century. Indeed, the post-Cold War period brought to light a reconceptualisation of the discourses of nation and nationalism, which were affected by questions of gender and sexual orientation that produce new intersections that displace the old discourses of nation, as featured by their phallocentric nature. The gendered and sexual dimension of the nation challenges the binary partition between public and private spheres, emphasises the interrelation between masculinity, femininity and the constitution of the modern collective; and finally, as Ranchod-Nilsson and Tétreault underline, evinces the historic and recurrent recourse to the female individual for national and state consolidation[2] (*Gender* 1-17).

This paper centres on the strategies deployed by two Canadian women's novels to reflect the sexual and gender bearing on the discourses of nation and community. These texts, as Benedict Anderson (2000) would put it, delve into the forms in which the communities with which they are involved are *imagined* to eventually assert the phallic structure underlying that imaginary. In Susan Swan's *The Biggest Modern*

Woman of the World (1983) and Margaret Atwood's *The Handmaid's Tale* (1996 [1985]), the space determined by the female body and sexuality is the scene for the proliferation of mechanisms of homogeneity and difference oriented to the national/communal regeneration, since as Zillah Eisenstein affirms, "national identities shift and change. The idea of a nation is a phantasmatic imagining that misrepresents the diversity that exists within the borders it names" (35). As shown in many Canadian fictions, gender and sexual orientation prove essential in the fabrication of the national entanglement, so that stereotypical configurations of gender and sexuality are oriented to the national perpetuation, whereas certain sexual practices and gender formations are reduced to a level of otherness. The creation of the national subject and its other is mediated by the articulation of regulating desires, which link homogeneity, difference and sexuality, producing a further intersection between the public discourse of nation and the private discourse of sexuality.[3] In this way, sexuality unveils "[...] much more than a facet of human nature, the seat of pleasure and desire. It has become a principle of explanation whose effects can be discerned, in different ways, in virtually any stage and predicament of human life, shaping our capacity to act and setting the limits to what we can think and do" (Glover & Kaplan xii).

As Judith Butler affirms, the tangibility with which sexual practices materialise on the body leads us to believe that its politics govern the material bodies of its inscription (*Bodies* 1-2). Accordingly, I intend to exemplify first the conversion of the female body into a limit for the human collective and the required subordination of gender and sexuality implied in this practice. In a number of Canadian fictions written by women, the body, an intimate physical domain, has been transformed into a public frontier, homogenising its difference for the benefit of the perpetuation of the masculine narrative of nation.[4] In the process, patriarchal ideology uncovers its fundamental role in the appropriation of the female body as a site of production and reproduction. "Reinvested in limits and impermeabilities, [the body] serves as the margin joining and separating the subject and the other, the inner and the outer [...]. It is this politics of the body's borders that determines the complex relationship of individuals to their bodies, to the bodies of others, to fantasies of the founding subject, and to the body politics" (Smith 269).

It has been almost forty years since the publication of Mary Douglas' *Purity and Danger: An Analysis of the Concepts of Pollution and Taboo* (1966), where the British anthropologist concluded the existence of an equation between the functioning of the human body and that of Western societies. Like the human body, society is manufactured in the popular imaginary as a permeable entity, and therefore, subjected to a plausible contact with any organism coming from an external sphere. This accounts for the relevance given by contemporary communities to what is located in their marginal areas, to any presence likely to break up the usual development of the social and implying a further alteration of its working. Hence the present interest, for example, in the contact zones (Pratt 6), where the threatening hybrid occurs. Likewise, a great deal of attention is paid to the frontiers of the human body, as Caplan points out, making of the orifices through which matter is incorporated and expelled the object of censorship enacted on a number of individual behaviours at levels as diverse as nourishing and sexual practice ("Introduction" 14). In turn, such censorship defines and creates a norm of social acceptance. Drawing on Mary Douglas, Judith Butler states: "If the body is synecdochal for the social system *per se* or a site in which open systems converge, then any kind of unregulated permeability constitutes a site of pollution and endangerment since anal and oral sex among men clearly establishes certain kind of bodily permeabilities unsanctioned by the hegemonic order." Thus, "male homosexuality," Butler concludes, "would within such a hegemonic point of view, constitute a site of danger and pollution" (*Gender* 132).

Consequently, those behaviours that the norms marginalises as pernicious are located beyond the edge of the human collective. The body is then turned into a metonymic frontier that may allow the entrance in the social realm of threatening others or into a threshold for social relations with what lies outside the communal. Traditionally, the practices to which the body is subjected have been allied to patriarchy to impose surveillance on the female body, a historical enclave in necessity of protection from outer threats. Such a condition is partially due to the female role of biological reproducer of the community (Yuval-Davies 27), to which I briefly turn now.

In Canada, such vigilance on the female body became apparent in the enactment of the Janet Smith Bill that forbade immigrant Chinese men to work beside white women. The origin of the segregationist decision was in the murder of a white woman, Janet Smith, allegedly committed by a Chinese, though never solved (Chan).[5] The promulgation of the act was a racist attempt to avoid the contact between the theoretically external to the community with the reproductive vehicle of the white sector that acquired in this way a presumed coherence in terms of skin colour. The same racial intertext is present, for instance, in any condemnation of miscegenation, which simultaneously strengthens the assumption that "nationhood is constructed in and through psychic identities that institutionalise difference." According to Kristeva, "[people] live and experience their identity through their bodies; the physical and psychic knowing of their sex, gender and race. Women are the boundary subjects defining this process" (35).

The appropriation of the female body for being the biological supporter of the collective exploits the purely reproductive dimension of female sexuality, while it denies or relegates the existence of any other. As a consequence, the need to reclaim the right to decide on the female subject's will to reproduction and sexual pleasure occupied the centre of the former feminist agenda (Yuval-Davies 22). Yet, in spite of being the element for the biological expansion of the collective, women have historically been constrained to the domestic space, a circumscription additionally determined by the husband's authority, which means that women have been doubly displaced, in the public as well as in the private sphere. The reason for this double submission can be found in a historical otherness of confusing origins, but contributed by several overlapping discourses like those of science and religion.[6] The obscure origins of this gendered otherness reside in the very genesis of patriarchy, whose cornerstone resides in biological difference; in other words, in women's capacity to bear children and in their minor physical might. Women do not form a minority group, or a religious or cultural community marked by its cohesion, neither do they have a similar ethnic origin (Darias Beautell 158; Balibar 56; Valcárcel).

The difficulty to identify the cause of female ancestral otherness and the subsequent oppression it engenders leads to think that it may be heir to the structural organisation of any primitive society based on the survival of the fittest. Within this schema women are automatically ascribed to the domestic, subjugated to male authority and, in parallel, cherished for their reproductive capacities. The necessity and denial of the female subject reveals the contradictory functioning of patriarchy, for which the female subject oscillates between the other and the same by means of a convenient movement of the fundamental categories of binary identification. Far from being permanently encapsulated in a hermetic otherness, the female figure fluctuates among positions, which allows for its situation as border and basis of the collective. This position illustrates the mutability and internal instability of the pair subject/other, and the transformation of otherness into similarity for the welfare of the nation; but also, once its difference is reduced, the conversion of the female body into a border zone regulating the communal interaction with the marginal presence beyond its demarcations. The pliability of those borders permits us to observe the complex, sometimes paradoxical, enclave occupied by women in the fictions under scrutiny.

The vested interest in female difference for the perpetuation of the national/ist zeal is dramatised in Susan Swan's novel *The Biggest Modern Woman of the World* (1983), where the fictionalisation of Anna Haining Swan's voice immerses us in an autobiographical narration of a vital period between 1846 and 1888, shortly before Anna's death at the end of the 19th century.[7] As she announces, her narration is frequently interrupted by fragments extracted from other discourses and interspersed with her personal rendering: perspectives provided by her friends, husbands or newspaper clippings, which, taken as a whole, come to decentralise the narrative domain of autobiography and come to constitute an angle for comparison and contradiction with the data Anna brings out when intending to ensure her authority and property of the enunciation. In this way, she tells:

> Now I am in full voice [...] blow my own horn [...] spieling the way I used to for P.T. Barnum, Queen Victoria and all the normals who came to my performances after I grew up into an eight-foot giantess who toured North America and the Continent. [...] What really happened to THE BIGGEST MODERN WOMAN OF THE WORLD in a never-before-revealed autobiography that contains testimonial and documents by friends and associates [...].[8] (2)

In the novel, the nationalist and mercantilist appropriation of Anna's body enters in conflict with her will to affirm her dominance on her own corporality. Clearly, Swan's *abnormal* bodily dimensions—"8'1" in bare feet" (2)—set her apart from her neighbours and brothers, who exploit her potential commercially and scientifically. As a child, her neighbour, the midget Hubert, turns her into the object of his erotic and perverse games, and, once Anna starts her pseudo-scientific worldwide talks, Hubert boycotts her by reproducing the impressions of his exploratory meetings with the child Annie. "Birth canal—seventeen inches—the longest in history!," claims Hubert once disappointed and despised by the giantess. "I barely tolerated Hubert," explains Anna, "who acted as if he had special rights to my friendship since he had taken my virginity with an icicle" (37).

Anna is always aware of her obvious difference, and, although at the beginning and the end of her narrated life, she intends to reduce that difference to accommodate to the dictum of the majority; she also employs that difference to articulate a personal space immune to the assimilative interest.

Whereas initially her unaccepted difference leads her to hanker after a man taller than her, later she drinks the Nelvana fraud-potion to diminish her height and be similar to her husband Apollo. On the contrary, her physical peculiarity allows her to reclaim back her sexuality unburdened by the national, reproductive will. The discovery and preservation of her sexual pleasure locate her on the margin of the masculinist national appropriation, which eventually makes irreversible prey to her as it also did of Anna's mother. Emphasising the relevance of her sexual joy, Anna temporarily reverts the power enacted on her by scientific and nationalist discourses intent on transforming her body into the basis of a new race of North Americans by means of her union with the US giant Martin Bates and the Canadian Angus McAskill. In the course of her life Anna does not find a man able to sexually please her, and conscious of her submissive role in any intercourse with her husbands, remains silent. Nevertheless, in incorporating such experience in her autobiography, she draws our attention to that evident silence and her no less evident lack of satisfaction with her bedfellows. Simultaneously, she differentiates her pleasure from any sexual act patriarchally conceived and oriented to penetration and reproduction, and very much the same does she with the concentration of her sexuality on a single organ, to favour instead a dispersed, multiple and more complex sexuality. "At fifteen, I didn't know that I was as much in charge of my sexual ecstasy as the man," Swan points out. "I imagined it was something the male of the species did to the female and I didn't connect it to the fumbling which Momma had surprised me at that night in the shanty. Had I known I had shown Angus how to rub me" (58).

In spite of her multiple attempts, seldom can Anna avoid the dynamics of the national appropriation of her body. The Canadian national discourse as much as the post-colonial discourse of North America envision Anna as the metonymic frontier of a new nation that tries to be different from the one that originated them (LeBihan). While in her British tour, Anna asserts: "for a nation that would fit into a Canadian lake, the Brits are an arrogant people" (229), which establishes an immediate parallelism between the Canadian geographical vastness, as opposed to the British reduced, metropolitan insularity, and Anna's physical dimensions, the giantess herself internalises the Canadian specificity to make herself distinct from her American husband and stop the neo-colonialist spirit of that place where she spends most of her life, the United States: "[w]e are a country of two nations," she reflects. "And we are not part of the American empire. The ability to function without a national consensus in the Canadas is a mystery who cannot fathom a system that isn't modelled on theirs" (265). However, while married to the irascible Bates, Anna assumes the role of the country where she was born in relation to the States, and thus:

> Anna [...] has been replaced by a wifely manipulator whose sole purpose is moderating the behaviour of her husband [...]. I feel I am acting out America's relationship to the Canadas. Martin is the imperial ogre while I play the role of genteel mate who believes that if everyone is well-mannered, we inhabit a peaceable kingdom. That is the national dream of the Canadas, isn't it? [...] Indeed, to be from the Canadas, is to feel as women feel—cut off from the base of power. (274)

Indeed, Anna loses the scarce power she might have wielded when she falls in Bates' hands and becomes the centre of his new North American nation. In an entry of "Species Development, or a Tract towards Continual Anatomical Wonders" written on 25th of April, 1875, Bates refers to his idea, and during Dr. Naughton's medical exploration of Anna, affirms: "Americans are destined to grow into a species of giants. [...] [Naughton] was impressed with my interest in the reproduction possibilities of the giantess and agreed to let me view the examination after we imbibed some bourbon in the smoker. 'The things I do in the name of science'" (170). However, despite the potentialities appreciated by Bates, Anna does not have children: in 1872, her daughter with Martin is stillborn, and later, in 1878, Anna gets pregnant by Apollo when married to Martin and their son dies shortly after being born. In this way, her contribution to the new race of Americans and their promising nation is non-existent.

The Biggest Modern Woman of the World shows three stages in the transformation of Anna's abnormal and feminine body into a national prop and a limit. First, the diagnosis of an evident difference and its following isolation; then, the nationalist and mercantilist exploitation of that difference, and finally, the use of Anna's body as a vehicle for the biological reproduction of the nation. Only the relevance Anna gives to her sexual pleasure, as independent from her role of a reproducer, partially neutralises the effects of those discourses that reify her body. On her physical domain, two contrary impulses coexist, sexualisation as exploited by Hubert, for example, and the pathologisation of Anna's sexuality and reproductive dimension concerning Apollo and Bates. Anna defies the actions of those discourses by means of her autoerotic practices, and turns her body into a refuge from them. Hence the similarities that she exhibits with Atwood's protagonist in *The Handmaid's Tale* to I pay attention in the following pages.

In *The Handmaid's Tale,* Atwood draws on the dystopian tradition started by George Orwell's *1984* (1949) and Aldous Huxley's 1958 novel *Brave New World* (Ingersoll 1998).[9] Gilead is a society restructured after a nuclear catastrophe, which has brought about a radicalisation of precepts like maternity. All in all, familiar values or the family as institution are a privilege exclusively enjoyed by those having a certain social status. Such is the case of the commanders in charge of any of the social units forming Gilead. What distinguishes Atwood's novel from Orwell's and Huxley's productions is a distinctly feminine standpoint, as the text centres on the patriarchal imposition of the maternal experience on women, and the national appropriation of the handmaids' bodies. After her arrival in the Commander Fred's house, the protagonist is renamed as Offred, a name that, as composed of Of- and -Fred, would indicate either her belonging to the commander (*Handmaid* 318); or as composed by of- and -red would point out the red colour that the handmaids compulsorily wear (Givner 59).[10]

The novel is divided in two distinct parts, whose relation to each other cogently evinces the struggle to homogenise the female individual and her body, and the articulation of personal resistance against the state's apparatus. In the first of them, Offred reconstructs her experience in Gilead and subverts in and by her narrative act her silence and subordination.[11] The Gileadean society of classes and coloured uniforms turns Offred into one of the handmaids destined to bear children, though lacking legal or affective rights on her offspring, as it also happens with her own body: Offred is forbidden to remember her marriage with Luke or their daughter; the legal code that Offred and her commander repeatedly transgress strictly bans love relations between members of different castes. Offred enters in the territory of Gileadean criminality in her meetings with the sentinel Nick, with the commander, and finally in accepting Serena Joy's, the commander's wife, bribery to let Nick impregnate her and deceive the similarly sterile commander.

In spite of all the contradictions in Offred's tale, hers is the only testimony that provides an insight of this society that deprives women of her will to turn them into reproductive bodies, an oppression partially accomplished by other women. From the *Wives,* like Serena Joy, to the *Marthas* or *Aunts,* all these women participate in the oppression of other women situated in an inferior social rank. Offred reverts this authority whose basis is the female body, by retaining her personal identity and crosses the frontiers of Gileadean society in several ways. First, she overlooks the social division into castes, and being a handmaid, gets in touch with the guards and the very commander, while disposing freely of her body. Although Villegas López holds that "[l]a única resistencia que Offred opone para frenar la disolución total de su identidad es su negativa a revelar su nombre, un secreto que se convierte para ella en una forma de supervivencia" (126), it seems that the handmaid enjoys certain agency, which goes beyond the almost passive resistance proposed. Her uniform notwithstanding, her individuality is clearly stated in several occasions (York). Offred never takes part in the cathartic acts like the *salvaging,* consisting in the public lynching of the criminals, and no less important, Offred escapes from Gilead, from its reproductive mechanics, despite of which the aseptic sexual intercourses have left an imprint in Offred and her text:

> My arms are raised; [Serena Joy] holds my hands, each of mine in each of hers. This is supposed to signify that we are one flesh. One being. What it really means is that she is in control, of the process and thus of the product. [...] My red skirt is hutched up to my waist, though no higher. Below it the Commander is fucking. What he is fucking is the low part of my body. I do not say making love, because this is not what he's doing. Copulating too would be inaccurate, because it would imply two people and only one is involved. Nor does rape cover it: nothing is going on here that I haven't signed up for. There wasn't a lot of choice but there was some, and this is what I chose. [...] Arousal and orgasm are no longer thought necessary; they would be a symbol of frivolity merely, like jazz garters or beauty spots: superfluous distractions for the light minded. Outdated. It seems odd that women once spent such time and energy reading about such things, thinking about them, worrying about them, writing about them. They are so obviously recreational. [...] He comes at last, with a stifled groan as of relief. Serena Joy, who has been holding her breath, expels it. The Commander who has been propping himself on his elbows, away of our combined bodies, does not permit himself to sink down into us. He rests a moment, withdraws, recedes, rezippers. He nods, then turns and leaves the room, closing the door with exaggerated care behind him, as if both of us are his ailing mother. (*Handmaid* 104-06)

In opposition to the investment in autobiographical authority in the first section of the novel, the second part is an analysis of Offred's narration as archaeological artefact. In a convention held on Gileadean life and customs, and in the course of a lecture whose proceedings we read, Professor Pieixoto offers a dissertation on the illicit recordings constituting Offred's narrative, already presented in the novel. Pieixoto attributes the denomination *The Handmaid's Tale* to a pun on words that, following Geoffrey Chaucer, his colleague Wade invented. Playing on the phonic resemblance between *tale* and *tail,* Wade relates Offred's narrative to the relevance given to the penis—the *tail*—in Gilead, "that being, to some extent, the bone, as it were of contention, in that phase of Gileadean society of which our saga treats" (*Handmaid* 313).

Yet such a parallelism obviates, the constricting role of the phallus in the organisation of Gilead, since as Elizabeth Grosz comments, "the penis takes on the function of the phallus because it is a mark or a trace that is able to signify, indeed, produce the exclusion of half the population" (121). All in all, thanks to Pieixoto we know that Gilead is geographically located in the area of New England, and that the recordings were done by one of the handmaids that fled through the clandestine escape route, "the Underground Femaleroad" to Canada (*Handmaid* 315).[12] Nevertheless, Pieixoto's text notably complicates Offred's autobiographical space, and, especially, the document's authenticity. First, in unveiling the problems of transmission implicit in the recorded text, Pieixoto breaks up the lineal consideration on the creation and circulation of historical data, which also does away Offred from the metafictive mood her text adopts; and then, Professor Pieixoto's words displace Offred's testimony to be centred on the commander's identity and personality, which reduces the handmaid and her experience to the silence of the dehumanising patriarchy of Gilead. Despite her escape, Offred and her text are prey to a different will to objectification by means of Pieixoto's concern with textual closure, as opposed to the woman's narrative.

In spite of the many differences that their respective texts present, Offred and Anna Swan are related to one another by the appropriation of their bodies articulated by the phallocentric narrative of nation. They witness how their sexuality is reduced to mere reproduction, as they both enjoy a questionable power to perpetuate the collective, biologically speaking. That power, however, enslaves women as an example of the contradictory working of patriarchy. Hence Offred's saying: "I am too important, too scarce, for that. I am a national resource" (*Handmaid* 75). In *The Biggest Modern Woman of the World*, Anna Swan witnesses how her evident difference is reduced to bring her to the position of supporter of a new race of Americans willing to dissociate themselves from their colonial linkage to the British mother country. Anna consents the grafting of this national will on her body, from which she partially releases in giving prominence to the pleasurable sphere of her sexuality detriment to her reproductive mission. Her pleasure distorts the appropriation of her body and neutralises the functioning of the national overwhelming power. Similar mechanisms constitute the basis of the social organisation in Atwood's Gilead, where personal identity and individual will are wiped out. Offred's individuality and that of her peers is destroyed by the homogeneous reduction provided by their reproductive commitment. Offred preserves her identity and partially recovers her body by trespassing the limits of the physical community and the limits between castes, by establishing sexual and affective relations with male members belonging to other classes. In Gilead, as Coral Ann Howells asserts, "sex and gender are made to coincide completely, and as a consequence instabilities of gender difference are suppressed as deviations from nature's norm" (64). The commander himself, while talking to Offred, reveals that the fundamentalist theocracy of Gilead is a reaction against the society that proliferated at the end of the 20th century, some decades which, according to Fred, "[...] were just an anomaly, historically speaking, [...] just a fluke. All we've done is return things to Nature's norm" (*Handmaid* 232). And, as the uncertain origin of patriarchy suggests, the commander's natural society adopts the survival of the fittest as motif, and in the resulting society, women, as the marked element of the binary opposition, aspire to reproduce biologically and perpetuate the source of their collective oppression.

In different forms, Swan's and Atwood's protagonists try to cease the national homogenisation of their bodies to transform them either into the biological bearers of the nation or into its limit. Anna Swan reacts with the discovery and preservation of her autoerotic pleasure, while Offred resigns the role given to her by Gilead and challenges patriarchy from inside and outside that society. The individuality that Offred preserves and treasures allows her to enjoy her sexuality and disregard a maternal imposition to finally leave Gilead, the instauration of homogeneity and the persecution of difference.

Significantly, the two texts employ autobiographical forms to uphold the individuation of their protagonists, to support their dissent as regards the national, gender and sexual homogenisation. Swan's memories and Offred's recordings register in addition the heteronormative attempt to mould the sexualities and gender configurations of the protagonists to agree with the purpose of national regeneration. Yet the autobiographical domain erected by Swan and Offred decides on preserving female sexuality from the national anxieties of reproduction. Aware of the individuation implicit in the act of writing autobiographically and the power it conveys, Offred, while handling the commander's pen in one of their clandestine meetings, says: "The pen between my fingers is sensuous, alive almost, I can feel its power, the power of the words it contains." To conclude later in a pun on words that resorts to Freudian psychoanalysis: "[P]en is Envy, quoting another Centre motto, warning us away from such objects. And they were right, it is envy. Just holding it is envy. I envy the Commander his pen" (*Handmaid* 196). Playing on *pen* and *penis,* Offred interweaves the act of writing, the maternal-filial relation and the girl's approach to the paternal presence. Realising the lack of penis on her body, the girl departs from the mother, blames on that figure her bodily lack and despises the maternal body for showing the same lack, while turning the father into the desired object. Once the girl notices that her lack of penis cannot be amended, in what Freud termed *penis envy,* the girl substitutes that will for the desire to have a baby. The thorough critiques that this definition of the female body as incorporating a biological lack gained for Freud notwithstanding (Mitchell; Chodorow), no one discusses, socially speaking, the importance of the penis to open or close access to the phallus, since the penis is not only a real organ, but "becomes an imaginary object dividing the sexes according to its presence or absence, possessed by some, desired by others." Hence, "[it] functions as a symbolic object [...] between the sexes" (Grosz 121). In her comment, Offred is aware of her place as other with respect to the essential signifier of the phallus. And in claiming her identity apart from this otherness, she, like Anna, interrupts the national phallocracy and its fierce assimilation of difference, while revealing its production of obligatory homogeneity.

NOTES AND REFERENCES

1. The incident is part of the conspicuously violent sexual politics of Findley's fictions. Thus, whereas the owner of the local supermarket molests the child Hooker Winslow in *The Last of the Crazy People* (1967), and in *The Wars* (1977) Robert Ross is raped by his fellow officers in the Canadian troops during World War I. In *Pilgrim* (1999) Da Vinci forcefully impregnates Elisabetta Gherardini and Jung does not censor his thoughts on raping his pregnant wife. Davey interprets these events as typical of what he terms misdirected sexuality (126), or the signifier that encodes the impotence of a homosexual world repressed by the dominant heteronorm, violence being the response to repression and a futile attempt of that world to highlight its existence. Nevertheless, I would rather agree, though partially, with Dickinson in considering it as part of a violent economy that materialises the phallus in the penis (49). In this context, the forceful possession of the other reinvigorates one's own identity. Dickinson's opinion is also problematic inasmuch as it overlooks the victim's and the criminal's sexual identities.
2. Yuval-Davies is more assertive when establishing the role of women in the modern national community as "bearer of the collective" (27). For Tracey Sedinger, the tension between feminist demands and the masculine hegemony in the discourse of nation has resulted in the tendency to imagine the feminine as a collective willing to part with the national consolidation (53).

3. In novels like Margaret Atwood's *The Edible Woman* (1969) and *Alias Grace* (1996) or Jane Urquhart's *Away* (1993) the atypical gender configuration into which the protagonist is encapsulated is the reason to displace her to a realm of otherness whose existence permits the binary masculine/feminine to survive on a postulate of normality/abnormality. In turn, such a precept is established on premises of sexual dissidence in fictions like Timothy Findley's *Famous Last Words* (1981) and *Spadework* (2001), or Wayson Choy's *The Jade Peony* (1995).
4. Significantly, whereas the narrative of national belonging is masculine and masculinist (Martin Lucas 163), the nation is usually produced as a female entity, a mother or a wife, a female body either in need of penetration or in need of protection not to be penetrated. "Woman has often represented in imaginary form the nation," Tracey Sedinger affirms, "but because women form a paradoxical class whose solidarity cannot be forged through symbolic identifications, the nation-trope remains unsuitable for the representation of women as a social collective" (54). The national construction in the feminine ensures the existence and preservation of an entity that can be mastered and likely to accept the imposition of male sovereignty (Eisenstein 35-53; Howells; McClintock; Yuval-Davies). In turn, Anthony Easthope states in this context, "[...] nationalism is masculine in the way it marks such a hard line between inside and outside, treating the body and the ego as fixed, self-sufficient." For him, nationalism "fits perfectly with the masculine ego and the masculine body, so that each overlaps and confirms the other" (56).
5. A number of fictions produced by the Chinese-Canadian community and chronologically situated in this period include references to Janet Smith. Such is the case of Sky Lee's *Disappearing Moon Cafe* (1990). The articulation of the law took place in a sexual and social context deeply influenced by the ideas put forward by Havelock Ellis. In the six volumes forming his *Studies in the Psychology of Sex* (1913), Ellis manufactured female sexuality as irremediably subordinated to the masculine one. Thus, pairs like agency/passivity and conqueror/conquered structured a heterosexual intercourse, the first element corresponding to a male ascription. Force is never delegitimated to consummate the conquest and there is a certain emphasis on the role of victim attributed to women,

who, nevertheless, enjoy being conquered. Much of the male arousal rests on this feature of submission of the female counterpart, according to Ellis (Jackson 57). Paternalism and protection underlie the promulgation of any similar law, which reifies the female body turning it into a centre of possession and pleasure, and adopting the narrative of the erotisation of female oppression (Jackson 52-81). This unveils itself as an entanglement of social and historical circumstances whose presence can be detected back to Rousseau's work and even earlier (Seidler).

6. Eva's consideration as the source of original sin in persuading Adam to eat from the banned tree directly influenced the negativity that the Catholic cult injected in women's subjectivity. The shadows of that delegitimation can still be perceived in the hierarchical structure of the Catholic clergy, whose more relevant posts are occupied by men. In turn, scientific discourses brandished physical might to situate women in a rank scale of inferiority. When Europe entered in touch with the so-called *New World,* Carabí highlights, "el camino para afirmar la supremacía de la raza blanca fue desvalorizar al 'otro,' conferirle un sentido de inferioridad y crear la mentalidad de esclavo" ("Construyendo" 16; Young 90-117). From that moment on, gender and race contrived a double axis of difference that strengthened the inferiority of non-white women. The sequels of this dangerous alliance were apparent sometime ago, when France authorised the return to South Africa of Saartjie Baartman's corpse. After the massacre of her people, the Khoisan, Saartjie was enslaved by a Dutch settler and later kidnapped by a British sailor, who in 1810 took her to London and presented her as a natural wonder for the *abnormal* dimensions of her body. After her death in Paris in 1816, the body of the Venus Hotentote was exhibited at several museums, in which her sexual organs, still missing, were the greatest attraction (Lamprecht).

7. In her preface to the novel, Susan Swan points out that the similarity between her surname and that of the giantess could unveil common ancestors beyond the frontiers of the British Isles from which their families migrated to Canada. Susan Swan's ancestors are Irish whereas Anna's are Scotch. Swan, however, affirms that the Swans settled in the islands after leaving Scandinavia, and through this transcontinental, transcultural and transoceanic genealogy the Swan-to-Swan

relation transcends the frontiers of Ireland, Scotland and Canada and materialises in a continuum of subsequent migrations.

8. Anna's acquisition of narrative consciousness is highly reminiscent of the picaresque tradition. First, she opens with a retrospective narration from the present and from a place of social stability; second, there is the promise of unveiling information so far unknown; and all this is done in a text that mixes mordacity and the poignant circumstances deriving from human exploitation (del Prado Biezma *et al.* 100-02). The beginning of Anna's narration tries to generate in the potential reader an interest that propels him/her to the capitalist consumption of the text, thus echoing the same capitalist zeal that has objectified Anna's body. As Steedman reveals, situating the lives of *pícaras* and women sentenced to prison as the first autobiographical attempts interrogates the presumed humanist origin attributed to this narrative mode by focusing on issues of class and gender.
9. Indeed the dystopian is a literary mode in which Atwood seems to be comfortable, as attested by her latest novel to date, *Oryx and Crake* (2003). Within one of its sub-plots, her previous fiction, *The Blind Assassin* (2000), also presents the dystopian society of Zycron, where ill-abused children become mercenary murderers, virgins are mutilated and eventually sacrificed and spiritual leaders maintained in a declining society under the siege of foreign barbarians.
10. *The Handmaid's Tale* has inspired a number of recent varied productions. In 1990, Volker Schlöndorff directed the movie based on the novel, starring Natasha Richardson, Aidan Quinn, Faye Dunaway and Robert Duvall as the Commander. In the film, Atwood's Offred is rebaptised as Kate, which diminishes part of the identity problematics found in the novel. In 1993, Paul Bentley transformed the novel into an opera in which Paul Ruders composed the music. The premiere took place in March of 2000 at the Royal Theatre of Copenhagen, in Denmark.
11. *Reconstruction* is the term that fits most into Offred's text. As Pieixoto explains, Offred's narrative has been recorded *a posteriori,* once the handmaid escapes from Gilead, and, consequently, much of it depends on her memory and her will to accurately reproduce the events. Offred indicates repeatedly

that the events might *not* have happened like she says, and never does she conceals her fabrication of the facts. Thus, after narrating one of her sexual intercourses with Nick, Offred states: "I made that up. It didn't happen that way. Here is what happened (*Handmaid* 273), but there is no certainty on the veracity of what Offred tells next, as she makes it clear (*Handmaid* 275). The same happens in some other occasions like Moira's presumed getaway from Gilead (*Handmaid* 262).

12. As Villegas López thinks, the novel is clearly founded on the conservative phanatism that invaded the USA in the 1980s, in the triumph of certain traditionalism and the decline of a number of feminist standpoints. Ronald Reagan's presidency witnessed the resurgence of the nuclear family as institution, an iron-fisted opposition to pro-abortion lobbies and the restriction of the female presence in the professional sphere. The novel also exploits the historical relations between Canada and the United States, and thus, the runaway handmaids seem to follow the tracks of the slaves that used the railway to leave for Canada in the 19th century. It is no accident either that the League pro-Women is in the novel established in Great Britain, which in the 1980s lived a remarkable outburst of feminisms. Finally, the geographical location of Gilead, somewhere between Massachusetts and Maine, reminds us of the Puritan zeal which led to the witch hunting (Howells 63). Atwood affirmed that the American society of the eighties inspired her project, and pessimistically concluded: "If you see someone walking toward a hole in the ground and you want them to fall into it, you don't say anything" (cited in Howells 57).

WORKS CITED

Anderson, Benedict. *Imagined Communities: Reflections on the Origin and Spread of Nationalism.* 1983. London: Verso, 2000.

Ashley, Kathleen *et al.*, Eds. *Autobiography and Postmodernism.* Amherst: The University of Massachusetts Press, 1994.

Atwood, Margaret. *The Handmaid's Tale.* 1985. London: Vintage, 1996.

——. *The Edible Woman.* 1969. New York: Anchor Books & Doubleday, 1998.

——. *Alias Grace*. Toronto: Seal, 1996.

——. *The Blind Assassin*. London: Bloomsbury, 2000.

——. *Oryx and Crake*. 2003. London: Virago, 2004.

Balibar, Etienne. *Masses, Classes, Ideas: Studies on Politics and Philosophy Before and After Marx*. Trans. James Swenson. New York: Routledge, 1994.

Butler, Judith. *Gender Trouble: Feminism and the Subversion of Identity*. London: Routledge, 1990.

——. *Bodies that Matter: On the Discursive Limits of 'Sex'*. New York: Routledge, 1993.

Caplan, Pat, Ed. *The Cultural Construction of Sexuality*. 1987. London: Routledge, 1991.

Caplan, Pat. "Introduction." Caplan 1-30.

Carabí, Ángels. "Construyendo nuevas masculinidades: Una introdución." Segarra and Carabí 15-27.

Chan, Anthony B. *Gold Mountain: The Chinese in the New World*. Vancouver: New Star Books, 1983.

Chodorow, Nancy. *The Reproduction of Mothering: Psychoanalysis and the Sociology of Gender*. Los Angeles (Ca): University of California Press, 1978.

Choy, Wayson. *The Jade Peony*. Vancouver: Douglass & McIntyre, 1995.

Cosslett, Tess *et al.*, Eds. *Feminism and Autobiography: Texts, Theories, Methods*. London: Routledge, 2000.

Darias Beautell, Eva. *Shifting Sands: Contemporary Theories and Canadian Fiction*. New York: Edward Mellen Press, 2000.

Davey, Frank. *Post-National Arguments: The Politics of the Anglophone-Canadian Novel Since 1967*. Toronto: University of Toronto Press, 1993.

Dickinson, Peter. *Here is Queer: Nationalisms, Sexualities, and the Literatures of Canada*. Toronto: University of Toronto Press, 1999.

Del Prado Biezma, Javier, *et al. Autobiografia y modernidad literaria*. Cuenca: Servicio de Publicaciones de la Universidad de Castilla-La Mancha, 1994.

Easinwood, Peter *et al.*, Eds. *Difference and Community: Canadian and European Cultural Perspectives*. Amsterdam: Rodopi, 1996.

Easthope, Anthony. *Englishness and National Culture*. London: Routledge, 1999.

Eisenstein, Zillah. "Writing Bodies on the Nation for the Globe." Ranchod-Nilsson and Tétreault 35-53.

Findley, Timothy. *Famous Last Words*. 1981. Markham (Ontario): Penguin, 1982.

——. *Not Wanted on the Voyage*. 1984. Toronto: Penguin, 1996.

——. *Pilgrim*. 1999. London: Bloomsbury, 2000.

——. *Spadework*. 2001. London: Faber & Faber, 2002.

Givner, Jessie. "Names, Faces and Signatures in Margaret Atwood's *Cat's Eye* and *The Handmaid's Tale*." *Canadian Literature* 133 (1992): 56-75.

Glover, David and Cora Kaplan. *Genders*. London: Routledge, 2000.

Grosz, Elizabeth. *Jacques Lacan: A Feminist Introduction*. London: Routledge, 1990.

Howells, Coral Ann. *Private and Fictional Words: Canadian Women Novelists of the 1970s and 1980s*. London: Methuen, 1987.

Ingersoll, Earl G. "Margaret Atwood's *The Handmaid's Tale* as a Self-Subverting Text." Mauguiére 103-10.

Jackson, Margaret. "Facts of Life or the Erotisation of Women's Oppression? Sexology and the Social Construction of Heterosexuality." Caplan 52-81.

Kristeva, Julia. *Nations without Nationalism*. 1990. Trans. / Intro. Leon S. Roudiez. New York: Columbia U.P., 1993.

Kroetsch, Robert. *Badlands*. 1975. Toronto: General Paperbacks, 1982.

Lamprecht, Andrew. "Saartjie Baartman." *Culture and the Arts* 3 (2002): www.saculturalheritage.org/amagugu2/baartman.htm

LeBihan, Jill. "Freaks and Others: *The Biggest Modern Woman* and the World." Easinwood 185-96.

Lee, Sky. *Disappearing Moon Cafe*. Vancouver: Douglas & McIntyre, 1990.

Martín Lucas, María Belén. "Mujer y nación: construcción de las identidades." Suárez Briones *et al.* 163-77.

Mauguiére, Bénédicte, Ed. *Cultural Identities in Canadian Literature/ Identités culturelles dans la literature canadienne.* New York: Peter Lang, 1998.

McClintock, Anne. *Imperial Leather: Race, Gender and Sexuality in the Imperial Contest.* New York: Routledge, 1995.

Mitchell, Juliet. *Psychoanalysis and Feminism.* 1974. London: Penguin, 1990.

Pratt, Mary Louise. *Imperial Eyes: Travel Writing and Transculturation.* London: Routledge, 1992.

Ranchod-Nilsson, Sita and Mary Ann Tétreault, Eds. *Women, States and Nationalism.* London: Routledge, 2000.

——. "Gender and Nationalism: Moving Beyond Fragmented Conversations." Ranchod-Nilsson and Tétreault 1-17.

Sedinger, Tracey. "Nation and Identification: Psychoanalysis, Race, and Sexual Difference." *Cultural Critique* 50 (2002): 40-73.

Segarra, Marta and Ángels Carabí, Eds. *Nuevas masculinidades.* Barcelona: Icaria, 2000.

Seidler, Victor J. "Reason, Desire, and Male Sexuality." Caplan 82-112.

Smith, Sidonie. "Identity's Body." Ashley *et al.* 266-92.

Steedman, Carolyn. "Enforced Narratives: Stories of Another Self." Cosslett *et al.* 25-39.

Suárez Briones, Beatriz *et al.*, Eds. *Escribir en femenino: poéticas y políticas.* Barcelona: Icaria, 2000.

Swan, Susan. *The Biggest Modern Woman of the World.* Toronto: Lester & Orpen Dennys Ltd., 1983.

Urquhart, Jane. *Away.* Toronto: McClelland & Stewart, 1993.

Valcárcel, Amelia. *La politica de las mujeres.* Madrid: Cátedra, 1997.

Villegas López, Sonia. *Mujer y religión en la narrativa anglófona contemporánea.* Huelva: Universidad de Huelva, 1999.

Young, Robert. *Colonial Desire: Hybridity in Theory, Culture and Race.* London: Routledge, 1995.

Yuval-Davis, Nira. *Gender and Nation.* 1997. London: Sage, 2000.

'A Body of One's Own': A Study of Violation of Women's Body in Arundhati Roy's *The God of Small Things*

6

JAYDEEP RISHI

Women's body has long been used as a canvas for painting the outlines of patriarchal domination. Women have generally been constricted to a reproductive and nurturing role within the familial sphere. Therefore, the patriarchal culture essentially identifies women in a biological context and recognizes them on their reproductive capacities. Women are thus socially enslaved by their own bodies and denied to play any part in the public sphere. "(W)e ... see woman's exclusion from public life operating on two levels. Woman is relegated to childrearing by biological fiat on an individual level, which is then reformulated through the formation of the state and the institutionalization of public-private domains on a political level" (Eisenstein 14).

The realization that the female body was the root cause of sexual subjugation shaped much of the second wave feminist thought process. Shulamith Firestone, Susan Brownmiller, Susan Griffin and Andrea Dworkin are all of the opinion that the exploitation of women's bodies is the edifice on which patriarchy is established.[1] Robin Morgan feels, "the patriarchal control of women's bodies as the means of reproduction is the crux of the dilemma" (Morgan 6). Andrea Dworkin writing in the same vein says, "Male domination of the female body is the basic material reality of women's lives; and all struggle for dignity and self-determination is rooted in the struggle for actual control of one's own body" (Dworkin 203).

The credit for bringing the body into the focus of the political debate, however, goes to Kate Millet. Emphasizing on the female body Millet underscores the patriarchal politics that goes to shape femininity. Commenting on the title of Millet's pioneering work Maggie Humm states, "Kate Millet's choice of the two terms 'sexual/politics' for the title of her pioneering book powerfully identified sexuality, not as some simple, 'natural' experience of women and men, but as being socially constructed with political consequences and as being politically constructed with social consequences" (Humm 260). Millet thus rejects biological determinism and highlights the social construction of womanliness as the root cause of female subjugation. Judith Butler goes another step forward and is not ready to accept the division between sex and gender. She argues that sex as well as the female body is a social construction rather than a biological phenomenon. "On some accounts, the notion that gender is constructed suggests certain determinism of gender meanings inscribed on anatomically differentiated bodies, whereas those bodies are understood as passive recipients of an inexorable law. When the relevant 'culture' that 'constructs' gender is understood in terms of such a law or set of laws, then it seems that gender is as determined and fixed as it was under the biology-is-destiny formulation. In such a case, not biology but culture becomes destiny" (Butler 8).

Arundhati Roy's *The God of Small Things* delves deep to expose the patriarchal control over the female body. The novel depicts women as subservient to the patriarchal ideology, so much so that they hardly have a space of their own. The male control in *The God of Small Things* is absolute and women hardly have any right over their own bodies. Therefore, the generational dialectics portrayed in the novel, featuring Mammachi, her daughter Ammu and granddaughter Rahel, gets reflected in the form of the different degrees of control over their respective bodies that these women enjoy and aspire for.

Mammachi's life seems to be controlled by Manu's dictum, "In childhood a woman should be under her father's control, in youth under her husband's, and when her husband is dead, under her sons. She should not have independence" (Doniger and Smith 115). Though we have no idea about the condition of her life under her father, her husband and her son proved to match each other in their domination over Mammachi. Married to the Imperial Entomologist, Pappachi, Mammachi was used to the bullies and regular beatings of her husband. Pappachi's professional frustration finds an expression in the torture he perpetrates on his wife and daughter. The more painful aspect of this torment is Pappachi's hideous double-faced attitude. Whereas he keeps a very respectable social posture by being honey-tongued to visitors, donating money to the orphanages and leprosy clinics, the "cold, calculating cruelty" (Roy 181) of the schizophrenic maniac towards his wife and daughter left them dumbfounded.

Pappachi's cruelty increased manifold with his retirement. His wife's success in the locality as a pickle and jam maker made him envious of his wife's vigour:

> Pappachi, for his part, was having trouble coping with the ignominy of retirement. He was seventeen years older than Mammachi, and realized with a shock that he was an old man when his wife was still in her prime. (Roy 47)

Mammachi finally escapes the physical torments when her son Chacko arrives on a vacation from England and sees his father beating her. Chacko, physically stronger than his father, overwhelms him and gives a stern warning, "I never want this to happen again" (Roy 48). But what Mammachi earns is not freedom from her servility; she can only exchange her master. Now it is her son to whom she must serve instead of her husband. And this she accepts without a grudge.

> The day that Chacko prevented Pappachi from beating her..., Mammachi packed her wifely luggage and committed it to Chacko's care. From then onwards he became the repository of all her womanly feelings. Her Man, her only Love. (Roy 168)

Mammachi has suffered immensely at the hands of the patriarchal forces. But the experience has not made her a rebel.

She only barters one form of slavery for another; her slavery towards her husband is replaced by her unquestioning subservience to her son. She has indeed picked up the voice of patriarchy in her relationship with her children. She is supportive of her son and adores and pampers him in all possible ways. She even gives away her new found economic independence to her son who takes over her pickle and jam factory. The transformation of 'Sosha's Tender Mangoes' and 'Sosha's Banana Jam' into 'Paradise Pickles and Preserves' has been a loss which Mammachi fails to comprehend. She is even supportive of Chacko's view about the family property: "What's yours is mine and what's mine is also mine" (Roy 57). Her attitude towards her daughter, Ammu, could not be more contrasting.

The anguish and torment that Ammu is subjected to since her childhood forces her to promptly marry the first man who proposes to her. Her marriage to a Bengali manager of a tea-estate involving an inter-caste, inter-community wedding was out of sheer desperation as her paternal family failed to be a recluse. However, marriage was never the Utopia that her fortunes promised her. The manager she falls in love with and marries without giving much of a thought proved to be a drunkard who was not unwilling to trade his attractive wife's young body to secure his position in the company he worked for. Ammu who hopes to escape from the violation of her body by her father finds only a greater transgressor of her body in the form of her husband. She has no option but to walk out of the marriage and return to her parents unwelcome, now burdened by her twin children, Estha and Rahel. The immensity of this neglect can be comprehended when Mammachi's approving gesture towards her son's homecoming is considered. It is important to note that like Ammu, Chacko too arrives devastated from a failed marriage which is also inter-caste and inter-community in nature. Chacko also marries away from home, the first woman with whom he develops a friendly relation. He does not even bother to let his family know about his marriage. And yet Mammachi receives him home with all the ambience and adoration possible. The disparity presented here blatantly points out to the contrasting social attitude with regard to the body defined on the edifice of gender. Whereas, a male body is considered sacrosanct even if 'defiled' with a union with one belonging to a different body and caste, no such allowance is admissible for the female body. Having no right over her own body a woman is considered 'polluted' if she for once dares to defy the dictum of her family or society.

Mammachi's special favour for her son at the cost of her daughter is again manifested in her views about sexuality and how much control one may exercise over one's own body. She embodies the voice of patriarchy and succumbs to the notion that what may be allowed to a male member in the family should be a taboo for the females. This behaviour of hers goes a long way in shaping the tragedy. Her perception of sexual promiscuity in relation to her son and daughter is obviously conditioned by sexist views. When Chacko is found to be involved in profligacy with the female workers of her factory, many of whom are 'untouchables,' she dismisses it simply as "Man's Needs" (Roy 168). She is indeed so considerate about his 'Needs' that she builds a separate entrance "so that the objects of his 'Needs' wouldn't have to go traipsing *through* the house" (Roy 169). She even secretly goes about paying these women to buy their silence.

On the other hand, Mammachi's reaction presents a blatant contrast to Ammu's 'needs'. Once she finds her daughter being involved in a sexual liaison with a Paravan, Velutha, Mammachi gets furious. Her very considerate self, which can understand the nuances of 'Man's Needs,' does not operate to feel her daughter's 'needs,' her emptiness, frustration, longing. Aided and abetted by Baby Kochamma she gives vent to the full fury within her. The anger is now directed to her daughter who, she believes, has ruined the family reputation for ever:

> Mammachi's rage at the old one-eyed Paravan standing in the rain, drunk, dribbling and covered in mud was redirected into a cold contempt for her daughter and what she had done. She thought of her naked, coupling in the mud with a man who was nothing but a filthy

> *coolie.* She imagined it in vivid detail: a Paravan's coarse black hand on her daughter's breast. His mouth on hers. His black hips jerking between her parted legs. The sound of their breathing. His particular Paravan smell. *Like animals,* Mammachi thought and nearly vomited. *Like a dog with a bitch on heat.* Her tolerance of 'Men's Needs' as far her son was concerned, became the fuel for her unmanageable fury at her daughter. She had defiled generations of breeding (The Little Blessed One, blessed personally by the Patriarch of Antioch, an Imperial Entomologist, a Rhodes Scholar from Oxford) and brought the family to its knees. For generations to come, *for ever* now, people would point at them at weddings and funerals. At baptisms and birthday parties. They'd nudge and whisper. It was all finished now. Mammachi lost control. (Roy 257-258)

The angst in Mammachi's thought pattern undoubtedly brings out how the patriarchal society views a female body. Ammu is at a fault not only because she gets involved in an illicit relationship with an untouchable Paravan, but also because her act defiles and desecrates her family in particular and her community in general. The female body is thus regarded as a procreative machine over which the individual has no control. The need for protecting the 'Touchable womb' from the 'Untouchable body' gains such prevalence that the 'Touchable Communists' and the 'Touchable Police' of Kottayam make it a common cause to teach Paravan Velutha a lesson. The clinical precision with which the Kottayam Police goes on maiming Velutha is not the by-product of any personal rage but of 'feelings of contempt born of inchoate, unacknowledged fear—civilization's fear of nature, men's fear of women, power's fear of powerlessness' (Roy 308).

It is no wonder that neither the family nor the society show any compassion for Ammu once her body is 'defiled' by the unlawful union. When Ammu visits the police station to clear Velutha's name of the false charges she is called and treated like a whore. Chacko, whose own profligacy knows no bound, does not allow her to stay with the family any more.

She is hounded out, separated from her children, and at thirty-one she dies lonely, desolate in a cheap hotel. The violation of her body does not stop with her death. Being excommunicated, her body cannot be buried in the church-side graveyard and has to be cremated in the Government crematorium, a funeral-receipt being her only memorabilia.

Despite her ignominy, Ammu is not the last person to challenge the 'Love-Laws'. Ammu's daughter Rahel, separated from her mother as well as her twin brother Estha with whom she shared a 'joint identity', returns from her exile to reunite with her brother and to understand and experience what her mother underwent twenty-three years ago. But once Rahel understands her mother, she has to reunite with her mother, to reaffirm her presence; and what better way to do that than to break the love-laws that Ammu had once broken.

When Rahel returns from America to meet her brother Estha, who has been re-retuned by their father, the similarities between her and Ammu are obvious. She has reached the age of thirty-one, an age in which her mother died. She has also been married and like her mother her marriage too has been a failure. A divorced woman from an inter-community love marriage Rahel returns to the Ayemenem family, unwelcome by Baby Kochamma, the only survivor from the past. She is only summoned to take care of and finally cart off her somewhat eccentric brother, who has stopped speaking altogether. She too is a burden to the household like her mother once was.

Rahel's intimacy with Estha is fuelled by a discovery that was so obvious and yet remained hidden for the entire life. The same is true in case of Ammu-Velutha relationship. Ammu and Velutha know each other for a life time. They grow up together. Though separated by the curse of untouchability, the two are not totally strangers to each other. Ammu as a little girl, received small gifts from Velutha, artefacts made by the Paravan himself. But after her return from her husband, on a fateful day, a gaze transforms the relation between the two. The forces of history are relegated to secondary places as biology takes over. The two of them discover each other to be man and woman (Roy 176-177). Ammu and Velutha dare to break the love-laws. Again, biology asserts itself as Rahel discovers her twin-brother in a different light. Once more, a gaze transforms the course of the relationship:

> Rahel searched her brother's nakedness for signs of herself. In the shape of his knees. The arch of his instep. The slope of his shoulders. The angle at which the rest of his arm met his elbow. The way his toe-nails tipped upwards at the ends. The sculpted hollows on either side of his taut, beautiful buns. Tight plums. Men's bums never grow up. Like school satchels, they evoke in an instant memories of childhood. Two vaccination marks on his arm gleamed like coins. Hers were on her thigh.
>
> Girls always have them on their thighs, Ammu used to say. Rahel watched Estha with the curiosity of a mother watching her wet child. A sister a brother. A woman a man. A twin a twin.
>
> She flew these several kites at once.
>
> He was a naked stranger met in a chance encounter. He was the one that she had known before Life began. The one who had once led her (swimming) through their lovely mother's cunt.
>
> Both things unbearable in their polarity. In their irreconcilable far-apartness. (Roy 92-93)

It is the various aspects of the relationship that strikes one most. Entwined in mind, physically separated at birth, the twins are forced apart from each other. Their physical union is in a sense a rebellion against this forced detachment. But their union is not merely a union of the bodies. Their union is also marked by the sharing of the same haunting memory from which they can hardly escape. The actual copulation between Estha and Rahel is preceded by their viewing of the *kathakali* dance, and the maddening frenzy of the dancers:

> There was madness there that morning. Under the rose bowl. It was no performance. Esthappen and Rahel recognized it. They had seen its work before. Another morning. Another stage. Another kind of frenzy (with

> millipedes on the soles of its shoes). The brutal extravagance of this matched by the savage economy of that.
>
> They sat there, Quietness and Emptiness, frozen two-egg fossils, with hornbumps that hadn't grown into horns. Separated by the breadth of a kuthambalam. Trapped in the bog of a story that was and wasn't theirs. That had set out with the semblance of structure and order, then bolted like a frightened horse into anarchy.
>
> (Roy 235-236)

The mad frenzy that Rahel and Esthappen had watched as children sent their life into a crazy whirlpool; unable to stop the violence they had accused themselves of being the perpetrators of the same violence, of setting everything into motion. The guilt has pervaded all their lives and added a tinge to their consciousness. Now face to face with the same fury, their life reaches another crossroad as they make a passionate outburst. This is almost a cathartic response to escape the frenzy, to protect them from the mindless violence that envelops their lives and over which they enjoy no control. It is because they can make no sense of this rage in the outside world that Rahel and Estha seek a world of their own. In this regard, they are akin to Ammu and Velutha, who too cannot cope with the vagaries of the external world and seek redress by coming together in search of solace.

As Velutha was once fascinated by Ammu's beauty, Estha too remains enchanted by Rahel. But to Velutha, Ammu was only a woman, apparently dangerous because of her family background, yet too desirable to be avoided. Estha on the other hand, not only sees a woman in Rahel, he also witnesses his twin-sister—a part of himself and more importantly his mother, Ammu. Rahel thus takes the role of her mother and helps to satisfy the Oedipus complex in Estha. It is noteworthy that Estha was once forced out of her mother's company when he was returned to his Baba. His union with Rahel stands out on a symbolic level to be a reunification with his mother. Naturally, Estha's visualization of his sister is in terms of Ammu.

> She was lovely to him. Her hair. Her cheeks. Her small, clever-looking hands.
>
> His sister.
>
> A nagging sound started up in his head. The sound of passing trains. The light and shade that falls on you if you have a window seat.
>
> He sat even straighter. Still, he could see her. Grown into their mother's skin. The liquid glint of her eyes in the dark. Her small straight nose. Her mouth, full lipped. Something wounded-looking about it. As though it was flinching from something. As though long ago someone—"a man with rings"—had hit her across it. A beautiful, hurt mouth.
>
> Their beautiful mother's mouth, Estha thought. Ammu's mouth.
>
> That had kissed his hand through the barred train window. First class, on the Madras Mail to Madras.
>
> *'Bye, Estha. Godbless'*, Ammu's mouth had said. Ammu's trying-not-to-cry mouth.
>
> The last time he had seen her. (Roy 299-300)

Estha's first observation of Rahel after they once again return to Ayemenem reminds him of his last moments there with his mother, Ammu. This may have to do something with the setting of the two scenes. It is the same room in which Ammu had packed Estha's belongings in a little trunk. Again, it is here that Rahel returns, rediscovers his brother, makes love to him. This visibly goes on to show the mantle with which Rahel is now on-stage, no matter what might happen she has to take on the role of her Ammu.

> The room to which, years later, Rahel would return and watch a silent stranger bathe. And wash his clothes with crumbling bright blue soap.
>
> Flatmuscled, and honey coloured. Sea-secrets in his eyes. A silver raindrop on his ear.
>
> *Esthapappychachen Kuttappen Peter Mon.* (Roy 227)

It is the uttering of the same words that goes on to establish the relationship between Rahel and Estha once again. Rahel approaches her brother; it is an advance which Estha cannot resist. But it is notable that even when they are involved in sexual consummation, Rahel takes the part of her mother.

> She moves her mouth.
> Their beautiful mother's mouth. (Roy 327)

And what they carry out is also a repetition of what happened in the past, of history being reiterated.

> Only that once again they broke the Love Laws. That lay down who should be loved. And how. And how much. (Roy 328)

It is a parallel to the events in the lives of Ammu and Velutha. Ammu and Velutha, two outcastes of the society, seek refuge in each other. Their coming together is as much influenced by their physical needs as by their necessity of being able to cope with the societal hassle that they regularly face. They find in each other the safe haven, a harbour where they can unburden their feelings. But it is not with great hope that they approach each other. They have only little hopes to share; the only immediate wish of being able to meet each other once again the next day, of being able to lose oneself in the arms of the other. So every day they part with a word of hope, a small promise, *'Naaley,'* tomorrow. But they are unable to keep their appointment. The brute social forces obliterate their love as they dared to defy the common norm. They fail in what they dared to achieve. But now after twenty-three years it is their loved ones, who once again appears in their role to enact the same drama. Where Ammu and Velutha fail, Rahel and Estha succeed. They carry on with the tradition of breaking the Love Laws, of rewriting the pages of history. If one looks at the physical relationship between Ammu and Velutha not simply as a sexual gratification of two individuals belonging to two different castes not allowed to mix freely but as a statement of protest against the social custom that encourages untouchability, Rahel's and Estha's relationship may be interpreted as an assertion of the very voices of protest once again. This voice of protest, which places greater value on the individual's wishes and fancies than the mere reiteration of social norms had once been subdued, but they can now be heard once again. Ammu and Velutha dared to break the greatest of the social taboos, the taboo of the body and pay dearly at the cost of their lives. It is now left to Rahel and Estha to mark their protest by breaking the taboo of forbidden relationships once more.

Virginia Woolf in her famous essay "A Room of One's Own" had given voice to the need of space and economic independence of women to help them be equal with men. However, the patriarchal society marginalises women and makes them prisoners of their own bodies. Arundhati Roy's *The God of Small Things* explores how these patriarchal forces work and voice a protest where the very body that is used for the violation of the women becomes a means of their protest.

REFERENCE

1. See Firestone Shulamith, *The Dialectic of Sex: The Case for Feminist Revolution,* London: The Women's Press, 1979; Brownmiller, Susan, *Against Our Will: Men, Women and Rape,* London: Secker and Warburg, 1975; Griffin, Susan, *Pornography and Silence: Culture's Revenge Against Women,* London: The Women's Press, 1981; Dworkin, Andrea, *Pornography: Men Possessing Women,* London: The Women's Press, 1981.

WORKS CITED

Butler, Judith. *Gender Trouble: Feminism and the Subversion of Identity.* New York: Routledge, 1990.

Dworkin, Andrea. *Pornography: Men Possessing Women.* London: Women's Press, 1981.

Doniger, Wendy and Brian K. Smith, trans. *The Laws of Manu.* New Delhi: Penguin India, 1992.

Eisenstein, Zillah. *The Radical Future of Liberal Feminism.* New York: Harper and Row, 1981.

Humm, Maggie, Ed., *Feminisms: A Reader,* Hermel Hempstead: Harvester Wheatsheaf, 1992.

Morgan, Robin. 'Introduction/Planetary Feminism: The Politics of the 21st Century,' in Robin Morgan (ed.), *Sisterhood is Global: The International Women's Movement Anthology*, New York: Doubleday, 1996.

Roy, Arundhati. *The God of Small Things*. New Delhi: IndiaInk, 1997.

Woolf, Virginia. *A Room of One's Own*. Harmondsworth: Penguin, 1945.

7

Feminism in Roy's *The God of Small Things*

R.S. JAIN

Let me clarify at the outset that just as every male writer does not possess anti-feministic view, every female writer does not necessarily depict feminine point of view. This is more than true in post-Rushdie writers like Shobha De and Arundhati Roy. There is a basic difference between female protagonist revolting against the age-old traditions and the female characters revolting against the pressures of married life. The first category of writers hold broader perspective than the second ones.

Most of the feminine writers in Indo-Anglian fiction have portrayed the individual woman's struggle to get free from male dominance in everyday affairs. They want to be paid attention; they want to have separate existence; they are opposed to Indian joint family system; early marriages and dowry system make them fight against the social evils. They are disturbed by family's negligence of women in the major decisions. Lack of participation in the matters of their own concerns, discrimination between male and female child are some of the major issues that the Indian English novels dealing with feminine theme contain.

Feminism in Western countries has an enlarged framework. The institutions of marriage, family and society are not only challenged by these feminine writings but also replaced. Their attitude forbids them from accepting the responsibilities emerging out of marriage. Many of them do not believe in the sanctity of marriage. In short, they believe they have destroyed the fundamental cause of their subjugation.

Can the Indian women follow the Western ideology of feminine independence in toto? Novelist like Kamala

Markandaya in her voluminous writings present the sufferings of a rural illiterate Indian women. These pictures extract pity and sympathy of the readers. Most of her novels end up with sad happenings like death. Writers like Dina Mehta, Anita Desai, Ruth Prawer Jhabvala have urban orientation. Their novels travel into the psychological terrains. Individual problems like alienation, unemployment, sexual exploitation, rapes, arising out of expanding urbanization are the topics of these writers. Jai Nimbkar in her 'Come Rain' presents the subliming picture of a Western woman in the traditional Indian society. Kamala Das, Shobha De, Gauri Deshpande are bold female writers in Indo-Anglian fictional world. They write openly about man-woman sexual habits, pre-marital and extra-marital sex, lesbian detours etc. According to them, man is the malicious factor in imposing surveillance on the women. To overthrow man's authority for them is the first step towards liberation. They advocate not only the economic independence but also the independence from man as an opposite sex.

The history of women in India shows that the girls in the past were considered to be feeble, that they needed man's protective sheath. They were deliberately looked down upon and were prohibited from having independent developmental channel. The family and the society always looked at them as secondary citizens. Recently, there is a change in the public outlook. Fifty years of Indian independence, continuous fights of the women's organization against their subordinate status, political gambit for reservation of seats of power, free education to girls, special legislations to safeguard the interest of women have together contributed to the improvement of their conditions to some extent.

But will the depiction of all these historical and social realities in the fiction of women writers make our feminine writers really feministic? Won't it be another form of propaganda to be detested from literary point of view? Should not our writers dive deep into the literary realities? How long should they hold man, family and the society responsible for their predicament? Won't it be woman chauvinism as against man chauvinism?

The above questions are not directed only to female writers alone but to the entire literary fraternity, who wish to see the Indo-Anglian fiction come up to the mark. We must give sufficient proof to the world that we are fully grown-up as writers and readers. We don't want to see our novels in the sociology section of the Western libraries any longer. I don't think we should vent only the terrible conditions of women in India as it is going to reflect not only on the men but also on the helplessness of the Indian women.

Feminism in traditional Indian society has many dimensions. A woman has to play a variety of roles in our society. She is daughter, sister, wife, niece, aunt, grandmother besides in-laws of different kinds. Indian social structure in rural areas particularly is such that a girl is the responsibility of the entire village. When she thinks about her liberation, she is thinking about the liberation from all the above roles and responsibilities that accompany these roles. In Western society woman is thought of in relation to a man and not in relation to various roles. Their concerns are limited to their 'men' only. Hence, their idea of independence covers limited ground.

Dr. Pashupati Jha has a point when he says, "That woman is not crude imitation of the western libber, but a lifelike figure whose sufferings win sympathy, whose victory instills courage."[1]

I would now turn my attention to Arundhati Roy's *The God of Small Things*. The novel maps five generation. The novelist does not say anything about the woman in the first generation. Aleyooty Ammachi is Pappaeni's mother. We do not know much about her except that she continued to live in an oil-portrait beside her husband Rev. lpe's painting. While Rev. lpe smiled, Aleyooty Ammachi looked more hesitant.

Baby Kochamma and Mammachi belong to the third generation. Roy makes us feel, hear and see Baby Kochamma in her novel. She fell in love with a handsome, young Irish monk, Father Mulligan when she was eighteen. The young girl and the intrepid Jesuit both were quaking with unchristian passion. She entered a convent in Madras after becoming a

Roman Catholic with special dispensation from the Vatican. She hoped that it would provide her opportunities to be with Father Mulligan. The love affair did not materialize. She was sent abroad for studies and two years later, she returned with a diploma in Ornamental Gardening. After fifty years she abandoned the gardening and fell in love with dish-antennae. These are the noticeable happenings in the life of Baby Kochamma.

She was snobbish in all sense and pretended that she had great knowledge of literary works like Shakespeare's *The Tempest*. She never forgot to lie about her age when she filled in application. She strongly believed in the theory that a divorced daughter had no position anywhere at all. A divorced daughter from a love-marriage was outrageous. A divorced daughter from an inter-community love-marriage was simply unbearable to her. That was why she never tolerated the presence of Ammu and her twins in her house.

It is interesting to note down the sentiments of one woman for the other. It throws light on the writer's idea of female characters in his or her works. Baby Kochamma who takes a drastic step of conversion in order to meet a man of her choice dislikes Ammu for the similar reasons. She allows her brother to have illegal sexual relations with unfamiliar women in order to satiate his hunger. But she frowns upon Ammu for thwarting the ethical boundaries of the family. This shows that Roy does not present her female characters as ideal ones. She is neither exploited by the man nor devastated by the customs in the society. She is solely responsible for the development or the otherwise of her character. This is where one likes to applaud Roy as a female writer of new generation.

Mammachi and Pappachi run a factory called Paradise Pickles and Preserves. After Pacchchi's death Chacko became the sole proprietor of the factory. Mammachi goes into the background and does not appear on the scene regularly. She belongs to the old generation that did not want to assert as Mammachi did not feel cheated by Chacko's moves simply because she did not see anything unusual in it.

She was unkind towards her workers but was meek with Chacko. She had a separate entrance built for Chacko's room, so that the object of his 'need' would not have to go traipsing through the house.

The fourth generation of women characters are Ammu and Chacko's alien wife, Margaret Kochamma. Ammu did not have good looks. Her father's retirement from a job in Delhi forced her to return to Ayemenem. Ammu went to Calcutta to attend a wedding of a distant relative and was attracted towards a stranger, Mr. Hallick. She got married with him, gave birth to a twin and returned to her father after her husband left for a job in Australia. She had sexual contacts secretly with Velutha till she died at an early age of thirty-five in Bharat lodge in Alleppey. The church refused to acknowledge her as Christian. Ultimately, her corpse was put into electric crematorium.

Rahel, Estha's sister and Chacko's daughter Sophie Mol belong to the fifth generation. Rahel returned from Calcutta with their mother without much din. Rahel and Estha grew up together. Sophie Mol had come back with her father from England. She died at an immature age of nine.

Arundhati Roy's female characters in *The God of Small Things* stand out as persons and not as role-players. Mammachi, Ammu, Margaret, Kochamma and Baby Kochamma have independent existence. Ammu and Margaret get married with the boys of their choice. There is no controversial discussion on their decision. Their marriages do not divide families among groups, one supporting the move and the other opposing it. Such inter-caste, inter-state, international marriages would have raised hue and cry in other Indo-Anglian writers. The other novelists would have spent dozens of pages in order to describe 'Marriage' in the Indian context to prove the Indianness of their writings, making it melodramatic. Marriages and divorce in many Indian novels occupy such a central position that one begins to doubt if there is anything else in the novel.

Ammu's sexual links with Velutha do not raise the question of high caste versus low caste. In fact their relationship is almost unnoticeable in the sense that except few occasional remarks by Mammachi and Baby Kochamma Roy does not spend pages after pages in the lucid descriptions of their sexual exploits. Nobody hates it; nobody likes it. Everybody knows about it as everybody knows that man has a penis and woman has a vagina. Such a natural presentation of relationship makes this novel more authentic and less pornographic. Roy's attitude demonstrates that, man and woman are bound to come together and there is nothing describable in it. Jasbir Jain's remark in this regard need to be quoted, "Women have been portrayed both by men and women writers as mothers and wives. It is within these roles that their new selves are born or can be born. The areas of relationships remain the same but the relationships change."[2]

Chacko takes over the responsibility of pickle factory after Pappachi's death. In other Indo-Anglian novels this would have been presented as a case of male injustice on Indian female. But Roy saves the incident from following into such jargons. Chacko does not want to strip Mammachi of her wealth through his action. On the contrary, he owns the financial responsibility of Mammachi, Ammu, Estha and Rahel. That is why he cannot attach theoretical tag to Mammachi-Chacko relationship.

I would like to draw readers' attention to a very significant incident in the novel. Estha goes to Abhilash Talkies along with other members of his family. The Orangedrink, Lemondrink, man makes Estha shake his penis feverously till his semen is ejected. Roy could have demonstrated it as a sensational case of rape on Rahel. But she abstains from it. This is where she excels. This makes her more reliable and acceptable than the propagandist female writers. The stickiness of semen upsets Estha in the theatre. Roy does not make it a public talk by repeating the incident in different forms later.

There are three sexual deviations in the novel. First one is Baby Kochamma's unfulfilled desire to marry Father Mulligan; second is Chacko's marriage with and divorce from Margaret and the third one is Ammu's sexual contacts with backward class Velutha. First one is a case of pre-marital love affair, the second one is the case of international marriage and divorce. Third one is the demonstration of extra-marital sexual behavior. The so-called love affair between Baby Kochamma and Father Mulligan is between the two separate sects of Christianity. Marriage between Chacko and Margaret is a case of international adventure. Ammu's sex with Velutha is between upper caste Hindu woman and lower caste boy. In spite of all this variety, Roy does not make them sensational cases of man-woman relationship. Roy does not make them unduly secret or disproportionately conspicuous. Though members of the family occasionally comment on their irregular sexual behavior, Roy does not overreact.

I would like to point out once again that Roy's *The God of Small Things* is feminine creation of unique nature. She does not deal with love, marriage, sex in the populist's fashion. She does not write about family and society working against the interest of the woman. She does not put an individual woman in squarely confrontation with her husband and male in-laws. She avoids writing about cultural conflicts, traditional viewpoints and treacherous customs. In short, she transcends the ordinary concepts of feminism and hence becomes more convincing.

At one place, Roy writes about the honest ration buyers who were tempted by "Cheap soft porn magazines about fictitious South Indian sex friends with glimpses of ripe naked woman lying in the pools of fake blood."[3] The cheap feminist writers might have given it a form of a conflict between exploited and exploiter. But Roy makes it a very casual tendency of ration buyers to satisfy their sex hungry eyes through such glimpses. What one likes about Roy is that she does not see opposition in all male-female encounters. Sometimes, as in above case, she finds a natural human impulse of both the sexes to be voyeurs.

REFERENCES

1. Jha, Pashupati, Ed. *Indian Novelists in English*. Delhi: Sarup & Sons, 2000, 102

2. Jain, Jasbir. *Problems of Postcolonial Literature and Other Essays*. Jaipur: Printwell, 1991, 33.
3. Roy, Arundhati. *The God of Small Things*. New Delhi: IndiaInk, 1997, 13.

The Nostalgic Note in their Flute: A Reading of Arundhati Roy and Jhumpa Lahiri

8

NANDINI SAHU

The critical attention that has been paid to the young Indian writers in the last two decades needs a critical inquiry. A re-reading of their staggering literary output adding tremendously to the tradition of the Indian literary scene—with special reference to Arundhati Roy and Jhumpa Lahiri—that is what is the essence of this paper. The intensity and the narrative technique, which both Roy and Lahiri use in their creative pursuits, are the matter of research and vital importance here.

In the post-colonial era, young Indian writers have succeeded in drawing the world attention with their psychoanalytical methods of characterization. Jhumpa Lahiri, Manju Kapur, Arundhati Roy, Gita Mehta, Shashi Tharoor, Pankaj Mishra, Rajkamal Jha, Geeta Hariharan, Amit Choudhury, Manila Suri, Mark Tully, Anita Nair, David Davidhar, Radhika Jha, Preeti Singh, Makrand Paranjape, Mrinal Pande have written masterpieces which can be termed as literature of encounter and synthesis both culturally and linguistically. The object of this study is to analyze how literature is a gateway for a meeting point of the world tradition through encounter of the cultures and an existential rediscovery. The semitic creativity is enhanced by a significant enrichment of the narrative in the hands of young experts like Arundhati Roy and Jhumpa Lahiri who employ their cultural, racial past as well as familial past as their recurring theme. The literature of exile is not peculiar to modern Indian, particularly the literature where recollection acts as a mode of redemption. So important is the past to both Lahiri and Roy that a consciousness of it colours their insistent preoccupation with living. Memory plays a vigorous, creative role in their writings, a preoccupation with their personal, familial past leads in the long run to a search for the racial roots.

Life is viewed as a nostalgic recollection through the eyes of sensitive, vulnerable and observant characters. These two writers do not write from the position of a distant observer, rather their writings reflect the perspective of someone between a paradisal past and a tormenting present. The oppressiveness of the present reality and the temporal time are the facts to accept here and now. The writers' efforts to bring out a meeting point for the past and the present have been intensified by their nostalgic representation of characterization. The dichotomy with which both these writers present the present existence is resulted by the aesthetic dilemma, which they perceive due to their nostalgic experience. In the context of the contemporary milieu, the lack of unity of being with the self is reinforced by the lack of unity of the past and the present, which is focused throughout. Their characters live in two worlds—one within and one without and the past keeps intruding into the present.

In the case of Arundhati Roy, she greatly concerns her writings with the necessity to regain her identity through language as a creative mode. Her lines contain open statements about her passage from alienation to the awareness of a sense of discovering the world and its values and roots. The knowledge of the world gives her the knowledge of herself. In *The God of Small Things* early euphoric adolescence of himself in the part of Estha works as a stepping stone towards his maturity. Rahel's unrestrained enthusiasm of everything around gives her a broad vision to narrate the picture gallery of life as a whole. Rahel, the persona of 31 years, "a viable diable age" is in a self-introspective mood crossing the border of youth on a way to maturity. Though her stance is detached and controlled, it is all the while infused with emotion. She recalls the years of mistakes they have committed, the years they have been deeply wronged, have been "more sinned against than sinning." In the process, self-delusion overtakes her, she gets distanced with her present self while evoking the moments of their past.

A sense of loss, non-fulfilment, of apparent failure, a desire for the oblivion, and a love for the small things, which, in fact, convey big things, find repeated occurrence in the novel. *The God of Small Things* is a story about love, death, lies and law, and hence the universal tale of love and tragedy. Through it, Roy pictures a child's view of the adult world, a tragic world of the feudal Christians, a barbarian communist who wipes his armpits with his terelene shirt, and a few sentimental untouchables. Love, that is erotic and cross-caste between a Paravan and Syrian Christian, and politics, an insight into the complicacy of Kerala, are the two mainstreams of the story.

Roy uses flashback technique for the narrative, memory being the source of narration in most parts. Her characters are lifelike, almost alive in each one of us. They are allegorical, sometimes they seem to be attributes rather than individuals. Baby Kochamma stands for jealousy, inferiority complex, Ammu for suppressed desire and hurt pride, Rahel and Estha for curiosity and unbounded love, Chacko for affectedness, Pappachi for male-chauvinism, Mammachi for inner blindness of a woman. About this deep concern for humanity in the novel, Roy says, "My work is not an academic, sociological study of untouchability but a human story that springs from love for human beings and a close contact with what happens to them."[1] Rahel, the narrator, is sometimes a stranger, sometimes the observer and yet some other times she is the performer. She expresses herself in the language of generic human emotion with its inevitable commitment to images, symbols, allegory, repetition, fluidity of language and the tension between the intense experience and its verbalization.

Early memories of life are suddenly activated years later when once again the siblings meet at youth. The memories of trivial things of childhood reveal how childhood impression years later add new meanings to those with an adult experience.

Roy's thematic strategy is exactly the right one for a writer of her situation, who loves her characters dearly.

The familial memories she employs are more of human interest at large, prone to social plane speaking of the higher values of life and complex human situation. Her small memories create a masterpiece of moving psychological fiction. Rahel remembers, though the "Little Man" Estha had always thought that "anything might happen to anyone, so it's better to be prepared" (118), yet he himself was never prepared for that anything in his life. Sophie Mol's funeral, the memory of her 'child sized', 'satin-lined', 'brass handled Shined' coffin, her go-go bag, yellow bellbottoms that made Rahel feel inferior, Baby Kochamma's expensive funeral saree, are haunting, picturesque. Other funny memories like the 'porket-munny' of children, their learning of pronunciation to impress Sophie, Kochamma's make-up, K.N.M. Pillai's sister's rendering of the poem "Lochinvar", Ammu and Baba's pushing the children to each other like billiard balls, "Et Tu, Kochu Mariye" to the housemaid, incidents in the Abhilash Talkies bathroom, the Orangedrink Lemondrink man episode add a lot to the storyline.

Rahel's sneezing a bead out of her nose, Ammu's "Lay Ter" Rahel's request to Mammachi to inherit her contact lenses after her death, children returned, and re-returned like library books—all these make one nearly laugh. But the underlying deep tragedy, mysterious like the Meenachal river speaks volumes of the deceptive simplicity of the novel. Nostalgia is the only motif throughout that plays a great role to arrange the present in a right order. Estha's story called "Little Ammu" that Rahel reads at thirty-one, Ammu's gifts of a pencil box and a comic book that reaches Estha when he is thirty-one after Ammu's lonely death leaving her death receipt No. Q. 498673, all these memories have big emotions to convey. Roy loves her characters, that is why they seem so lifelike. When the producers propose her for the picturization of the story, she would say, "It may sound silly, but I could not bear the idea of seeing actors play Eshta, Rahel, Velutha... it would kill me. I love them too much. I always will."[2]

Roy's tone gets satirical whenever she mentions the politics of contemporary Kerala. Comrade E.M.S. Namboodiripad is referred to as "Kerala's Mao Tse-Tung", about whom Roy satirises writing: "He broke the egg, but burnt the omelette" (281). Similarly, comrade K.N.M. Pillai is an opportunist who pretends to forget the past and his role in Velutha's murder. Similarly, the pickle factory 'Paradise pickles and preserves,' the jam, the jelly, the river Meenachal, all these bear bigger significance to the plot. The small things have made Arundhati Roy the winner of the big Booker Prize. Observing life from all directions, blending the past, present and the future in the single thread of life, she makes the storyline timeless. Roy's concern is with memory and the way it establishes or falsifies the relationship in a challenging world. She is neither a nostalgic traditionalist nor an advocate of modernization, she is the product of both and her novel reflects a personality conscious of change, and also aware of memories, which form her inner self as the foundation. For her, past is a time before Fall, she can be viewed as a writer on cultural crossroads.

Following the publication of three of her stories in the *New Yorker* in 1998, Jhumpa Lahiri's reputation was established among both critics and readers alike. When *Interpreter of Maladies* was released in 1999, it received a flurry of reviews. In an interview with Vibhuti Patel, Lahiri commented on her first career progression from scholar to Pulitzer Prize winner, saying: "Its all been a surprise—getting an agent, an editor, a book contract—it was all so fast. I feel extraordinary gratitude and amazement. Writers need time, some money and a little encouragement. This book has given me just the right amount of all three."[3]

Jhumpa Lahiri concerns her writings with the consciousness of the need for regaining roots in the tradition of India and a rueful nostalgia towards that. Her quest for identity is a consciousness towards exile, the dynamic force working to bring about this quest is a point of active engagement between two cultures—Indian and Western. This collection is a 'confessional piece', speaking of the pattern of hope and disenchantment arising from the predicament of the writer placed between two traditions, neither of which she can wholly accept or renounce. Like all expatriates, it sounds as if the Western culture forms a part of her intellectual and rational make-up whereas Indian culture is a part of her emotional make-up. She writes about how the English culture produces disenchantment in the minds of the expatriate Indians, and how they find themselves crushed under the burden of alienation and rootlessness. There is a sense of loss of identify with their own culture, therefore, the need for roots. There is an aesthetic continuum in her writing. The stories present the writer's intercontinental journey during which she gets herself accustomed to both the cultures—by her long stay abroad and regular trips to India during every summer. The realization that is dawned on her is about the possibility of affirming the identity of her Indian self. It seems that for Lahiri, East is the symbol of intellectual alertness and West is of emotional poverty. An identification of herself with either one is a frustrating experience, the artistic self is at war with the collective consciousness of both. Her stories seem to attempt to bring meaning to the present by reassessing the past and by giving shape to the accumulated waste of experience of the character's past prior to the period of Westernization. With every detail of the experiences of both first and second generation of Indian immigrants, the topics of the stories range from emotional struggles of love to immigrants battling in a new world. The stories draw upon the racial past of India, Indian cultural heritage, the topics of communication, relationships. She is an interpreter of maladies of people "Who think in a way they can't fully express."[4] About her Indian past, she speaks to Rediff.com, "India is the place where my parents are from, a place I visited frequently for extended time and formed relationship with people and with my relatives and felt a tie over time even though it was a sort of parenthesis in my life to be there."[5] Her writings are scattered with the details of traditional Indian names, food, flavor and wardrobe giving shape to her stories. Her representation of Indian culture is inherently present without exaggeration. Even her characters belong to different ages, nationalities and religions. Lahiri's characters demonstrate the universality of real life experience. In a story 'Mrs. Sen's', an eleven year old boy in an American college town watches his baby sister Mrs. Sen with her eccentricities, from chopping vegetable with a "blade curved like the prow of a Viking ship" to applying a fresh streak of crushed vermilion to the parting of her hair with the head of a thumbtack while recollecting the life she reluctantly left behind in Calcutta. Lahiri manages to portray so well the confusion and despair a young Indian wife feels so far from home. Her anxiety for letters from her kith and kin from her motherland, her Indian dishes—fish curry, family members' voice on the tape recorder during her farewell and many other things reflect the pathos of an expatriate Indian. In "This Blessed House" Sanjeev can barely stomach his young wife's glee at finding and displaying garish Christian objects—a typical Indian Hindu mentality. In "A Temporary Matter" the characters live with the memory of their lost love, and during the power failures, they remember India, Shobha's granny's house, where during such power failures each has to say something like a joke, a story, a little poem. This leads towards the confession game, and the catastrophe. "When Mr. Pirzada come to Dine" is an emotional story. Here, there is the flashback of Pakistan civil war and the partition, its history, geography. Lilia's mother recollects her past in India during the Independence, the crisis, the power failures, the light of kerosene lamps, the pressures, the English tutors, the constant examinations, and facts secure about her daughter's life in the US. Still Lilia would never chose to distance herself from her roots, store her chocolates in her grandmother's sandalwood box, the only moments of a grandmother she had never known. The predominant tone of the story is nostalgia with Mr. Pirzada's memory of his wife and seven daughters living in Dacca. Ultimately, after Mr. Pirzada's departure, Lilia could realize "that is meant to miss someone who was so many miles and hours away, just as he had missed his wife and daughter for so many months" (42). The title story "Interpreter of Maladies" deals with the racial past of Indians with a vivid description of the Sun Temple at Konark, and the confession of Mrs. Das about her past before Mr. Kapasi, the interpreter. In "A Real Durwan" for Boori Ma, the protagonist, the memory of her royal youth is the only source of remaining alive in her old age. She "Exaggerates her past at elaborate lengths and heights" (73). The story "Sexy" is about identity crisis. Dev is an expatriate Bengali boy. Miranda is born and brought up in the US. Dev talks to her about the Taj as "the everlasting monument to love", speaks of the Indian significance of her name Mira. Goddess Kali, Indian food, Indian spices are mentioned all over the plot. "The Third and Final Continent" is a touchingly transparent story, it speaks of the protagonist's past with Mrs. Croft.

There is an ardor of empathy in the stories where she displays a steadfast curiosity about human behaviour and a healthy respect for its mystery. She literally makes the readers share the character's tragedies, their nostalgic experiences. She does not point out the loss of their cultural identity directly, her characters seem to be relieved when they adjust to the new world and are regretful at the separation from their original culture. Indian food, spices, flavors are a talisman in the stories, a reassuring bit of the homeland to brood over. She doesn't filter life through the single, steady voice of a young satirist, instead she writes about Indian American experience from all angles in indelible, lifelike stores who cling to memory as a source of living, she herself being the interpreter of human maladies.

In her perception the journey of the Indian becomes an aesthetic continuum reading the Indian landscape as a foreigner would read it. The characters look back to India satirically celebrating their freedom or asserting their biculturalism, look skeptically and wryly on their new homeland as outsiders, with a feeling of something being lost, a sense of longing a loss that often comes with the life of an immigrant. She confesses to Elizabeth Farnsworth in an interview, "I think that, in part, it's a reflection of what I observed my parents experiencing and their friends, their circle of fellow Indian immigrant friends. It's also, in part, drawn from my own experiences and a sense of...loss from my parents that was so palpable all the time while I was growing up, the sense of what my parents had sacrificed in moving to the US."[6] The character's ability to accommodate and absorb the other culture without losing the consciousness of being Indian marks the major concern of Lahiri. She pictures how life abroad is exciting, a bit absurd and often lonely.

Through Lahiri's stories, we learn bits and pieces about Indian life and how they fit into lives in America. In the title story, an Indian family from New Jersey who are every bit "ugly Americans" hire an old-fashioned Indian guide Mr. Kapasi who knows nine languages. The dual theme of love and duty in the story emphasises on the word interpreter. Mr. Kapasi wants "to get to the heart of the matter." Getting to the heart of any matter is the best thing that Lahiri does through the themes, love, fidelity, tradition and alienation. In a conversation with Arun Aguiar, she talks about one of her Indian characters, Bibi Haldar, "...from going there and observing people. For that story I took as my subject a young woman whom I got to know over the course of a couple of visits... she lived in the same building as my aunt and uncle....I learnt from my aunt that she had some epileptic like disease." When asked about the reaction of the Indian readers to her stories, she says, "When I read for a predominantly Indian audience, there are more questions that are based on issues of identity and representation. That also happened in England last week. Some Indians will come up and say that a story reminded them of something very specific to their experience."[7] Prof. R.K. Kaul writes about her, "Out of nine stories in this volume, at least six or seven have a touch of magic. The author has narrative skill which captures the reader's attention immediately. Unlike the other women writers, she is not interested in problems of gender, race or colonialism. Only the story 'A Real Durwan' arouses our awareness of the callousness towards a woman sweeper. Whether the setting is in Bengal or in the US, she creates a probable world where human relations are all that matter."[8]

"There is something to be said for exile," says R. Parthasarathy, "your learn roots are deep."[9] The illustration of this truth may be best found in the writings of Jhumpa Lahiri. In spite of the slightly ironic tone employed throughout her descriptions, the final impression is that of an obsession with and an admiration of Indian traditional culture. Arundhati Roy and Lahiri prove it wrong that a language a writer uses must be his or her own, and it must mean everything to him. There is a feeling of buoyancy for the language in their writing and they are comfortable with it despite their alien experiences with life. Even if there is any discomfort, it is purely intellectual. The use of private experiences, especially the inner world of memories and the continuities with the past can be seen on the basis of their writing. They are not attempts to intellectualize and make moral choices; their writings are a retrospective photoflash. Along with these intimate portrayals their vocabulary is touchingly Indian. The Indian phrases and syntactical patterns transplanted in the English milieu in their writings add a new flavour to the English idiom itself. Their writings convey the whole range of feelings—from the ecstasy of transcendence of emotions to the drugged mildless trance of passion, from the feeling of being cleansed by love and sex to the poignant bitter sweet memories of the loved and lost, their flutes play the nostalgic note from their heart and intellect. In the writings of both Roy and Lahiri, the protagonists search for the symbols of collective past and their attempts to resensitise their sensibility through their communion with past, with heritage is obvious.

REFERENCES

Primary Sources

Roy, Arundhati, *The God of Small Things*, IndiaInk, 1997.

Lahiri, Jhumpa, *Interpreter of Maladies*, Harper Collins, 1999.

Secondary Sources

1. *The Indian Express*, October 18, 1997, p. 1.
2. *Frontline*, Jan. 19, an interview with N. Ram, 17.

3. *Voices from the Gaps*, Deptt. of English, 207 Lind Hall, University of Minnesota, Minneapolis, 55455 I, 38.
4. *Ibid.*
5. *Ibid.*
6. *Ibid.*
7. *Ibid.*
8. Kaul, R.K. "Twinkling Interpretations of Bengali Characters." *Indian Book Chronicle*, July, 2000, Vol. XXV, No. 7, 3.
9. Parthasarathy, R. "Exile." *Ten Twentieth Century Indian Poets*, Delhi, 1976, 75.

The Letter and the Image: India in Jhumpa Lahiri's *The Namesake*

9

MANISHA SHARMA

I have, in this paper tried to analyze the way India has been projected in *The Namesake*, explain the reasons behind, and thus lay bare the effectiveness of the images. The content related to India is a reflection of an entirely different culture with a distinct language transcreated into English.

An image certainly conveys something beyond the literal word. The works of James Joyce, D.H. Lawrence besides many others are classic examples of the use of imagery in fiction. Ironically enough, this term is as vague and confusing as it is concrete and vivid. Chris Baldick calls imagery "... a rather vague term covering those uses of language in a literary work that evoke sense impressions by literal or figurative reference to perceptible or 'concrete' objects, scenes, actions, or states, as distinct from the language of abstract argument or exposition."[1] Ranging from mental and visual pictures in the mind of the reader to those that are sense appealing, involving metaphors, similes, symbols all fall under the blanket term image. A multiplicity of images spread throughout a work, conjure up a larger image. Food, the trips to Calcutta, Ashima's nostalgia and her memories combine to form a larger image, an image of India in *The Namesake*.

But is it really an image of India that the book draws? The answer to this question lies in the understanding of few essential facts about the country and its people. India is, perhaps the only place in the world where people professing multiple religions, speaking 22 languages and unknown number of dialects, following numerous customs and traditions cohabit. It is amusing as well as astonishing to discover the similarities and differences about them.

Looking from a macrocosmic point of view, *The Namesake* does offer glimpses of or about India but, a microscopic scrutiny would class the novel primarily as the spokesman of a middle-class Hindu Bengali family in particular, the Hindu Bengali community, their traditions, customs, cultural beliefs and social set-up. For the sake of clarity in understanding, I have divided the discussion under four headings: food, society, mythology, customs, traditions and language. But before embarking onto the points of each heading, I would like to illustrate how each of them is an integral part of culture; hence the image of India in *The Namesake* has been inspired and has its genesis in the particular culture. Probal Dasgupta in his book *The Otherness of English* says, "A community represents itself to itself via several types of mediations—the food it eats, the land it works on, the houses it inhabits, the machinery it uses."[2] Thus, all that goes on in a community is their culture and the language of a community is the thread that binds them and ensures the perennial nature. Language then, is an indivisible part of a community.

Let's begin with the most prominent cultural feature in the novel, *Food*. India is a poor country classified as a developing nation among the Third World countries. The fact dictates optimum use of resources produced in a region by the people of that area. Thus we see that rice and mustard as are cultivated in plenty in West Bengal that lies in eastern India, becomes the staple diet of the inhabitants. In the novel, Ashoke and Ashima Ganguli hail from Calcutta, the capital of West Bengal. Perhaps we now know the reason behind Ashima's wistfulness to make her recipe without mustard oil in the opening sentences of the novel. The climate, type of soil and rains allow mass cultivation of rice in Bengal, hence an all pervasive presence of rice in the meals and ceremonies of the Ganguli household. Puffed rice is thrown into fire when a marriage ceremony takes place. The first time Gogol, their son, is fed with *anna* — the closest translation of which is food grain, rice. At one point in the novel, Ashima thinks it her good fortune of having shared rice in a foreign land. It is suggestive of the fact that rice is not just a food item to satisfy hunger, but, has greater, weightier significance attached to it.

She cries because there is no rice left in the house and then borrows it from her neighbor but on finding it is brown not white rice, throws it because white rice is the variety of rice eaten in India. Samosas, halwa, rasogullas, curries, shrimp cutlets fill up the tempting descriptions of food in the novel.

India is associated with vegetarianism because in certain states where droughts are a common feature, it makes sense not to eat animals, but feed the cattle and use their by-products. A restriction on eating beef follows the same suit. On the other hand, there are certain states where people consume meat because the geographical conditions allow that to happen. The novelist suggestively makes an attempt to shed this illusion about vegetarianism and India. Judy and Alan, the Gangulis neighbours have also been invited to Gogol's annaprasan ceremony. "Judy eyes the buffet, bites into something that turns out to be a shrimp cutlet. "I thought Indians were supposed to be vegetarian," she whispers to Alan."[3] Because Calcutta lies on the belt of Ganges, a sacred river that is also home to fish, Bengalis eat fish which actually contributes to the economy of the state. There are no rivers in most states which explains why people don't eat fish or meat there. While Ashima was going to the United States, her parents, relatives advised her not to eat beef but her grandmother was not fearful of such signs of betrayal. Eating beef is considered a sin in most parts of India. Cow provides the bulk of dairy products to the country and mythology too, places cow on a high altar. Soon people started to venerate cow. It was also associated with vehicles of gods and so cow became the holy cow. When the word spread as a religious canon, people followed it.

Shifting focus from food to society, it will be safe to say that Lahiri has picked characters that belong to the huge mass of middle class. Arnold Kettle quotes E.M. Forster from *Aspects of the Novel*, "The novelist deals with personality, with characters wearing their *personae* or social masks."[4] Next to the huge poor class, is the middle class in India. The Indian novelist in English has quite successfully employed his pen in drawing realistic descriptions of this middle class, perhaps because he too is the product of the same. Lahiri presents a perfect picture of the middle-class household when she talks about Ashima Ganguli's life before marriage. She was a girl of 19 studying to get a college degree and also tutoring school children in her Calcutta neighbourhood. Their house, a middle-class house, is whitewashed with limestone dissolved in water and not painted with expensive paints. The novel when talking about Ashoke and his parents who come to see Ashima as a prospective bride for their son says, "The man was sitting in a rattan chair, his parents perched on the edge of the twin bed where her brother slept at night."[5] It is the same space that served as a bedroom for her brother at night and living room during the day. The mention of the Ganguli's relatives in Calcutta, their houses with clay, concrete or terrazzo flooring and their amazement on seeing pictures of the carpeted bathroom of the Gangulis in the United States all refer to social life in India.

Ashoke and Ashima have an arranged marriage agreed upon by their parents. It is here that the family comes into purview. Against the individual, the whole family is a unit in an Indian society with the eldest living member being the head. Besides very few exceptions, the male is the head of the family in most Indian societies. It is his responsibility to provide for the basic needs which is a lifelong struggle. In such circumstances, it is impossible to imagine living on one's own for the children when they are adults or for that matter to marry by their choice. In the novel, it is Ashoke's father who does all the talking when they come to see Ashima. Ashoke is too shy even to raise his eyes to her. In a society that has evolved with values of respect and submission to the wishes of elders, it is usual for Ashoke and Ashima, later in the novel, to avert their gaze when Maxine, their son's girlfriend runs her hand through Gogol's hair or for that matter Ashoke's reticence and no public display of emotion between the husband and wife. Since a woman in an Indian society takes care of the children and the house, it is appropriate for Ashima's mother to brag about her daughter's accomplishments. She says, "She is fond of cooking, and she can knit extremely well. Within a week she finished this cardigan I am wearing."[6] Back in the 1960s and 70s there were very few women in the Indian society who ventured out to work but things have changed a lot now. It is no wonder that Ashima learns the name of her husband after engagement. For Lydia and her family a visit to their parents is a pleasure trip, a sense of duty for Ashoke and Ashima.

Marriages are an expensive affair in the Indian society and with a daughter in the family, a father's worries start right from her birth. The financial status of Ashima's father could afford men who were widowed with children or handicaps for his daughter. It was Ashima's and her family's good fortune that these men had rejected her. That Ashima had no say in the choice of her husband is sufficient indication of male superiority and female subjugation. Though winds of change have been perceptible over the years, it is the concept of family as a unit that lies at the foundation of arranged marriages too. Since both Ashima and Ashoke are products of this system, they are quite indifferent to their America-born and raised son when he confronts them, "I'm 18 now."[7] A Hindu Bengali wedding ceremony is described hastily in a short paragraph in the novel.

Besides the projection of the financial state of a middle-class family in India, the novel also offers a panoramic view of the economic imbalance of a culturally rich and varied country. The always on the go city of Calcutta, its railway station lined up with uniformed porters carrying heavy luggage on their heads with no signs of complaint, railways the heart beat of the country, means of local transportation draw the busy life of Calcutta. Besides taxis, there are rickshaws pulled by men to earn their livelihood. Poverty peeps in the mention of people whose houses are the side walks where they shampoo their hair and boil rice. The busy city of Calcutta never sleeps. Each city has its own character and so Calcutta cannot be characterized as representing India in its entirety. Both Ashima and her daughter Sonia remove their gold ornaments before boarding a train in India. Ashoke wears a special garment to hold money. The mention of Bihar, one of the 28 states in the Indian territory, is emblematic for notoriety in criminal records. The incident of a man robbed and stabbed in the train stands as a testimony and is a strong contrast to another incident in the novel. Ashima in a haste and excitement forgets the shopping bag full of things she had bought for relatives in India in the subway. She is surprised to find the bag intact after some time. On sharing her amazing story with other Bengali friends, she hears them saying that such a thing could only happen in the United States. The two incidents should be seen in an unbiased light, a reflection of the economic status of both countries.

Since India is a poverty-stricken nation, human labour is cheap and the divide between classes rigid. Ashima is at first reluctant to buy stuff from yard sales but on knowing that her husband's boss also buys from yard sales, there is a reversal of her opinion. Because of poverty, providing three meals a day is a lifelong struggle, the mother in an Indian family takes pleasure in cooking and feeding her guests and family, cooks and serves at the same time so nothing goes waste. In the novel Ashima is seen preparing elaborate meals and is the last one to eat. There is no customary laying of food on the table. The novelist also presents a contrast in the way an American and an Indian family greet and feed a guest.

Mythology contributes in culture and the resources are collectively found in the literature of a country. Eliot's *Wasteland* is blank, devoid of its mythological framework. We have in the discussion so far, an inkling about the Indian way of life, where family comes before an individual and the social conditions that run things the way they are. People's actions are influenced by mythology, customs, traditions and beliefs.

Ashima doesn't pronounce her husband's name. She even learns his name for the first time after they are engaged. She is conscious of writing his name on the Christmas cards. There runs a belief among Hindus that if a woman pronounces her husband's name, she contributes to the lessening of his age. No one would dare to deny the word because in most houses the male head of the family is the sole bread earner. Besides the geographical and climatic relation of rice to Bengal, it also refers to an episode in Hindu mythology. Rice is considered an eternal donation. According to Hindu mythology, earth, water, fire, wind and sky are the five elements that are pious and revered. Each of them is god for Hindus. In the novel, the bride and the groom in a marriage ceremony pledge the vows of matrimony by fire and throw puffed rice into it as donation to the fire god. Food grain is also god for Hindus. There is a ceremony when the child tastes *anna* or food grain for the first time known as *annaprasan*. This ceremony is one of the 16 *samskars* translated as impressions that an individual goes through, starting when the child is in the mother's womb. Beliefs about graveyards as visiting places are also contrasting. Taking the students for a field trip to the graveyard is seen in a very critical light by Ashima. Graveyards are forbidden places for Hindus. The dead among most sects of Hindus are burned rather than buried. There are no tombstones for the dead. Their bodies merge into the five elements of which they are constituted, says the Hindu belief.

There are three attributes that determine a man's behaviour or *swabhava* in Hindu mythology. One of these attributes, Rajas is associated with activity and passion symbolized by red colour. Vermilion is a representation of that. Only a married woman decorates her parting with vermilion. The dot or *bindi* on a woman's forehead is also an extension of the same, though even unmarried girls apply dots on their foreheads in some states and also as part of fashion. If the wife survives the death of a husband, her vermilion is erased, she no longer wears bracelets. What runs behind all this is that a woman lives for her husband and once the husband is no more, there is nothing to look forward to for her so whom would she dress up or look beautiful for. Long ago religious and social reformers raised their voices against this system and path was paved for widow remarriage. Ashima's and her mother's vermilion is washed after their husbands pass away.

Anyone elderly is either a relation called by the particular noun appropriated to that relation or if not a relation simply by adding a pronoun to the name which can be appropriated to sir or madam in the English language. Ashima was startled that Maxine addressed her and Ashoke by their names because according to the Indian customs, you are ruled by relations.

Getting on to the most significant aspect of culture, language, I would like to quote from the book, *Colonial Discourse and Post-Colonial Theory—A Reader* edited by Patrick Williams & Laura Chrisman, "Written literature and orature are the main means by which a particular language transmits the images of the world contained in the culture it carries.... Language carries culture, and culture carries, particularly through oral tradition and literature, the entire body of values by which we come to perceive ourselves and our place in the world."[8] In the case of an Indian novelist writing in English, he constantly has to struggle in appropriating an alien tongue, English to an entirely different culture and social inheritance. Sentences like this one addressed by Ashima to Ashoke "Are you listening to me?"[9] are mere translations that fail miserably to convey the complete intended meaning. Ashima uses words ten finger and ten toe because she has directly translated the Bengali words into English. In such instances, the real meaning never gets conveyed. Examples from the novel like a Bihari couple drinking water from the same cup without putting their lips to the rim, or Ashima touching the dust of her grandmother's feet face two obstacles. They refer to acts that are either absent in the English language or do not have an appropriate equivalent and by actually trying hard to convey the closest meaning, the narrative is robbed of what masters of the art have called 'a painting in words' reducing it to some description of a scientific experiment. The aspect of culture that lies at the very genesis never comes to the surface. Bill Ashcroft sums this failure as "[The] 'intolerable wrestle with words and meanings' has as its aim to subdue the experience to the language, the exotic life to the imported tongue."[10] Piri, dal, payesh, ajowan, chanachur are some of the Hindi and Bengali words that the novelist has used unitalicized and proper nouns like relations or desh magazine are italicized. Whether it is a linguistic strategy to incorporate the unitalicized into the English language or are the Indians writing in English pressing a disguised demand that words from their native tongue be incorporated into the English language with pride as certain Greek, Latin and French words are, is a topic of research.

In conclusion, I'd say that the India Lahiri has portrayed in *The Namesake* is the India of 1960s, 70s which, as most societies are now, has undergone a sea change and the findings in this paper are generalizations with equal respect for exceptions. Her major focus has been on the middle-class Hindu Bengali family. We see more of Calcutta and Hindu Bengali culture than India. By making Ashima the carrier of most cultural ideas, she has put forth the pivoting yet subjugated position of woman in Indian Hindu culture. As an Indian living in the United States for the past three years, I can associate myself with Ashima most of the time. Besides all this, language has and will remain a bone of contention, an obstacle for the Indian writer in English.

NOTES AND REFERENCES

1. Baldick, Chris. *The Concise Oxford Dictionary of Literary Terms*. New York: Oxford University Press, 1992 (a reprint), 106.
2. Dasgupta, Probal. *The Otherness of English*. New Delhi, London: Sage Publications, 1993, 56.
3. Lahiri, Jhumpa. *The Namesake*. A Mariner Book, Houghton Mifflin Company, Boston, New York, 2003, 39.
4. Kettle, Arnold. Ed. *The Nineteenth-Century Novel*. London: Heinemann Educational Books Ltd., 1972, 26.
5. Lahiri, Jhumpa. *The Namesake*. A Mariner Book, Houghton Mifflin Company, Boston, New York, 2003, 8.
6. *Ibid*. 7.
7. *Ibid*. 107.
8. Williams, Patrick and Laura Chrisman. Eds. *Colonial Discourse and Post-Colonial Theory: A Reader*. New York: Columbia University Press, 1994, 441.

9. Lahiri, Jhumpa. *The Namesake*. A Mariner Book, Houghton Mifflin Company, Boston, New York, 2003, 2.

10. Ashcroft, Bill, Griffiths, Gareth and Helen Tiffin. *The Empire Writes Back*, Routledge, New York, Great Britain, 2002, 24.

The Theme of Indian Marriages in Cauvery Madhavan's *The Uncoupling*

10

SHUBHA TIWARI

I

Those who love to relax with a novel may find Cauvery Madhavan's *The Uncoupling* enjoyable. It is the story of a South Indian couple, Balu and Janaki. They are middle-aged. Their son Ram, who lives in London, arranges a sixteen days all European tour for them. As the tour begins, so begins the uncoupling. Balu is a typical Indian *manly* man and Janaki, as the name suggests allegorically as well, is the very picture of modesty, forbearance, and docility. But as the journey starts, Balu's Right-Wrong, Appropriate-Inappropriate Indian standards look oppressive and tiring. Old injuries, the trouble lock of any marriage, begin to surface themselves. To begin with, Balu has a very clear cut idea of 'the wife stuff' and 'the hot, wild stuff, implying thereby the impossibility of a wife being hot and wild. A wife has to be totally *Satvik*, pure with no animalism or graceless craving for physical pleasures. On the other hand, the hot, wild stuff is what dreams are made of—film heroines, models, TV news readers. This is a broad *loose* category of women for Balu. Those whose wives are not educated or educated cosmetically and are not working find solace in the chastity and non-availability of their prized possession. The working women lot is happily pushed to the *loose* group. Our Balu is reaping all the fruits of a conformist's life. He has the upper hand in marriage. He unhesitatingly takes decisions on his wife's part, speaks for her before she can, defends her when feels like it, and also insults her according to his sweet will. When co-tourists urge Janaki to sing, Balu says, "My wife hasn't the confidence... Oh, she sings, but you know ordinary, mainly devotional songs... Perhaps some other time, not in this—you know-hotel setting," (151) Mark 'hotel setting.' It hints at all the things associated with a hotel. But it is Europe and people want a word from Janaki's own mouth. "I'll sing." Janaki looked at the surprise on their faces. "I have the perfect song for the occasion" (151-152). Then she sings a traveller's prayer song *Yatri,* her father's favourite. She even explains the meaning of the *bhajan* to fellow passengers—Europeans, Americans, and of course, the British Indian couple, the Singhs. After this, there is no going back for Janaki. Her personality grows and changes before our very own eyes. With every passing event of bravery and Balu's reaction to it, Janaki becomes another person, liberated and thinking. It is a tough ride for Balu. With a growing 'wild' wife, his own pent up sexual urges itch him hard. With European climate of open sexual display in shops, red light areas and restaurants, our Indian Balu is only short of getting insane, he is flabbergasted, shocked, repulsed, attracted, aroused. He does not know as to what is happening to him. Amidst extreme confusion his wife sips brandy one night. But Balu did not know then that her taking brandy would prove to be a blessing in disguise for him. Once in bed, Janaki is almost unconscious as the effect of alcohol is so strong on her. She has no idea as to what Balu is doing to her. With this sleeping partner Balu unleashes his suppressed lust. He looks at his wife the way he would have looked at the "hot, wild stuff." He does all the 'disgraceful' things happily musing that Janaki would never know that her 'dignified' husband did all those 'chhi chhi' things to her. And she never knows. Next day Balu uses every trick in the book to make his devout Hindu wife drink. He succeeds. Again he realizes all his newly found sexual dreams. But the third day onwards the Indian wife puts her foot down. Howsoever hard Balu may plot, maneuver or conspire, she refuses to be inebriated. The stimuli of the memory of having seen his wife in forgetful sexual ecstasy nag him to no end. His lusting after his own wife, watching greedily his wife of thirty-three years is so funny. And to intensify his desire are exotic European locales where open sexual display is quite common. In market artificial male and female organs are on display. Sales boys and girls are advertising them freely. Even cuckoo clocks wake with sighs of orgasm. Balu's world goes topsy-turvy.

Janaki is on a tour of a different type. She recalls the events of her life, evaluates Balu and his behaviour. There is a sort of a feminist brewing in her. She recalls her failure to do a college degree. She realizes that Balu, like most Indian men, has been merely 'tackling' her all these years. Indian men have this deep-rooted sense of intellectual superiority over women. When it comes to intricate affairs, women howsoever wise or educated fall short for them. I am reminded of Sandhya Mulchandani's analysis, "This enhanced sense of freedom, self-worth and non-accountability for their actions and manipulation of their families make men the decision makers—the man in charge, so to speak...What a man is in love with is everything that makes him look like a man. This is in effect a man's ego which is about being seen as a male—brave and strong...Masculinity is synonymous with being in charge; so it's usually the man who orders a meal in a restaurant, checks in at the airline counter, drives the car and balances the cheque book" (28-29). This one up manship takes away the elements of companionship, and sharing in relationships between Indian men and women, something common in dealings of Western men and women.

Janaki, while on a life review ride, remembers her failure to do a college degree. She decides to do something useful in her life, rebuild her broken confidence and find meaning in life beyond husband and family. But before that she knows that she will have to put an end to the oppressive ways of Balu. The novel describes a number of 'war tools' that operate within a marriage between a husband and a wife. Balu, for example, never voices his grievances clearly. He tries to impress and register his annoyance through indirect ways. His favourite tool is being over kind to his wife, thereby reminding her of her supposed faults and wrongs and also of his own goodness. The undeclared ongoing war between Balu and Janaki hint at lack of openness, honesty and sincerity within Indian marriages. Balu does not want Janaki to think of education and career. He goes about it saying that there is an age for everything, that a woman's world is her 'home sweet home', that there is no need and he is providing so well for them and so on. The victory for Balu is not far. It is a different matter that in this victory lies his defeat. He is denying himself the love of his wife. When Janaki is finally faced with the question of what would she like to do or what were her areas of specialization, "... she was stumped for an answer. He was waiting to move in for the kill, to quash her ideas for once and for all, confident in the knowledge that she wouldn't be able to think of anything at all. How right he was!" (199) This is the extent of Janaki's self denial and loss of identity that even for her own hobby she'll have to ask her husband and then decide. Imagine the words, "O lord, tell me my hobby. Tell me about my temperament, my likes and dislikes. And also tell me as to what should I do in order to develop my decision making power." Janaki has been reduced to straw.

But then as we said, Janaki is changing. She is in no mood to entertain Balu's censorious behaviour. She enjoys her trip thoroughly with four rich divorced women of America, the two nuns, and her, closest friend on tour, Romi Singh. When Balu loses his passport while rapt in the erotic sounds of cuckoo clocks, he is forced to stay back in the city to get a duplicate one. Janaki decides to go on with the tour and not miss her chance of seeing the world. Janaki has no idea of the dilemma in Balu's mind, of his newly awakened appetite for physical pleasures, and of his sprees with her own body. How symbolic is Janaki's ignorance of all carnal affairs! How innocent she is! Just mark the irony of it all. An Indian woman does not have any right over her own body. Cast in the Sati Savitri model, she cannot enjoy this part of life even with her own husband. Can a Sati lust? No way! Secrecy is working is poisonous designs. Balu decides not to disclose his fantasies to Janaki. An Indian wife may be serving, docile, obedient and passive but she is never the soul mate, the true companion. As the joke goes that once a husband saw his wife going with another man and enjoying, he fell off with shock, "I never thought my wife could be so much fun!" The standard wifely attributes leave out surrendering of self, and opening up of innermost dreams. Marriage has gone down to become a matter of habit and ritual. The Sati Savitri model to which Cauvery refers again and again gives no space for sensual joys. A Sati can only submit her body to her husband because it is her religious duty to do so. The whole thing is vulgar in its hypocrisy.

II

In *The God of Small Things,* Ammu says that a woman has no choice in choosing between a father's or a husband's name. The situation of an Indian feminist is not different. Between an Indian brand of life and Western feminist model she is left with hardly any choice. Both the paradigms are equally hurting. Only a little searching reveals that somehow the male Indian mind over the centuries has selected certain myths. For its convenience, it has (cunningly?) pushed the uncomfortable myths into abyss. Passivity and womanhood is a forced and unnatural combination. As A.L. Basham writes in his classic *The Wonder That Was India,* "The literature of Hindu India, both religious and secular, is full of sexual allusions, sexual symbolism and passages of frank eroticism" (170). And again, "Sexuality was not looked on as a mere vent for the animal passions of the male, but as a refined mutual relationship for the satisfaction of both parties" (171). Basham's whole discussion on marriage in ancient India and its essence is centred around mutuality, reciprocity, and active participation of both man and woman in social, cultural, religious as well as physical domain. If we look at the plethora of myths, the active woman myths far outnumber the passive woman myths. Adyashakti, Agni, Mohini, Shakuntala, Kali, Urvashi, Vidula, Kunti and Draupadi have been put aside. With centuries of practice Sati Savitri, Sita and Ahilya have gained currency as ideal for womanhood and wifehood. Moreover, in reality, women of the latter group stand for an intense *interiorization* of mental energies and thought processes rather than passivity.

On the other hand, when the four American divorcees recount the pleasures of separation to our native Janaki, it is difficult to keep one's post-colonial consciousness at bay. The binaries are so obvious. Janaki is the third world model while the Americans are naturally first world specimens. This *first* and *third* are used here for want of better terminology. Remaining in marriage, it follows, is Janaki's inability (therefore fault) to come out of this old ritualistic bond. The first world women have successfully broken the barriers, succeeded in getting thick sustenance amount from their ex-husbands and are now happily enjoying the singlehood sans any liability, touring around Europe and, pitying the condition of poor Janaki. They have used the other gender in getting material benefits and have then gone on to oust it from their world. The Westerner urges, prods, entices, pities, insults the Easterner to enter the game by their rules. You are not free if not free by their standards. A Hindi phrase beautifully sums up all techniques, *sama* (friendship), *dama* (monetary reward), *dunda* (punishment), *bheda* (division) that are used to operate their scheme of things. This sickening type of feminism is as bad as going for the misinterpreted Sati Savitri model. Leela Gandhi writes, "Wherever she goes, the native woman is required to exhibit her ineluctable difference from the primary referent of Western feminism: It is as if everywhere we go, we become someone's private zoo" (Trinh 1989, 82). This voyeuristic craving for the colourful alterity of native women seriously compromises the seemingly egalitarian politics of liberal feminism. The consciousness of difference, identified by Trinh, sets up an implicit culturalist hierarchy wherein almost inevitably the native woman suffers in contrast with her Western sibling. By claiming the dubious privilege of preparing the way for once more unfortunate sisters, the Western feminist creates an insuperable division between "I-who-have-made-it and you-who-cannot-make-it" (85).

When I urge for an Indian brand of feminism, I imply a more socially welfare oriented scheme. The Indian feminist ought to be talking of female foeticide, malnutrition of the girl child, poor education for girls ('My son's at St. Stephen's doing commerce, my daughter's cozily doing M.Muse. at Mahila Mahavidyalaya), child marriages, the risks of child bearing, insincere treatment of girls ('in parents' home I'm a guest about to be disposed of in marriage and in in-laws' home I'm an outsider—where do I belong?'), dowry and related deaths, gender discrimination at workplace, double standards of working men ('my wife's a housewife—pure, chaste AND not available while those who work with me are entertainers') etc.

But with our Macaulay made minds, what we talk instead is liberation of V, subjugation of P. We love to talk about same sex sex, redefinition of the age old institution of marriage, its destruction if possible, single motherhood, gay marriages, living together arrangements and so on. With half of the society malnourished, we can hardly afford to talk like this. Our discourse!! becomes meaningless if it does not have at least a remote relevance to the society we live in. As teacher-critics, (or we may employ more grandiose and narcistic terms like scholars, intellectuals etc.) we must be part of the society. It sustains us and has every right to expect something from us. Criticism, of course, cannot be reduced to direct social service like dropping pulse polio drops but it must be sensitive to social conditions. Then only it can claim to be relevant. Once you start aping others, you hardly know what to think. As it is the commands from the West are ever so fluctuating. So smashing marriage and thereby disintegrating society will not lead us anywhere. A study is required of the mindset that produces the endless queue of novels by women of Indian origin written on the same beaten track where marriage stands for bondage, husband for villain, liaison for enlightenment, divorce for freedom, children for burden, home for fight and so on. As I wrote elsewhere, "Western feminism separates man from woman, and mother from child. It results in divorces, estrangement, and a feeling of vacuum in life. How many women in India will agree to be freed from their biological fate, i.e., giving birth to a child? A feminist of the Western orientation of mind goes on doubting. She sees a plot, a design, a conspiracy in everything...When I read novels by Indian women, I get acutely aware of the persistent Western influence on their perception. 'Husband', 'poor husband', I am inclined to say, is the target number one. He is the enemy number one...In Ruchira Mukherjee's *Toad in my Garden,* there are two women: the young Megha and the middle-aged Damyanti. While Megha's life is ruined by her uncle, Nilu, Damyanti finds her doom in her husband, Beni Madho. Then comes a bright, young chap called Ashwin who with his modern ideas transforms these sleepy things into real women of substance...While a husband is funnily named Beni Madho, the lover is stylishly called Ashwin. I want to ask Mukherjee that if enlightenment has to come through a man, why not let it come through the husband himself?... So many young minds are being denied the possibility of finding happiness in domestic life by this kind of literature. Various T.V. serials, and novels have created a kind of atmosphere where urbanized, half Westernized girls and boys are entering the nuptial life with suspicion and a militant attitude. Marriage in their minds is a battle and the house of the in-laws a battlefield" (317-320).

The most interesting point to note is the persistent male referent, a judging attitude by male standards. That unarmed, believing attitude of the remote Indian past has faded so badly that even its memory is blurred. Feminism of the negative sort turns even good things into bad. Balu did not take dowry in his marriage. The money earmarked for Janaki's marriage was diverted towards her brother's education. But that brother shamelessly demanded dowry in his own marriage. Later, it was found that his wife had a sixth finger on her one foot. For hiding that deformity, that brother kept demanding money from his wife's parents for next ten years. They paid him too! Now our hero, Balu gets a rough deal. Although Janaki's family is for ever grateful to Balu, Janaki herself is not. While on tour, Janaki remarks, "Yet I sometimes feel that it is better for the girl's parents to give as much as they can. Why be beholden to the boy's side for ever?" (171) For Balu, this is indeed painful, "To insinuate that he had expected or wanted her family to be grateful to him for the rest of his life was, he thought, a grossly unfair accusation. Is that what she was trying to say after all these years? What had come over her?" (172)

The Uncoupling, however, ends on a positive note. Balu and Janaki return from England, Balu *lets* Janaki start her tailoring school and in the very last lines suggestions of sensuous joys between the husband and the wife are suggested. But the best part is the lesson that Balu takes from his European tour, "But Balu is not at all keen on traveling abroad any more. India is good enough, he says" (236).

When as critics we comment on the thinking of the author and accuse her/him of Westernized approach, or biased attitudes, or just anything else, some injustice is done to the author. *The Uncoupling,* for example is a casual piece, meant to be enjoyed. And such novels are needed as well. But then each reader (the critic is also a reader) uses, misuses, even abuses the vehicle provided by the novelist to express her/his own ideas. Things are twisted and turned to suit the inclination and intention of each reader. This is unavoidable. This is part of the reading process and should be taken like that. A feminist will see gender injustice everywhere, be it Shakespeare, Austin or Kalidasa. A structuralist will search for patterns. Rukmani Bhaya Nair writes correctly, "Story-imports are formulations of the intention of the storyteller. Inferences from stories are made, on the other hand, by the listener and are structurally derivable from the listeners' knowledge of typical story-schemata' (65). The remarks of the second part of this paper may be taken in this light.

WORKS CITED

Basham, A.L. *The Wonder That Was India.* London: Macmillan, 1954.

Gandhi, Leela. *Postcolonial Theory: A Critical Introduction.* New Delhi: OUP, 1998.

Madhavan, Cauvery. *The Uncoupling.* New Delhi: Penguin Books, 2003.

Mulchandani, Sandhya. *The Indian Man: His True Colours.* New Delhi: Picus Books, 1999.

Nair, Rukmani Bhaya. *Narrative Gravity: Conversation, Cognition, Culture.* New Delhi: OUP, 2002.

Tiwari, Shubha. "Women on Crusade: At War with Themselves. A Look at Feminists in India" in Basavraj Naikar Ed. *Indian English Literature,* Vol. IV, New Delhi: Atlantic Publishers and Distributors (P) Ltd., 2003.

Shades of Life in Usha K.R.'s *The Chosen*

11

SHUBHA TIWARI

Over the years I have realized that it is easier to write on books that one does not like completely and it is difficult to write on books that one accepts, assimilates, and identifies with totally. I did not expect when I first picked up *The Chosen* by Usha K.R. the pleasant surprise that awaited me. To begin with, it is a good novel. Nagaratna, the heroine, the soul of this novel comes from a lower middle-class background. She and her mother from a village in Karnataka come to live in the outskirts of Bangalore where Nagaratna's brother Satya and his wife Pushpa are already staying. The girl is especially right from the beginning. The indefinable thing called 'personality' is her asset. 'Personality' is not physique, not looks, not complexion, not clan, not even education, but something all of these and at the same time above these. And of course, it can be cultivated and improved upon. But here we are talking about the original brightness of a child, growing into adolescence. In some measure, it can be referred to as intelligence. But intelligence itself can be very oppressive at times. Nagaratna carries a head of her own over her shoulders. She thinks, she does not copy the style of her classmates, not even of the most charming and beautiful of them, Shylaja. She is self-composed, every bit an original. I am reminded of the Freudian concept of psychic energy. In fact, throughout our discussion in this paper we will need psychological, and para psychological viewpoints to demystify the text and build our understanding of it. Mental energy is energy in the physical meaning of the word, i.e., probably something that can be transformed into another kind of energy analogous to the transformation of mechanical into thermic energy. Energy is not perishable—it can be accumulated, preserved, discharged, dissipated, blocked—but it cannot be annihilated. This postulate of preservation of mental energy, its transformability, its functioning in a close analogy to physical energy, is one of the guiding principles of psychoanalysis.[1]

Nagaratna or let us call her Naga is no meteor but she certainly is quite a person, especially keeping her age in mind. What I like most about her is her observing power. She carefully looks at people, compares and contrasts, and draws her own conclusions. The big thing is that she wants a better life. She is not satisfied with the mundane, low, cheap, inconsequential existence. She has that necessary hunger, that sparkle that makes one move forward in life.

When Naga enters the school, there is an undeclared war of nerves between her and Shylaja, the most beautiful girl of the class. "In Nagaratna, Shylaja recognized an original. All she usually saw around her were pale imitations of herself. When she wore a pair of earrings or bangles, or the latest hair clip, the very next day half the class would be wearing the same thing. They also tried to copy her laugh, she knew, and the way she looked up from beneath the flip of hair across her eyes. But Nagaratna continued to plait her hair tightly. When all the girls were swarming around her, admiring her latest hair band, Nagaratna would not even ask her where she had bought it. To Shylaja, Nagaratna had the appeal that the elephant with its lumbering grace has for the dear."[2]

The two girls work as a contrast only to show what the other is not. Eventually, they become friends or 'best friends' in their adolescent terminology. To the world of adolescent girls where style of hair, dress, feminine charms, lisping, eyebrow depletion, sideway glances and a touching faith in one's own attracting power are everything, Nagaratna by and large, remains an outsider. She is the only one in her class to know that the plural of mouse is mice and the correct way to end an application is 'yours faithfully'. With her sound knowledge of English grammar, she stands first in her class. Ultimately, she is accepted by her mates, accepted being such an important factor in any individual's life, particularly in the transforming age of teens.

Two girls, Shylaja and Nagaratna, choose two opposing directions. When the shorthand tutor, NPP Sir, writes a letter of admiration and invitation to Nagaratna, she decides not to go. Instead, Shylaja goes and hooks him as we come to know quite late in the novel. Nagaratna wants a job. She wants a neat and clean home like that of one of her neighbours, Nirmala. Even amidst such hustle bustle Nirmala manages to live with some grace. Her children are clean and tidy. Her home is peaceful. This is the promise that life holds for Nagaratna, a ray of hope, a distant possibility.

Then come life, real life drama, and experience in worldly affairs. For all her psychic energy, her personality, and her good English, the system does not see Nagaratna any different from countless others with a B.Com. degree and a diploma in shorthand. Her sandals wear out. Her confidence is on the brink of falling into the abyss of depression. She is desperate for a job and a job is not in sight. Her state at this stage depicts the fate of so many young men and women in our country who are bright in their own way. Unemployment, underemployment, and unsuited employment turns them sour, their life energy freezing, their attitudes becoming cynical, and their potential going to the dustbin. Among all crises structures of youth, this one is the most poignant, urgent, and painful. As a renowned psychologist, Prof. Durgadas Sinha writes, "This period of crises, whether it be in the life of an individual or that of a whole generation of young people, is often reflected in certain kinds of strains and stresses and has been variously described as generation gap, vocational and social disorientation, alienation, ambivalence and identity confusion... As experienced subjectively, it means a feeling of fragmentation, of indecision, and of isolation from social and interpersonal contacts."[3]

As we shall see, Nagaratna is saved from this crises only to return to it more acutely at a later stage. She gets the job of an office assistant in an ashram school. The cacophony of Saikrupa Apartment in Vithala Colony where Nagaratna lives and the expansive, cool, soothing peace of the ashram premises where she works, are two opposing and most drastically different facets of human existence. The school sprawls across acres. Disciples of Swami Mukteshwaranand, popularly known as Guruji, run it. The present heir is Tejas Pandit. His daughter, Ms Damyanti Pandit runs the school. Tejas Pandit lives in another ashram at Muttu. This world of spirituality-cum-social service is new for Nagaratna. She is drawn to it as magnet does to iron. She is fascinated and impressed by the graceful living and thinking of Ms Pandit, her nephew Priyam, her friend and benefactor, Vasant Chandra, and Tejas Pandit and his entourage. They are a colourful batch. Some odd foreigners, some whimsical natives who are stinking rich and have denounced their wealth—such people make Tejas Pandit's band. Theirs is a life of no demands. They have everything. Their minds are free to venture into abstract territories of thought. Life is so easy for them. The world is an unrestricted and overflowing source of energy. Naga takes this world of spiritual luxury for what it apparently looks. Salary does not matter to her; only work does. She works sincerely, day and night for 'her' school. It becomes her life. She has a brief period of closeness to Ms Pandit and thereby influence in school. Things appear only too correct for Naga. To top it all, Vasant, a trustee of the school, son of a big businessman makes romantic advances towards her. Our Naga is on seventh heaven. She is happy.

Then comes her fateful visit to Muttu, the Ashram headquarters, where the great Tejas Pandit lives. The need of a spiritual guru is fundamental to human nature, just as love, hate, deceit, friendship or bigotry is. There is no escape from it. Since the very beginning, people have gone to and assembled near the wise one, the radiant one, the most compassionate one among them and have relieved themselves of their anguish, their failures, and frustrations. And frustration is also fundamental to human nature. No one, howsoever successful has escaped from it. Sudhir Kakar writes, "To be approached in awe and reverence, he (the guru) is someone who makes possible the disciple's fateful encounter with the mystery lying at the heart of human life. He is also the Rasputin look-alike, with piercing yet warm eyes, hypnotic and seductive at once, a promisor of secret ecstasies and radical transformations of consciousness and life. The guru is also the venerable guardian of ancient, esoteric traditions, benevolently watchful over the disciple's experiences in faith, gently felicitating his sense of identity and self."[4]

Naga's encounter with Tejas Pandit and of many others with him resembles the above description. Dumped and buried by the trivialities of life, cheap talk and dirty politics, the guru's touch and look is like an unlocking of the spiritual reservoir. "He simply held her hands in his and smiled at her and she felt a sudden liberating gush of happiness, as if a secret valve had opened in her heart to let the blood through. It was his eyes that locked you in—serene, luminous, and very, very kind as if they had instinctively divined your uncertainties and your troubles and would provide all the answers" (194).

The necessary imperfection of an individual's life, the burden of owning the doership of all actions, being held responsible and accountable for all one's deeds, being in continuous tension of performing and succeeding and all such pressing psychological demands create an urgent need in an individual to 'let go' of everything. One wants to let go, let loose of all credits, discredits, successes, failures, expectations, memories, hopes, everything. All that one wants to be oneself To 'be' is to live. The guru is one door, one altar, one entrance that invites you to do that. The guru is there; s/he will take care of everything. The guru takes the responsibilities of all your efforts, your good or bad actions. This is the psychotherapeutic value of gurus. Thus we have this spate of gurus, and healers of all grades and statutes around us. We can cry before our guru. There is no pretension, no ego, nothing to prove before our guru. Being devoted to the guru with 'tana, mana, dhana', nothing as such is expected from us. All of a sudden, the burden of living goes off.

But then, there is another side of the coin as well. Tejas was marked for his 'tej' (radiance) right from the beginning. Swami Mukteshwaranand chose him to be his heir, the inheritor of his spiritual legacy. He sidelined the old timers like Biswas (Mauni Baba) and Chandana (Tejas Pandit's first wife and Damyanti's mother). Now, this selection of one and rejection of others is a tricky business. It gives birth to what we have in *The Chosen*, a parallel text or story. One story is what is usually accepted and propagated by Tejas Pandit and Damyanti. But Mauni Baba's daughter, Shyamoli tells Naga a story not known to the world, the suppressed, and ignored story. "I could never say this in front of my father. But Guruji himself was not free from flaws," she said slowly. "My son in spirit, he called him and loved him like a father—blindly, unconditionally. Of the three of them, equally worthy, he decided that only Tejas would be sent to Shantiniketan. 'Pandit', he called him, and the innocuous H.R. Tejas Kumar became Panditji. Chandana felt it keenly, but Guruji said that he could not spare my father and her, they were the backbone of Muttu. But even as he came to depend more and more upon them, he had eyes only for Tejas. My grandmother always said, she sighed audibly that good looks eventually pay and that appearances are always deceptive—and he *looked* so spiritual" (243). So looking spiritual is more important than being spiritual.

There are bundles of hints all along that suggest that all is not well in the ashram. In the present times (or who knows, it might have been the same in olden days), spiritual conclaves have been badly marred by reports of bad moral conduct. Spirituality, 'the preparation of soul curry', has become a profession just like any other profession. The sheer intensity and totality of a devotee's surrender before the Guru paves way for perversion. It is very difficult to overcome the temptation when you are surrounded by beautiful, attractive males and females of all ages, sizes, and shapes. Chandana, Tejas Pandit's wife, objects to his spending private moments with his secretary. Then follows his punishment to his wife. He neglected her so completely, so perfectly, so wholeheartedly that her existence itself zeroed. She did not exist for him. He drove her carefully and calculatedly to commit suicide; Shyamoli says, "... the Pandit is too clever—yes, very clever—and that's the last thing you expect a guru to be... I can forgive him anything, but not the way he treated her, his wife. She practically ran the ashram, along with my father. Chandana will take care of that, Biswas will see to this, their names were always on everyone's lips, but he did not see them. He has that remarkable quality of not seeing what he doesn't want to see and of making people feel worthless when they don't agree with him... She committed suicide... But he drove her to it" (245-46).

This is the sidelined, parallel tale. There is a big gap between how the Pandit is perceived by the world as a spiritual guru and the cunning maneuverer that he actually is. The last bit is also cemented in the whole scandal when he finally marries his secretary, Suguna. Damyanti, his daughter is thrown out of her mind. She has remained a spinster just to take over the spiritual legacy. She felt to be 'a team' with her father. But the 'tilism', the chimera, the charisma, the myth is broken for her and for the reader as well. For Damyanti, the most painful thing is not the relationship but the act of marriage—marriage for her being 'the most common, most middle-class thing' in the world. But then, this is all part of the spiritual game—the risks that a guru-devotee relationship usually runs into. I cannot help quoting from Sudhir Kakar's *Essential Writing* again, "These idealizing projections are subversive of the guru's self-representation, constitute an insidious assault which a few gurus... are not able to successfully resist. A regression into omnipotent grandiosity is one consequence, while in the sexual sphere a retreat into sexual perversion has been reported often enough to constitute a specific danger of the guru role. It is sad to hear or read reliable reports about 70-year-old gurus who become Peeping Toms as they arrange, with all the cunning of the voyeur, to spy on their teenaged female disciples... The sexual aberrations, however, have not only to do with pathological regression in stray individual cases, but are perhaps also facilitated by the way the fundamentals of healing are conceptualized in the guru-devotee encounter. For instance, given the significance of a specific kind of intimacy, there is no inherent reason (except cultural disapproval) why intimacy between guru and devotee does not progress to the most intimate encounter of all and be seen as the special mark of the guru's favour; why the merger of souls does not take place through their containers, the bodies" (160).

> So much for our spiritual leaders, gurus, babas, yogis, sanyasis!

The Chosen evokes ideas in many other spheres as well. The very words 'the chosen' suggest the looming fate of human lives. You do not do a thing, you perform no role on your own—you are chosen to do it. Tejas is chosen for the guru role, Naga is chosen to have a glimpse of sophisticated life, Damyanti is chosen to act as an inheritor of spiritual legacy. It is the destiny, the preplanned scheme of things that chooses some, discards others, and how it discards after choosing. It is more painful to be cast off after being chosen. Damyanti receives a jolt from her father; and Naga from Damyanti and Vasant. Without a word or hint, without any reason or rhyme, Naga is left in the lurch, as though she is nothing, she does not exist, she is of no importance to anyone. She is rejected just as husk is separated from grain and blown into the wind. Naga is simply dropped out of scheme of things. After roaming in the town with Naga, after offering flowers to her, after showing her concept shops where food, junk jewelry, and artifacts are all available in one sweep, Vasant leaves Naga without any explanation, without even a word of formal excuse. It is appalling to our middle-class sensibilities. She followed him around and stood on the fringes, burning, distracted, carrying herself in both hands, as if she were a fragile, precious offering which unfortunately was of little use to the intended one. This was not what she wanted, not the apologetic half glance, the secretive half-smile, but an avowal, an acceptance, an uninterrupted half-hour, a sign that made it clear that she mattered most.

> But it was not to be. (260)

As if to seal her tragic fate completely, Naga is thrown out of the school as well. Damyanti, disappointed by her father, leaves school and goes abroad to her sisters. Damyanti's nephew, Priyam is the new man in command. And it is told to Naga that just as a US President goes for his own team, every Principal also needs her/his people to man the system. Naga tries to commit suicide and fails there too. She is nursed back to health and brought back to Sai Krupa courtyard amidst the realization that she has no job to return to and the "nursing home bill has eaten into the rest of the nest-egg her father had left for her wedding" (321).

The lower middle-class existence is so pathetically brought out in this novel. The street described in the novel seems directly coming out from the phenomenal tele serial by Aziz Mirza, *Nukkad*. Spirituality is personified by Nillakai Swami, the healer of the poor. There is a matching centre, a barber's shop, a grocery store, as also the goddess, Plague Amma, who came into existence in some remote past when plague had hit the area. The sheer congestion in homes, the forced proximity of one home to the other leaves no space for privacy. Tears are public, so is laughter. There is no possibility of thought except crude generalizations ruling or better, overruling human life. Naga has her 'private' space in the living-cum-drawing room near the window overlooking the street where she sits and combs her hair. The stairs of the apartment, and the common space downstairs servers as a courtyard to all the occupants of Sai Krupa—children do their home work there, women take nap, clean grains and pound masalas. Everything is discussed out in the open—honeymoon of someone, someone else's efforts to get pregnant, daughters and their marriages—everything is out for public display. There is no such entity as an individual in Sai Krupa. All vows, the ills of life are hurled at Shani, the evil planet. Petty affairs and trivial talk are the order of the day. I am reminded of Dominique Lapere's words when in *The City of Joy,* he calls the dwellers of Anand Nagar slum as sub-humans. Although, the conditions here are a shade better than Anand Nagar but the roughness, the thick skinned attitude is sickening indeed. Lemon lamps are lighted to appease gods. Naga's exposure to the fine aspects of life are of no meaning to Sai Krupa residents as well as to members of her family. What is the meaning of a job if it does not pay you well? What is promotion without increase in the salary? Naga, in her airy, seventh heaven days is fed up of this obsession with money. She declares, "Anyway, you wouldn't understand" (95). The same Naga, when faced with the bitter truth of being used and thrown off, decides to talk about a pay hike. But then, it is already time for her to leave the school. After the betrayal and humiliation, knowledge comes to Naga in painful pangs. She cannot escape the truth of her birth, her family, and surroundings. Her fate clings to her very closely.

Amidst all these dreary affairs, life goes on uninterrupted. Births, heroic deeds, love affairs, and survival—everything moves on smoothly. For example, Indramma, the owner of the apartment, is a single woman with a son. She runs her catering business from her own kitchen, serves and packs for office goers, school and college goers, earns a somewhat dignified existence. These are unsung, unrecognized heroines of the lower rung of the Indian social matrix. A millionaire's daughter goes for charity work in her white starched handlooms, and the whole world goes mad at her goodness, kindness and gives a standing ovation. And here are women, exploited and abused, struggling hard to hold their heads high. The book pricks the sensibilities of the reader continuously as the two worlds, one exuberant and elegant, the other, decayed and poor, are juxtaposed. It is a unique experience to see life in two stratas, two hues, two compartments only to realize in the end that the apparently better one is actually more dirty. Perseverance, comradeship, and companionship are found in lower strata. The human virtues, the godliness, is not in ashrams; it is in chawls, slums, and apartments like Sai Krupa. Our Naga is no ordinary woman. At twenty-one, she has all the necessary experience to face life. And the miracle is that she is not dumped, not stumped. Life goes on unabated. Happiness and zest also go on. The very last sentence of *The Chosen* says, "But today, Naga knows, though it is neither a festival nor a birthday, today there will be a row of ghee lamps on the God shelf" (321).

'Sinner and saint, beloved and betrayed', in Kamala Das's terminology, at the tender, young age of twenty-one, Naga begins her innings in life. Das writes and I conclude with her lines:

> I am sinner, I am saint.
> I am the beloved and the betrayed.
> I have no joys which are not yours,
> No aches which are not yours.
> I too call myself I.[5]

REFERENCES

1. Woleman, Benjamin B. *Contemporary Theories and Systems in Psychology:* New York: Harper and Row, 1960, 208.
2. Usha K.R. *The Chosen*. New Delhi: Penguin, 2003, 15. Subsequent references to the text of the novel are from this edition.
3. Sinha, Durgadas, Sudhir Kakar Ed. *Identity and Adulthood.* New Delhi: OUP, 1997, 56-57.
4. Kakar, Sudhir, "T.G. Vaidyanathan" Ed. *The Essential Writing of Sudhir Kakar*. New Delhi: OUP, 2001, 141.
5. Das, Kamala. *Poems Old and New*. New Delhi: Macmillan, 2002, 178.

Psychological Exploration of Women: The Indian Literary Context

12

R.K. MISHRA

In the galaxy of Indian novelists in English, Indian women writers too shine luminously like their male counterparts by their significant contribution to enrichment of Indian English novels. The women novelists, who have risen to celebrity and won global recognition in literature are Cornelia Sorabji, Iqbalunnisa Hussain, Kamala Markandaya, Anita Desai, R.P. Jhabvala, Attia Hossain, Nayantara Sahgal, Santha Rama Rau, Kamala Das, Rama Meheta, Shobha De and Arundhati Roy. These novelists seem to have derived inspiration and influences from British novelists in respect of art and device in writing novels. They resemble to a great extent Jane Austen, George Eliot, Brontë sisters, Mrs. Gaskell, Dorothy Richardson and Virginia Woolf in the art of characterization and portrayal of psychic mind of women. Like these British women novelists Indian women writers surpass their male novelists both qualitatively and numerically in exploration of inner mind of women and thereby assert their own identity. They further differentiate themselves categorically from the group of British women novelists in the thematic exploitation of Indian life, scenes and culture and externalization of interior region of Indian women's mind.

Since this paper seeks to focus primarily on the psychological exploration of inner mind of Indian women in Indian novels in English, there is a need and relevance to dwell briefly on some of the novels of feminist significance with a view to substantiating this issue.

Among the Indian women novelists Toru Dutt, Krupabai Sathianathan, Shevanthi Bai Nikambe, Cornelia Sorabji, Iqbalunnisa Hussain, R.P. Jhabvala, Anita Desai, Rama Mehta, Shashi Deshpande, Shobha De, Kamala Das, Mahasweta Devi and Arundhati Roy are primarily concerned in their novels with the psychological crises in the lives of Indian women who are subjected to physical and psychological torture in a male dominated society. The novelists have exploited their skill in projecting convincingly the agonized mind of the persecuted women. Their portrayal of women characters in the novels invariably hears authenticity to their feminist approach, outlook and perspective. Their keen observation of the life of Indian women and their interest in the study of their inner mind are evidenced by their vivid and panoramic portrayal of their plight. The women novelists focus in their novels on the existential predicament and travails of the subdued women in a male dominated society governed by rigid traditions and restrictions. These writers being women dive deep into the inner mind of the repressed women by virtue of their feminine sensibility and psychological insight and bring to light their issues, which are the outcome of Indian women's psychological and emotional imbalances.

The last quarters of the 19th century was a landmark in the history of Indian novels in English on account of the emergence of a host women novelists, who gave a new direction in the writing of fiction in English. Their novels distinctively assume feminist significance for focusing on the inner mind of Indian women in the feministic perspective.

The first Indian women novelist who made a pioneering efforts in writing novels of profound Psychological significance was Toru Dutt. Although she is pre-eminently renowned as a poet for the versification of a substantial number of poetical work yet she is recognized as a novelist for her fictional work like *Le Journal de Mademoiselle d' Arvers* written in French, *Bianca* or *The Young Spanish Maiden* written in English. These two novels are self-projection of her own agony and anguish of life. The Marguerite in French novel and Bianca in English novel are self-portrayals of Toru's own personality attended with tragedy. Toru's typical attitude, feelings and sentiments, which are characteristically Indian in all respects, manifest in the character of her heroines. Example can he cited of Bianca's commitment to sacrifice her interest for the sake of her departed sister. Bianca feels it her moral duty to treat her sister's fiancé with affection and not with love. She realizes it her moral duty to confide her father that her lover has kissed her. She deliberately turns down Henry's offer to ingratiate with her father. All these sequences contribute to configuration in reader's mind the image of an Indian woman rather than that of an English or Spanish woman. The portrayal of the woman characters lead us to infer that Toru remained invariably an Indian woman in her temper, temperament and outlook. She has given her novel *Bianca* an inward direction.

Another woman novelist, who has projected her own Indian sensibility and attitude through women characters in her novels, is Krupabai Sathianathan. Her novels *Kamala: A Story of Hindu Life* (1894) and *Saguna: A Story of Native Christian Life* (1895) reflect on her sentimental reaction resulting from the impact of conversion of her family to Christianity. These novels are also self-revelatory of her inner life of sorrows and anguish. Whereas Saguna is the portrayal of her earlier life, Kamala is the story of her later life written in her bedridden circumstances. As Prof. Karakal observes, "The faithfulness of Krupabai's narrative and the sincerity of her purpose become vividly clear in the story of Kamala the heroine. The novelist delineated that any sensible reader might infer that Kamala's sorrow is the sorrow of many Indian women."

Shevanthi Bai Nikambe is another woman novelist who is not less renowned than her predecessors Toru Dutt and Krupabai. As a champion of feminism, she combated injustice and ill-treatment meted out to simple, sober, unsophisticated housewives. She focussed particularly on the tragedy of unsuccessful marital life and of widowhood.

She advocated the freedom, liberty and emancipation of women in order to extricate them from obsequious servitude and in human torture to which they were subjected by their husbands, mothers in-law and others. Her novel Ratnabai is a novel with a feminist perspective. It portrays the agony of a girl named Ratnabai who is persecuted by the relatives of her father-in-law for going to school for higher education. This novel espouses and voices the need of emancipation and education of Indian women and hence its reformist objective is foregrounded in the novel.

Another woman novelist of the pre-Independence India was Sorabji, a feminist and a social reformer. As an advocate by profession she championed the causes of Indian women and exposed in her stories the deep mental agony of the married and unmarried women. *Love and Life behind the Purdah* (1901), *Sun Babies* (1904) and *Between the Lights* (1908) are the stories that focus realistically on the inner mind of the suppressed women living behind purdah. The first one is a collection of ten stories each seeking to evoke pity and sympathy for the socially and sexually tortured women who dare not raise their voice for deliverance from persecution. These stories are an attempt at exploration into the deeper chamber of the mind that reacts passively and timidly to various forms of oppression.

Sorabji too depicts the tragedy of the child marriage, child widowhood and sterility in marital life. "Greater Love" is a story that describes the psychological torture inflicted on a childless wife by all except Kamala a kind-hearted hostess. "A Living Sacrifice" is a story that delineates how Dwarki lays herself on the funeral pyre of her brother-in-law and sacrifices her life with a view to saving her twin sister Tani. Another story entitled "Between the Twilights" depicts the predicament of Indian women behind the curtain. It seeks to draw readers' attention to the silent reaction of the oppressed women in the male dominated Indian society that denies them the right to live with freedom. The story "India Calling" presents the bizarre picture of an Indian women placed forcibly on the funeral pyre with her legs dangling in the water of the holy Ganges. The lady was forced relentlessly to lie in the same posture of discomfort till she died after three days of physical affliction. This is illustrative of how women were tormented in the past without remorse and compassion.

Sorabji also describes the plight of co-widows in joint families. She focusses on the miseries of Giribala Dasi, the young widow, who is isolated in a family on the ground of her widowhood. She also recounts the gruesome story of Anarkali, the child daughter-in-law relentlessly forced to face the ordeal of 'Sati.'

Swarna Kumari Ghosal is different from her contemporary women novelists in respect of her adoption of themes for her fictions. Her fictions *The Fatal Garland* (1910) and *An Unfinished Son* (1913) are historical romances that deal with the theme of love rather than the tragic life of fettered women. Madam Ghosal is not at all concerned with the psychological suffering of Indian women behind purdah. She seems to have fallen back upon the traditional Victorian device of exploiting the theme of love and romance. From this viewpoint she can not be compared with those women novelists who wrote with a feminist perspective.

Most of the Indian women living in an orthodox and conservative family feel inhibited to raise their voice against aggressive dominance of the male persons of the society owing to their inferiority complex and rigid code of conduct imposed on them. Their ambitions, desires, sense and sensibility are faithfully expressed in the novels of the women novelists of the late 19th and early 20th centuries. Their novels show how such women in spite of being highly educated undergo psychological suffering due to inferiority complex and deep sense of inhibitions. They depict the image of the new women waiting for emancipation and liberation in a fast changing world. The Indian women novelists mentioned above belong to the pre-independence period during which both Hindu and Muslim communities in India were being governed rigidly by their traditions. Since India has been a tradition bound nation, its women are also shackled by numerous social and religious customs and conventions that render them incarcerated behind curtains. In view of their miseries, the women novelists of feminist perspective committed themselves to fictionalizing women's cause with a view to ameliorating their position and releasing them from the state of traditional servitude. With the increasing awareness of feminism as a new revolutionary idea, the trend of feminist writing persisted in Indian literature even after independence. The novelists of the post-independence period, who highlighted the causes of women, are Anita Desai, Rama Mehta, Shashi Deshpande, Arundhati Roy etc. Their main focus was on the undesirable dominance of men over women.

From the viewpoint of the theme of the novels and objectives of the novelists, we notice a sharp contrast between Kamala Markandaya's fictions and those of earlier and later writers. In Markandaya's novels we find an ideological clash between the East and the West, between the concept of ancient India and that of new modern India. Her novel *Nectar in a Sieve* deals with the themes of rural India and focusses on the miseries of the oppressed peasantry. This novel is reminiscent of Lal Bihari Dey's *Govinda Samanta* in respect of depiction of the life of Indian peasants. Similarly, Markandaya's *Some Inner Fury* and *Possessions* are also not at all concerned with the inner landscape of Indian women. They are on the other hand preoccupied with the theme of the East-West encounter, which forms the basis of Santha Rama Rau's novel *Remember the House* and Nayantara Sahgal's *This Time of Morning*. However, the theme of psychological suffering and traumatic experience of Indian women is exploited by feminist novelists like Iqbalunnisa Hussain, Anita Desai, Rama Mehta, Shashi Deshpande and Arundhati Roy.

Iqbalunnisa Hussain as a feminist writer has brought to limelight the tragic life of Indian women in her fiction *Purdah and Polygamy: Life in an Indian Muslim House* (1944). The novel unveils the silken curtain of Purdah and unmask the agonized mind of housewives living like encaged birds in the orthodox Muslim families. She has panoramically portrayed the evils and abuses of customs and traditions that had enslaved the married women and rendered them practically helpless and voiceless. She upholds the reaction of women and shows how Indian women endure physical and psychological suffering simply by virtue of their womanliness. Her novel *Purdah and Polygamy* thematically approximates to Cornelia Sorabji's stories of *Love and Life behind Purdah*.

Anita Desai like Joyce and Woolf is widely recognized as the pioneer of psychological novel in modern Indian English literature. The most conspicuous feature of her art is the portrayal of characters. She penetrates psychologically deep into the inner working of women and externalizes their passive reaction. In this respect she approximates to Dostoevsky, Proust, Virginia Woolf, James Joyce and Henry James.

Cry, the Peacock (1963) is the story of an Indian woman Maya who undergoes considerable traumatic experiences obsessed by forebodings and mental tension. In this novel Anita explores the turbulent emotional world of the neurotic protagonist Maya who is constantly haunted by a presentiment of her husband's death on account of her belief in astrological prediction. She desperately looks for someone to ward off the shadow of imminent death but none realizes her exuberance of sentiment, emotion and tension. Even her husband Gautam, an insensible and unsentimental youth hardly shares in her psychological suffering. On the contrary, he treats her as a spoilt child. *Cry, the Peacock* (1963) begins with Maya's reaction to the death of her pet dog and husband's total indifference to her. Anita projects the psychic mind of an Indian woman in the tone of Maya. She says, "Something slipped in my tear hazed vision, and shadowy something that prodded me into admitting that it was not my pet dog's death alone that I mourned to-day but another sorrow unremembered perhaps as yet not even experienced and filled me with despair." As the prophecy of the astrologer obsesses her mind she utters, "I am dying and I am in love with living, I am in love and I am dying, God let me sleep, forget, rest. But no I will never sleep again. There is no rest more only death and waiting." These spontaneous utterances evince her traumatic experiences. Maya absorbs herself in her inner world of tragic vision.

In the second novel *Voices in the City* (1965), Anita Desai psychoanalyses the inner mind of three characters, Nirod Ray and his sisters Monisha and Amla. These characters feel utterly frustrated like Maya of the novel *Cry, the Peacock* (1963). They profess a mysterious longing to return home in Kalipong and enjoy the solitude and serenity of jungles but they are forced to live in Calcutta which is a city of despair and death for them. Since we are concerned in this paper with the psychological exploration of women's mind we turn our attention to the character of Manisha and Amla; Monisha, who is married against her will in a joint family of rich middle-class Philistines, is haunted like Maya by her morbid musings about death. She morbidly deplores the futility of marital life, she reacts in the following words, "They put me away in steel container, a thick glass cubicle and I have lived in it all my life without a touch of love or hate or warmth on me." In order to release herself from the life of captivity she resorts to committing suicide.

In her other novel *Where Shall We Go This Summer* (1975), Anita follows the track of Brontë sisters, who chose to study the heart and mind of women from women's point of view. Their novels provide glimpses into the tortured souls of their heroines. In like manner, Anita too portrays the tragic intensity of her women characters with a feminist perspective. The novel *Where Shall We Go This Summer* depicts the tragic life of Sita who leads a life of isolation and loneliness in her husband's house. Her unmitigated suffering drives her to a state of madness and desperation. Desai portrays her women characters as sentimental and introspective under the influence of British women novelists—Meredith George Eliot, Virginia Woolf and Richardson.

The next novel *Fire on the Mountain* (1977) explores the inner emotional world of Nanda Kaul and Raka. Anita Desai draws a picture of the tragedy of Nanda leading a segregated life like a recluse in a lonely hill hut. In the *Clear Light of Day,* Vimal's attitude is more or less similar to that of Nanda in the sense that she too prefers to lead a solitary life in a decaying house. In this novel Desai penetrates into the hidden depth of mind of her characters, who are obsessed by nostalgic reminiscences of their past life and events. Thus Anita Desai heralded a new era of psychological exploration of inner mind in the novels.

Another novelist who traverses along the same path of study of psychic mind is Rama Mehta. In her novel *Inside the Haveli* (1977), she like Cornelia Sorabji and Iqbalunnisa depicts how Geeta, a city-bred girl of Bombay, well to do and educated, has to marry a young man of Udaipur and live in a tradition bound haveli. She has to struggle much to carve out her own identity in the male dominated Indian society. The novel also focusses on the conflict between tradition and modernity. In the novel, the haveli represents Indian tradition and the girl Geeta represents modernity. Rama Mehta's *Inside the Haveli* presents a vivid picture of the traditional life of the women in the haveli. The novel seems to be thematically a compromise between tradition and modernity. A modern sophisticated girl of a modernized city of Bombay is brought into a tradition bound family in the form of matrimonial negotiation. She lives as a daughter-in-law in a family that circumscribes all her thoughts and activities and imposes on her all traditional restrictions. In defiance of these impositions she grapples to introduce the modern concept of values with a view to protecting and promoting the interests of the new women of India. The conflict between tradition and modernity imparts the dignity of a feminist novel to *Inside the Haveli.*

The novel seeks to delineate the various possibilities of synthesizing two different antithetical concepts of tradition and modernity and amalgamating these heterogeneous ideologies. Geeta's objective is sociologically significant in rebuilding Indian society and family life by wedding these two concepts. The haveli represents tradition, narrowness, servitude of women and shackles of freedom. Geeta represents modernism, rationalism, new outlook and emancipation of woman.

She also synthesized in her novels the two contrary concepts. This is evident from her dealing and attitude. For example, she behaves with her husband in the spirit and outlook of a modernized wife, whereas with other members of the family she copes with them as a traditional daughter-in-law, in keeping with the traditional code of conduct of the family.

She touches the feet of the elders every morning and veils her head and responds to them and in a humble tone of servitude asks for "Hukkum". While her husband's attitude and outlook are rooted in the tradition of Udaipur, her own sensibility and sentiments are influenced by the modernity of Bombay city life. However, the novel seeks to paint her as a new woman living in a world of tradition with her unconventional and modern outlook. The conflict between tradition and modernity is resolved only by Geeta, by her sense of adaptability, compromise and forbearance. Thus we find an excellent amalgamation of two concepts in the novel.

Similarly, Shashi Despande too reveals with a feminist perspective the revolutionary sentiment of an unusual women character Sarita. The girl revolts against the age-old traditions of orthodoxy and conservatism in order to assert her independence and identity. Her novels also tend to suggest a conflict between tradition and modernity. Her other work *The Binding Vine* (1992) is a novel of feminist significance. It presents woman as a spineless wooden creature subjected to male dominance. In the novel *That Long Silence,* Shashi voices her feeling in favour of emancipation of women from the grip of conventional male control. In all her novels she concentrates on the portrayal of pathetic and heartrending condition of Indian women in the male dominated society.

As a feminist par excellence, Shashi Deshpande depicts how her protagonists instead of rebelling against male, adapt themselves to a male dominated society. This patriarchal ideology and dominance are denounced. The age-old tradition of subordinating women to men is foregrounded as a stigma in the society. Simone de Beauvoir is of the view that the history of humanity is a history of keeping the women in subjection and silence. Feminists deprecate such masculinity and treatment meted out to women. Feminist literature tends to espouse the cause of the women and denounces everything that circumscribes the liberty of woman.

The Binding Vine (1992) gives an insight into the psychological suffering of Urmi and Mira, the women characters of the novel. It shows how an Indian women loses her identity after her marriage and birth of children. She is recognized either as a wife of somebody or mother of someone. After reading the doleful verses written by Mira, Urmi realizes the tragic intensity of Mira's suffering in which she herself feels pity for Mira forgetting her own suffering. Her personal diary is the mirror of her suffering and tortured life. The novel convinces the readers as to how a woman suffering in life can realize the plight of another woman by virtue of her womanly instinct and sensibility but man cannot realize because of his spirit of masculinity and his traditional ego or gender superiority. Mira's poems reveal this male dominance over women. She writes these poems in reaction to her husband's obtrusive imposition of a code of conduct.

> Don't tread paths barred to you/Obey, never utter a 'no.
> Submit and your life will be a paradise.

Similar is the reaction of Saru, the protagonist of Shashi Deshpande's fiction *The Dark Holds No Terror* (1980):

> A wife must always be a few feet behind her husband.

Another incident that illustrates the psychological infliction meted out to women by men is Venu's disparaging remarks on the poetic talent of Mira. When Mira asked Venu, the budding poet to read some of her poems, the latter commented, "Why do you need to write poetry. It is enough for a young woman like you to give birth to children. That is your poetry. Leave the other poetry to us men." This harsh disparagement on Mira agonizes her and dampens her creative talent. This is an example of how the male often torture women psychologically. The novel also exposes the anguish of other women characters like Kalpana, a girl who is sexually tortured. She is in the words of Doctor "neither dead nor alive". The novel further exposes the traditional Indian concept that emphasizes the marriage of girls for the safety of their life and chastity. We get the picture of the mental agony of Kalpana who is raped by Sulu's husband Prabhakar. Sulu, after knowing how her husband molested Kalpana, became agonized and committed suicide in a state of mental tension. Likewise Urmi, Mira, Shakutai, Kalpana and Sulu are all victims of male dominance. Shashi Deshpande has drawn out the women characters of this novel from women's point of view and has imparted feminist significance to this novel. *The Binding Vine* deserves to be treated as a feminist novel for its focus on the interior mind of the shackled Indian women characters. They are projected as educated, independent, rebellious and modern in outlook. Her women characters are no more like Toru's Bianca or Sorabji's Owarki nor are they encaged like Rama Mehta's Geeta. Her women characters are the replicas of the modern city-bred girls of metropolis.

Another revolutionary women novelist is Kamala Das who projects in her poetry and novels her own inner mind without inhibition and hesitation. She revolts against the male dominated Indian society and reveals her feeling in a confessional mood. Her novels *Alphabet of Lust* (1980) and *A Doll for the Child Prostitute* (1977) are the ironic expression of the various physical and psychological harassment meted out to married women. Her *My Story* (1976) is also an autobiographical novel in which she reveals her reaction in support of women and against male as a class of people. These novels are a study of the inner mind of an Indian woman.

Manshi, the heroine in *In the Alphabet of Lust* (1980), is a replica of Kamala Das. Manshi voices the sentiments and feeling of the author. The heroine of this novel is an unhappy and frustrated wife of Amol Mitra, a government official who looks old enough to be her father. He remains engaged all the time in the official work being indifferent to his young wife. Consequently, her marital life is disrupted and she is compelled to search for an identity. Manshi says, "We are not suited to each other. He is busy with his files all the time. I like people, some conversation and some show of affection." Manshi acts as a mouth organ of Kamala Das in the projection of her own state of agonized mind.

Kamala Das's next novel *A Doll for the Child Prostitute* (1977) deals with the same theme of psychological torture inflicted on women. In the context of this novel Anisur Rahman comments, "It may be treated as an expression of personality and not an escape from it. Her characters in fact like their creator crave as it were for an escape from their predicament and fall in its snare again and again pathetically, almost tragically." *A Doll for the Child Prostitute* adopts the theme of search for liberation and identity. Mirathai known as Mira secretly marries her student client in order to assert her liberty and identity as a woman but her marital joy and happiness dissolves into sorrow and despair as she is betrayed by her husband. This tragedy compels her to fall back on her past profession as a prostitute. The same quest for identity is also revealed through the character of Rukmini, a child prostitute. Her mother instead of giving her a doll to play with, sells her to Laxmibai, the keeper of a brothel. She is forced into the profession of prostitution.

In these two novels Kamala Das vividly delineates the helplessness of Indian women and indifference of society to their plight. None bothers to ameliorate their situation. These novels are poignant ironic criticism of the social status of Indian women. By her portrayal of women's predicament, Kamala Das has given a new direction and dimension to Indian novels in English.

Gita Hariharan is a novelist who uses her novel as a vehicle of her protest against male dominance over women. In her novel *The Thousand Faces of Night* (1992) she denounces the subservience of Indian women and advocates their emancipation from the bondage of male domination. She depicts the tragedy of women, who in their inner mind react to this kind of subjection and persecution. Devi is the central woman character in the novel *The Thousand Faces of Night* (1992). She like Ammu in Arundhati Roy's *The God of Small Things* (1997) has to endure all persecution in her social life. This novel presents a vivid picture of patriarchal dominance in social life. It also strikes a note of feminist approach in the theme of women's psychology.

The other feminist novelist who won the Booker Prize for literary achievement is Arundhati Roy. In her novel *The God of Small Things* she seeks to evaluate the abnormal psychology of men and women in the typical Indian social clime. She unfolds the inner working of some of the major characters in the novel. She focusses on the traumatic experiences of Ammu who is terribly shocked and upset due to her foolish marriage with a Bengali young man. She develops a contempt for her drunkard husband and falls in love with another man Velutha. Her frustration in marital life provokes her terrible psychological reaction, which manifests in her mental reflection and rumination. Roy has used the psychoanalytic theory of Freud, to unveil the agonized mind of her women characters. A study of her novels can convince the readers as to how they assume feminist significance by reason of her concentration on the portrayal of women characters.

Another woman novelist who projects a new vision of Indian women in her fictions is Manju Kapur. In her novel *Difficult Daughters* (1998) she portrays her women characters as woman of new modern outlook. The protagonist of this novel is Virmati who is a traditional women but her cousin is a Westernized lady. Unlike others she is inspired by Swami Dayanand's concept of women education. Manju Kapur denounces the persistence of the traditional idea that marriage is essential for women. She, therefore, depicts deliberately the characters of two girls of two different attitudes. They are Virmati and Shakuntala. The former is of traditional outlook whereas the latter is of modern outlook.

Shakuntala is an M.Sc. in Chemistry working at Lahore. She is intelligent, independent, sophisticated and above all rebellious in her attitude. She deprecates the concept of marriage as the summum bonum of life and reacts to this traditional idea. She speaks to Virmati with the following words, "but women are still supposed to marry and do nothing else." She advises her to live like a free bird and says "times are changing and women are moving out of the house, so why not you?" This reaction expressed by Shakuntala evidences Kapur's rebellious attitude against the servitude of women. She uses this woman character as her own mouth organ and advocates freedom and education for Indian women and their participation in national reconstruction. What authenticates this advocacy is Swarnalata's involvement in freedom struggle. In her novel *Difficult Daughters* (1998), the novelist portrays

Swarnalata as a committed women activist and a dedicated freedom fighter.

Manju Kapur unmasks the reacting mind of Virmati who is upset by the betrayal of her lover; her agonized mind is revealed in her utterances of the following lines, "Here I am in the position of being your secret wife, full of shame, wondering what people will say if they find me out, not being able to live in peace, study in peace and......why?" She refers to Swarnalata's statement about this selfishness and dominance of men over women. Swarnalata states, "Men take advantage of women." Virmati holds the conventional view of the purity and chastity of woman's body. "She was his for life, whether he ever married or not. She could never look elsewhere, never entertain another choice." This is her identity as an Indian woman of ideal womanhood. The novel presents a contrastive study of the mind of two Indian women who think differently in their Indian way of life.

After making a brief survey of all these Indian novels of feminist interest, we can look back to English novels by British women novelists in which women characters have been drawn out with psychological insight and feminist objective. Jane Austen was the first one to pioneer this venture in feminisation of the themes of novels. David Cecil aptly remarks in this context, "She represents a feminisation of the English novel." The other women novelists who reflect on woman's mind in their fictions are Mrs. Gaskell, Brontë sisters, Richardson and Virginia Woolf etc. Brontë sisters presented in their novels a sketch of women characters in their deep anguish. They portray these characters of women from women's viewpoint. Brontë's female characters Jane Eyre, Shirley and Agnes are fine studies of the plight of women. The British women novelists who were concerned with the exploration of the inner mind of women highlighted the various social, emotional and psychological phenomena that agonized English women in their social and familial situation. The novelists portrayed the plight of women with a feminist objective. The women in Great Britain are never socially or traditionally bound like Indian women. They are not subjected to ill-treatment and humiliation by the members of the family. Besides, their psychological suffering is not so intense and heart-touching like that of Indian women because of the liberty they enjoy. They can break away from any kind of bondage to revolt against any kind of persecution. Hence, they have no such cultural concept of subordination of women to men. Thus, the spectacle of suffering of women in English fictions is not so heart-rending as that of Indian women in Indian English novels. Similarly, the women novelists of other countries also cannot conceive of such inhuman torture meted out to Indian women. The pictures of the predicament of the women of Britain and America are entirely different. Hence, we hardly come across in their fictions the portrayal of extreme misery of women in their social life.

Jane Austen, who is upheld for her feminist approach in her novels, depicts only the problems of marriageable girls looking for worthy husbands of their choice. The themes of her six novels are identically the search of the mothers or aunts for grooms for their daughters and nieces. All events in her novels centre round the affairs of love, engagements, festivities, picnics, frustration and disappointments in marital life. Her characters in their state of disappointment never undergo deep psychological agony, which the Indian women experience in their male dominated families. Jane Austen presents the picture of the English women from a feminist viewpoint. In this context Baker points out, "In each one of her six novels, a young woman, witty, sensible, discerning and charming, is the pivot of interest and attention. In her novels we find ourselves in an intensely feminine atmosphere and from this viewpoint she stands in sharp contrast to Fielding who portrays male characters from men's perspective."

The Victorian women novelist Mrs. Elizabeth Gaskell (1810-1865) attempted novels of psychological significance and sought to explore and expose the inner mind of women in her masterpiece *Cranford* (1853). In this novel, Mrs. Gaskell presents the scenes of poverty, evening parties in a village dominated by the Amazons, widows and spinsters. The commonplace trivial incidents in the life of women are faithfully presented with a deeper psychological insight.

Her other novel *Ruth* is a study of the inner life of a young girl with focus on her intense psychological suffering resulting from her being seduced and betrayed by her lover. The novel presents the picture of the psychological crises experienced by the heroine Ruth.

Likewise, Brontë sisters also aimed in their novels at unmasking the feminine heart and anguished mind of women characters from women's point of view. They were not interested in the depiction of scenes of mystery and horror that characterized the Gothic novels by Horace Walpole (1764-1823) and Miss Clara Reeve (1729-1807) nor were they interested like Jane Austen in the portrayal of the beauty and elegance of country life. Never did they present sketches of pastoral beauty of rustic life. The Brontë sisters on the other hand impressed on the readers a new conception of the heroine as a woman of vital strength, courage and passionate feeling. Jane Eyre, Shirley and Agnes are the fine studies of feminine psychology from feminist viewpoint.

Another psychological novelist of the Victorian period was George Eliot (1819-1880). She was the first women writer who intellectualized English fictions by dealing with exalted and sublime thoughts of spiritual and psychological significance. Like Browning she was profoundly preoccupied with the exploration of inner struggle of human mind and soul. Her feminist interest is foregrounded in her portrayal and treatment of women character.

George Eliot's *Adam Bede* (1859), *Mill on the Floss* (1860) and *Silas Marner* (1861) are the novels of psychological interest and significance. She was basically a novelist of inner life engaged in delving deep into the souls of her characters from an intellectual and feminist point of view. She exhibited rare insight in the presentation of female characters. Richardson was another woman novelist who surpasses others in depicting feminine psychology. As an advocate of women movement, she is widely read and admired by women readers. In the same context of exploration and study of women's mind, Virginia Woolf stands unrivalled. She experimented and exploited both the theories of stream of consciousness and psychoanalysis. *Her Voyage Out* is her maiden journey into an unknown world. In her other novels *Mrs. Dalloway* (1925), *Jacob's Room* (1922) and *To the Light House* (1927) Virginia Woolf has portrayed the inner mind of women as an accomplished psychologist and keen observer of human characters.

Dorothy Richardson is another woman novelist, though inferior to Virginia Woolf yet influenced the latter and other writers of her time. In her novel *Pointed Roofs* (1915) she presents the subjective and objective biography of a young woman Miriam Henderson. Like Marcel Proust in France, Richardson was also concerned primarily with the inner perceptions of her chief characters particularly the women who were psychologically afflicted. In her novel *Pilgrimage* (1915) Richardson draws out the mental history of Miriam Henderson, whose impressions are recorded from moment to moment to convey the sentiment and feminine consciousness of a woman. She abandons homely life in England and begins a new life as a teacher in school in Hanover. Her professional experiences and feelings rising from her association with a strange unfamiliar world, form the theme of this novel. Richardson perceives all the activities of Miriam and interprets all her psychological impressions with a feminist insight. She treats every trivial incident of her woman characters from a woman's point of view. A male novelist would have ignored all those incidents as unmentionable. Miriam as a character occurs in Richardson's other novels such as *Back Water* (1916), *Honey Comb* (1918), *The Tunnel* (1919) and *Dead Lock* (1921). The other novels *Revolving Lights* (1923), *The Trap* (1926) and *Oberland* (1928) present further study of Miriam's consciousness as a woman and her sensuous exploration of the life around her. Thus, we find Miriam Henderson as the unique creation of a woman and remarkable manifestation of feminine sensibility and consciousness.

Another woman novelist who is preoccupied with the psychological exploration of the mind of women is Virginia

Woolf. Her novels are overtly psychoanalytic study of the hidden motives and reaction of women. In order to unveil their veiled mind, Woolf exploits with subtlety the new technique of interior monologue and stream of consciousness. She depicts women characters with a profound feminist perspective. She is primarily concerned with the relation of women with women and women with men. Like Richardson, she too perceives all activities and behaviour of women from her own angle of vision as a woman. Her novels *The Voyage Out* (1915), *Night and Day* (1919) and *Mrs. Dalloway* (1925) tend to explore the inner mind of men and women with particular emphasis on the study of women's mind. Woolf's *Mrs. Dalloway* is a study of the life of a cultured woman who remains engrossed in the contemplations of personal emotional affairs. The novel is a portrayal of the personality of a woman, whose feelings and thoughts are *laid bare* from a psychological perspective. All the impressions of Mrs. Dalloway relating to the incidents of a day are delineated in the style of Dorothy Richardson with a spark of novelistic trend of Joyce. Mrs. Dalloway's sentimental reactions can be studied from her moods psychologically poised and emotionally self-restraint on the evening of her celebration of 50th birthday party. Her various psychological reactions are expressed by Woolf in terms of interior monologue.

The Voyage Out (1915) is a narrative about a young girl, who is thrust suddenly out of a backwater into the whirl of life. Rachel Vinrace is the central character, a young girl who comes in contact with large number of people and gains variety of experiences in her life. She falls in love with Terence Hewet and as she emerges into the life of a normal young woman, she falls ill and succumbs to attack of tropical fever.

A contrastive study of the novels by Indian women writers and those by British women writers brings to light the basic differences in the portrayal of women characters. The differences result from sociological, psychological and cultural heterogeneity between two different classes of novelists—the Indian and the British.

The disharmony in various aspects of their respective national and social life engenders conceptual and perceptual differences in the depiction of the tragedy of women. Hence, the objective and approach of the writers in the treatment of women characters in their novels tend to be different. Unlike the portrayal of women in Indian fictions by Indian women writers, British women novelists present characteristically a different picture of women who figure in their novels conspicuously smart, bold, unsentimental and inhibited in their marital life. Indian women on the other hand appear strikingly simple, sober, sentimental, shy, submissive, self-restraint, docile, devoted to superiors and tolerant to all forms of torture. The apparent and distinctive unlikeness between English women and Indian women in respect of their psychic, mind sensibility and sentiment is due to the influences of their own tradition, culture and mode of living. Thus, the conception and depiction of women in these two classes of fictions, strike a note of difference and distinction.

In the light of the contrastive study of the novels by Indian women writes and those by British women as illustrated above, we draw a conclusion that the former are considerably concerned with the psychological exploration of the interior mind of Indian women. As the women novelists of India were moved emotionally and psychologically by the plight of the depressed women, they felt impelled to externalize their repressed psychic mind and highlight their issues in the novels with a view to arousing public consciousness in favour of women's emancipation and amelioration of their condition in the prevailing social situation. With this noble feminist motive and objective Indian women writers exploited their novels as a vehicle of social reform. Hence their feminist approach in the novels is surfaced in the delineation of travails and tribulations of women and in the depiction of their inner mind. Thus, their writings are remarkably representative in character on account of the faithful, vivid and candid revelation of issues that concern Indian women. In this feminist perspective they gain vide recognition as psychological study of Indian woman and their inner mind.

At the conclusion, it is established that the fictions by Indian women novelists occupy in Indian English literature a unique place as invaluable work of feminist significance.

WORKS CITED

Allen, Walter. *The English Novel: A Short Critical History.* London: Penguin Book Ltd., 1970.

Asnani, M. Shyam. *Critical Response to Indian English Fictions.* Delhi, Mittal Publication, 1985.

Devid, Cecil. *Early Victorian Novelist: Essays in Revaluation.* Ludhiana: Kalyani Publishers, 1934.

Durret, T.D. *The Modern Indian Novels in English: A Comparative Approach.* London: Brussels, 1966.

Friedman, M. *Stream of Consciousness: A Study in Literary Methods*, London: OUP, 1962.

Iyengar, K.R.S. *Indian Writing in English.* New Delhi: Sterling Publishers.

Mehta, P.P. *Indo-Anglian Fiction: An Assessment.* Bareilly: Prakash Book Depot, 1968.

Prasad, Amarnath. *Indian Women Novelists in English.* New Delhi: Atlantic Publishers and Distributors (P) Ltd., 2001.

Singh, Bhupal. *A Survey of Indo-Anglian Fiction.* London: Oxford University Press, 1960.

Singh, Sushila. *Indian Novel in English.* New Delhi: Arnold Heinemann, 1980.

Tompkins, J.M.S. *The Popular Novel in England 1770-1800.* London: Coy & Wyman Ltd., 1975.

William, Raymond. *The English Novel from Dickens to Lawrence.* London: Chatto and Windus, 1966.

Breaking of the Silence: The Novels of Shashi Deshpande

13

URVASHI SINHA AND GUR PYARI JANDIAL

> If I were a man and cared to know the world I lived in, I almost think it would make me a shade uneasy—the weight of that long silence of one-half the world.[1]

In the context of literature related to women, "silence" is used as a metaphor for submission and lack of self-expression. Moreover, silence in the context of the Indian woman is the most important characteristic feature of the code of conduct. It symbolises the woman's state in history and her conformity to tradition.

Much of our rich heritage of folk tales and folklores, myths and epics, sagas and history shows the Indian woman as the epitome of endurance, and silence as her strength. Tradition has taught the Indian woman to have a muted existence. From her very childhood the girl child is taught to accept her place in silence. She is often expected to accede to the distinction between herself and her brother without any objection. Her few efforts to raise a voice are checked early as she is told repeatedly that the behaviour of a girl must be submissive. As she grows she is forced to accept that helping in household chores is her responsibility. Her desire to study or her need to play is considered insignificant compared to more important things like helping in the kitchen.

Even in her relationship with her family members she is taught to be timid and tolerant. Often she grows up in awe of male members like her grandfather, father or uncles, with whom she is taught never to raise a voice, rather never to speak unless asked to. With her brother, her relationship is that of giving and sacrificing, in which it is accepted that she would amicably submit to his demands. Her conduct with her mother and the other female members of the family is of silent assistance.

The advent of puberty and the process of growing up pushes her further into a state of silence. The hushed up introduction into the world of womanhood where she is supposed to be unclean, embarrasses her. She is forced to deal with the changes in her body secretly. It becomes a subject never to be discussed and the tension, pain and discomfort is to be dealt with in silence.

Thus a girl's freedom of speech is never encouraged. Even in rare cases when the mother or a sympathetic member of the family lends her an ear—the advice usually rendered is a reminder of the tradition that has straight-jacketed a girl to be passive and inarticulate. In this way women in India have silently maintained the permanence and stability of its tradition and the consistencies of its ethos.

All this need to be enduring and sacrificing is emphasised specially in the context of marriage. The habit to remain silent is inculcated in the girl child as a preparation for marriage. Her need to speak for herself is viewed as a sign of indiscipline and lack of culture. Even in the choice of her life partner she has no say as the parents usually make the decision. At times she is forced into child marriage or married to a man twice her age. Financial crisis at home or some physical irregularity becomes her handicap, because of which she has to silently accept her parents' choice even if it means marrying a widower with children.

Marriage inadvertently re-affirms the quality of reticence in a woman. The traditional image of a demure and enduring wife looms large over her. The fact that she must mutely follow her husband's will leaves her with little choice. In a new atmosphere full of unknown people, her hesitation and the traditional expectations make her a voiceless member of the family. Her relationship with her in-laws is also dominated by the age-old expectations from an obedient daughter-in-law. Thus the little voice she had as the daughter of the house is lost once she becomes the daughter-in-law and enters a new house. It is taken for granted by one and all that she will silently accept all the decisions and the lifestyle of the family. The girl also begins her marital life tight-lipped, as she remembers that her slight disagreement or decision to voice her views will earn her a bad name and perhaps the wrath of the family. She fails to have control even over her own life. She lives by the dictates of the husband and his family. She loses the right over her own body, as she has to silently fulfil her husband's needs. Her unwillingness to have a child because of her tender age is never voiced and even after years of marriage she fails to express her desire not to have another child. She is unable to speak for herself and is often treated as a breeding animal. Besides, in case she fails to beget the much-awaited son of the family she also has to silently endure the abuses and curses of the family members.

Hence for ages the Indian woman has lived an inarticulate life. The cases of bold women in history are few and rare. As Indira J. Parikh and Pulin K. Garg in their book, *Indian Women: An Inner Dialogue* remark, "A woman rarely talks of herself. In normal circumstances she talks only of her role, her family and the traditions of society. She may talk of her reactions once in a while, but she keeps her real feelings hidden."[2] This glorification of silence in a woman has caused the ultimate suppression of woman. Denying her the right to speak and the assumption of her agreement inadvertently leads to her subjugation.

However, at this juncture it is important to accept that even though the silence maintained by the Indian woman is culturally conditioned it can be extremely articulate. There is much more that remains unsaid and unspoken. The silence maintained by the Indian woman speaks in many voices—each distinctly different. What the coy silence of the bashful bride says is very different from what is communicated by the nervous silence of new daughter-in-law or the frightened silence of the ill-treated wife. The defiant silence of the angry woman conveys messages that are quite different from the resilient silence of the woman who has learnt to endure. The eloquence of each of these is enhanced by the accompanying body language—for instance the light steps that convey confidence and joy, in contrast to the entire body cowering in fear, the shoulder drawn in apprehension or slouched in apathy and despair, the lowered gaze, the movement of the feet and of the hands. Social workers, counsellors and others who work with women who are traumatised and terrorised are now learning to listen carefully to the silences of their clients. It is only silence that confronts them in cases of rape, family violence, sexual abuse or even death.

This deafening silence had engulfed the Indian woman for centuries but independence, education, Westernisation, urbanisation and a number of social changes have contributed in bringing a change in the status of the woman. For once the Indian woman's voice was not stifled into silence. Education gave her a new outlook towards life, as for the first time the world of knowledge was opened to her. She became a more aware person and with it found her voice in stating her opinion about things. But the general patriarchal attitude remained the same. The expectations of the family and the society that the woman would unquestioningly accept her traditional role incorrigibly imposed silence upon her. Thus even today silence that signifies endurance and submission is the bitter reality of the life of the Indian woman.

'Silence' in the context of this thesis implies the suppression of women by denying them the right to express their feelings. It also implies the traditional expectation that the women will silently fall into the role strait-jacketed for them. The phrase 'breaking of the silence' connotes revolt against the traditional suppression.

Shashi Deshpande through her novels has highlighted "the weight of the long silence," which connotes the very world of the Indian woman. She brings out through her works the imposition and the effect of silence on women of different age groups and social stratas. Almost all her female characters either find themselves coerced into following this traditional sanction or are simply unaware of any other way of life. Deshpande shows through her novels how silence has been the most common strategy of survival for the Indian woman.

Her novels present a plethora of minor characters who spend a lifetime in muted existence while her educated and intelligent heroines, stifled under the weight of silence are waiting to break it. Anuradha Roy in her discussion of repressive forces, talks of silence as a strategy for survival. She stresses that the silence that predominates the world of Deshpande's women is not that of peace and tranquillity rather it is an amalgam of their pain, anger, frustration, defensiveness and rejection. Silence takes various shapes in her works. There is the unthinking silence; the resigned silence and finally the one bristling with suppressed anger.[3]

Almost all of Shashi Deshpande's female characters can be categorised into one or the other category of silence. Unthinking silence is that of the conformists, who unquestioningly make silence a habit. These are women rooted in patriarchal traditions and contribute to their transmission too. They imbibe the traditionally ordained qualities of a woman from their very childhood and aspire to become the ideal self-effacing and enduring wives. They are unaware of any other way of life.

The resigned silence is the result of the hopelessness in life. It symbolises the despair that overcomes the consciousness after being rejected or suppressed for a very long time. It is adopted as the will to fight is given up. This silence is haunted by the despondency of life without any hope and has a strong sense of defeatism. The imposition of traditional behaviour and the continuous suppression of self-expression had forced the women of all ages into a resigned silence—an acceptance of the patriarchal dominance.

Silence suppressed with anger shows the inability of the woman to accept unquestioningly the injustice that is a part of her daily life. It is mostly seen in the new woman who has a mind of her own and finds it difficult to lead a resigned life of silence. It is this kind of silence which must one day break. However, it had existed only in adherence to the traditional code of conduct and often to maintain peace and harmony in the family. But as the woman becomes aware of an identity of her own, free from the stereotyped roles of daughter, sister, wife or mother, then she must break her silence and perhaps re-organise her life differently.

Some of the reasons why women adopt silence of any kind and choose to be martyrs can be traced to traditional norms and customs which dominate the upbringing of a girl child, fear of social ostracism and the desire to maintain peace and harmony in the family.

Shashi Deshpande uses silence as one of the important mediums through which she highlights the state of suffering of her characters. By dividing her characters into three categories we realise how important silence is in their lives and how deeply it affects their sense of self.

The women, who conform to the patriarchal traditions, themselves adopt unthinking silence as their resort. They abide by the rules as they had seen their predecessors do it. Unaware of the changing times these women become the carriers of stale traditions and pose an obstruction in the acceptance of new thought. They passively accept subordination and subsequent non-existence because "they had schooled themselves to silence."

Such is the life of Kusum in *That Long Silence*, whose sole aim was to become an ideal self-effacing woman. Trying to achieve it she often emphasised her femaleness with exaggerated modesty. The way she pressurised herself into pleasing people and her failure to do so, proved to be a great setback for her. Her unthinking silence results in her madness. Her longing to be with her family and their indifference towards her affects her mental equilibrium. She inflicts herself with torturous silence, which increases her fear of being abandoned by her family and succumbing to it she jumps into a dried well to end her life. Regarding Kusum, Mukta Atrey and Vinay Kirpal write, "Deshpande also employs Kusum's character to illustrate the helplessness of the traditional woman who, unable to give a voice to her suppressed self, turns her aggression upon herself. Kusum's suicide may also be interpreted as an aspect of destruction focused 'inwards.'"[4]

Saru's mother in *The Dark Holds No Terrors,* herself adapts to this unthinking silence because of her firm belief in traditional norms. In spite of her domineering nature she maintains a rigid silence regarding her problems and ailments. Her slow approaching death by stomach cancer could have been averted. When Saru learns about her condition she wonders about such women whose lives are enveloped in a deafening silence that cannot be broken even in case of extreme pain. Saru feels:

> The myriad complaints, the varying symptoms, she thought, if put together it would provide a world of data for a treatise on the condition of women [...] all the indignities of a woman's life, borne silently and as long as possible [...]. Everything kept secret, their very womanhood a source of deep shame to them. Going on with their tasks, and destroying themselves in the bargain, for nothing but a meaningless modesty. Their unconscious, unmeaning heroism, born out of the myth of the self-sacrificing martyred woman, did not arouse either her pity or her admiration.[5]

Saru is astonished to see how easily her friend Smita mutely accepts the new name given to her after marriage. Her husband's strict control over the family purse leaves most of her desires unexpressed but she remains silent.

Nayana, the sweeper in *That Long Silence*, continues to get pregnant in the hope of giving birth to a male child. In her unthinking silence, she gives in to her husband's demand for a son, even though she truly loved her daughters and was happy to have them.

The unthinking silence adopted as a part of life is also revealed through Mohan's sister, Vimala in *That Long Silence*. Her childlessness makes her silently listen to her mother-in-law's taunts. Her suffering that results from an, "ovarian tumour with metastases" because of which she bleeds to death, never finds a voice. She silently endures the pain and resigns to death without even giving herself a chance to live. As Jaya recalls Mohan saying, "'Why didn't she tell us? Why didn't she write to me?' Mohan had cried out; but Vimala never gave us an answer, even to that question. She sank into coma and died a week later, her silence intact."[6]

Jaya's maidservant, Jeeja too surrenders to unthinking silence, which helps her to go on living. Married to a man who turns drunkard and batters her for money, Jeeja accepts all this brutality with a stoic silence and single-mindedly goes on living. Jaya fails to understand her silence as she says, "There had been days when she had come to work bruised and hurt, rare days when she had not come at all. But I had never heard her complain. What had surprised me then, what still surprised me, was that there seemed to be no anger behind her silence."[7]

In *That Long Silence*, Jaya's Saptagiri Ajji, also lives a life of unthinking silence. Strictly adhering to the traditional code of conduct of a widow, she had chosen a life of severe abstinence from comforts and luxuries. Silence dominates her life as she spent her days in the confines of her room. Her refusal to lead a normal life shows her conformity to the age-old traditions, which expect a woman to give up all comforts and pleasures of life after her husband's death. Jaya as a child was uncomfortable in her company as she describes her as:

> *Ajji*, a shaven widow, had denuded herself of all those things that make up a woman's life. She had no possessions, absolutely none, apart from the two saris she wore. Her room was bare, except for the large bed on which my grandfather had slept, a bed which, ever since I knew it, was unburdened by a mattress [...]. *Ajji* herself sat on the bare ground and slept on a straw mat at night.[8]

She even silently bears the hurt of seeing her youngest and best-loved son, Jaya's father, leave the house to make a separate home. As Ramukaka told Jaya, "that was the one time, the only time, I saw our mother in tears. I remember the day he cleared out his cupboard [...] his was in her room [...] she sat there watching him, she didn't say a word, she didn't make a sound, but the tears just poured out of her."[9] In silence and tears, she accepts her son's decision, and keeps her disappointment and grief to herself.

Jaya's neighbour in the Dadar flat, Mukta also maintains a stoic silence. After her husband, Arun is killed in a train accident, Mukta devotes her life in maintaining harmony between her sharp-tongued mother-in-law and her rebellious children, Nilima and Satish. She silently endures the jibes of her mother-in-law and the complaints of her outspoken daughter. Her own self has no importance and she never expresses her loneliness and frustration.

However, Ghulam Hassan's wife presents the ultimate picture of unthinking silence as her strategy for survival. Having deserted her for many years, Ghulam Saab carries on an illicit relationship with Savitri Bai. He even fathers a child, but when he returns to his wife she accepts him quietly. The years of struggle and the bitterness of being an abandoned wife are all left unexpressed.

However, in Shashi Deshpande's novels a greater place is occupied by the women who resign to silence as they think there is no hope for them. Mohan's mother in *That Long Silence,* best represents this silence. She is a woman caught in a hopeless situation wherein she is verbally, physically and sexually abused by her husband. Tired by his irrational demands like wanting his rice "fresh and hot, from a vessel that was untouched" even at midnight, she slogs the whole day in front of the fire. Even though her lungs and eyes are choked with smoke yet she could not speak a word in protest. One such night she mutely witnesses the food thrown at the wall for there was no fresh 'chutney'. She wakes up Mohan and asks him to get fresh chillies from the neighbours. In the middle of the night she begins preparing the food again. Unfortunately, to her son, Mohan who had seen his mother toiling everyday to keep up with the demands of her husband, she was tough—tough because she had silently endured. But it is Jaya, his wife who understands her mother-in-law better, even though she had never seen her. She is surprised by Mohan's reaction and feels, "He saw strength in the woman sitting silently in front of the fire, but I saw a despair. I saw despair so great that it would not voice itself. I saw a struggle so bitter that silence was the only weapon. Silence and surrender."[10] So great was the hopelessness of her situation that even when Mohan's father kicks Mohan while he was ill with fever, she rushes to console the child but does not speak a word of complaint.

The silence in Kalyani's life speaks of her resignation to her husband's will. When her mother is told about a boy's interest in Kalyani while she was in school, Kalyani's life changes. Unable to defend herself Kalyani's terrified silence over the issue is taken as the proof of her guilt. Manorama in her domineering way forces the young and innocent Kalyani into a marriage with her brother, Shripati. Kalyani silently gives in to her mother's wishes and is thus pushed into a loveless marriage which is "doomed from the start."

The absolute hopelessness of Kalyani's marriage surfaces when she returns home abandoned by Shripati for losing their mentally retarded son. Since that day Shripati inflicted silence as 'a weapon and a punishment' on Kalyani, and she endured it without complaint.

The unusual relationship between Kalyani and her husband also affects their daughters, Sumi and Premi. Sumi recalls once seeing Kalyani banging the door trying hard to be heard. "It is Kalyani she sees standing before the closed door, banging on it with her open palms, shrieking out something, slumping at last on the floor, her head resting against the still closed door. All the sounds fading away, finally leaving a silence that enclosed the thudding of a heart."[11] Like a terrified child Sumi blanks the incident and she and Premi never discuss the unnatural setting at their home. For the first time Premi talks about it when she tells Aru the story of Kalyani's life. Aru is shocked at the enormity of the punishment and Kalyani's silent endurance. She often wonders at Kalyani's silence and finds it inexplicable. We are also told by the author that Kalyani will later break her silence:

> She will, later, much later, and it is to Aru that she will speak. But even then she will not be able to bring herself to speak of that act of public desertion, of those long hours on the station platform with her children, surrounded by curious strangers, as if that is a memory

> so painfully blotted out that to bring it back to life would be as painful as the process of childbirth.[12]

Akka in *Roots and Shadows* and Mira in *The Binding Vine* undergo the physical trauma of rape within marriage but endure it in silence. Akka, however, survives because her husband dies. Mira after undergoing a short and intensely unhappy and traumatic marriage dies in childbirth.

Sulu in *The Binding Vine* makes silence her strategy for survival and endures the mortification of seeing her husband lust over her niece. Her knowledge of his obsession for Kalpana, makes her suspect him to be Kalpana's rapist. The day her suspicion is confirmed she tells her sister of his lust for Kalpana. She talks of his attempts to molest Kalpana when she was only fourteen and on his regular demand that she gets Kalpana for him. Saddened by Shakutai's outrage she ends her life of self-abnegation, humiliation and despair in suicide.

However, the power of silence, which allows women to ruin their lives and live in despair, is best revealed through an incident in *The Dark Holds No Terrors*. Three sisters suffering from syphilis are brought to the hospital where Saru worked. Saru is shocked at the silence of the sisters, the youngest only ten, and their mother's matter of fact reply that the father was responsible. "He had tried the ancient prescription for his own disease, [...] that of having intercourse with a virgin [...] the virgins being his own daughters. And then frightened by what he had done, he had disappeared."[13] Deshpande through this incident gives an example of the horrific tales of exploitation that remain muffled in the name of family honour. The silence of these girls is that of absolute hopelessness. Robbed off their innocence by their own father and inflicted by a disease, their lives are over even before they had actually begun.

In her novel *Small Remedies,* Deshpande brings out the injustice silently endured through the widowed cousin of Leela's father, who is raped by him because she was dependent on him. This woman's muted acceptance of her fate shows her despondency. It is only when she is pregnant with his child that the wife comes to know the truth. But she too, muffles her displeasure in the name of family honour. Thus both the women are forced into a life of hopelessness where silence is the only answer.

Similar is the plight of Atya in *Roots and Shadows*. A penniless and childless widow, she returns to her natal home where she is given shelter by the rich matriarch, Akka. But her status in the family is that of a subordinate and silent member. Her life is spent in helping her sister-in-law in household chores and looking after the children of the family. As Indu realises, "What else can a childless widow expect? Her in-laws had, true to tradition, ill-treated her after her husband's death. And then, grandfather had brought her home. Her home, where she worked from morning to night, every day of her life, expecting nothing."[14] Thus Atya resigns to her life of dependence and silence, keeping her feelings unexpressed.

Mini also resigns to silence and agrees to marry "an illiterate man with heavy coarse features and crude mannerisms." The problems and frustrations that her family experiences in finding a match for her make her agree to marry any man who is willing.

Inni in *The Binding Vine* resigns to silence and nurtures a lifelong guilt of having failed as a mother. But her husband in spite of his love and understanding fails to recognise her silent longing for her daughter. It is her desire to get rid of her guilt that after years she confesses her innocence. But Urmi realises, "[...] the scars of an old cruelty have shown me how hopeless, how utterly hopeless it is? Because I've seen how bottomless the chasm is, how impossible to bridge?"[15]

Akka, Urmi's mother-in-law, is left with little choice, when she crosses the marriageable age. She silently accepts her parents' decision to marry her to a man madly in love with his dead wife and who agrees to marry her only because he wanted a mother for his son.

Even Vanaa, Urmi's friend and sister-in-law, leads a life dominated by resigned silence. Her muted surrender to her husband's decisions infuriates Urmi who feels, "it irritated me terribly at first, her constant refrain of 'Harish says.' She says it less now, but her submissiveness, her willingness to go along with him in whatever he wants, makes me angry."[16] As always Vanaa resigns to silence when Harish rejects her desire to have another child by quoting population figures.

The silence that Saru notices in the wife of Manu's colleague is that of surrender. It speaks of the suffering of women who are crushed under the weight of a male dominated and tradition-bound society.

> She came in silently, unobtrusively, like a shadow and went out in the same way, her husband's conversation not interrupted even by a fraction of a second by her presence. He did not introduce her to us, and so strong was the man's disregard of her presence that we ignored her too. We ate our food, sipped the tea and gulped the water as if they had been brought to us by a nameless waiter in a hotel.[17]

Even Saru's effort to bring out the person behind the self-effacing, expressionless wife, fails. Her silence remains intact as she had completely submitted to her husband's desires. To Saru she reminds of the lines, "[...] If I cast no shadow, I do not exist."

Hence the woman's silence makes her a voiceless shadow. The silence in the life of all these women is a proof of the hopelessness and despondency of their lives. Their awareness of the lack of choice in their lives makes them silently pass the days. However, this attitude results in their subordination and helps in establishing tyrannical patriarchal patterns. As Deshpande in her essay "No Man is an Island" writes, "To be silent is to abet it."

Almost all the women in Deshpande's novels who fall in this category are bogged down by the misfortunes of their lives. But what is sad is their silence and passive acceptance of the situation. Through these women Deshpande reveals the suffering that goes unexpressed. She does not draw an unrealistic picture that—by speaking up these women could change their lives overnight. She emphasises that suffering in silence has been forced on women. And to achieve one's true 'self' women will have to break away from the tradition of enduring in silence. It is important to bring out in the open what lies in the heart of the Indian woman. Her feelings and needs are as important as those of others. Therefore, she will have to speak in order to create a place for herself and to affirm life.

However, there are two characters in Deshpande's *Small Remedies* whose silence is different from the types mentioned above. Savitri Bai and her daughter Munni consciously adopt silence as a way to erase certain phase of their lives, hence it cannot be called resigned or unthinking silence. Savitri Bai's silence regarding her personal life when she reaches the pinnacle of success is a means to cover up her rebellious days. Presenting herself as the traditional woman Bai once again appears with the *mangalsutra*, and takes the help of silence to erase her illegitimate relationship and its product, Munni. Bai avoids talking about Ghulam Saab and their illegitimate daughter, Munni even to Madhu, her biographer. This shows the influence of tradition that relates a woman's respectability to her marital status. Bai's desperation to attain a respectable position in the society seems to be the cause of her sudden withdrawal from her lover and her daughter. The conscious silence that she adopts as a means to negate their presence is viewed by Madhu as, "She has drawn a line through Munni's and Ghulam Saab's names and erased them from her life. This is something she did long back, when she turned to respectability, when she began her journey to success and fame. Perhaps she thought that to attain these things, this denial of her lover and daughter was necessary."[18]

Similarly, her daughter Munni too resorts to silence and detaches herself from her mother and everything she stood for. Once again Munni's silence is the representative of the traditional mindset which identifies respectability of a woman with her marital status. Her craving for respectability which an ordinary woman gets as a homemaker makes her bury her background under the self-imposed silence.

The heroines of Shashi Deshpande's novels grow up surrounded by women who mutely endure the injustice done to them or resign to a life of hopeless despair. Educated and intelligent, her protagonists refuse to submit or resign to an unquestioning life. Besides, the injustices done to women in the name of tradition, angers them. However, most of them find themselves unable to revolt initially. But the silence suppressed with anger in Deshpande's all protagonists differentiates them from most of the other characters. Amongst all the characters it is only these few strong women who show the capacity of breaking the silence. For them silence is a temporary state as the anger brewing inside them is bound to make them speak.

Saru, the heroine of *The Dark Holds No Terrors*, adopts silence as a means to hide her guilt and confusion. Her little brother Dhruva's death by drowning into a pond, when they had secretly gone out to play terrifies Saru. The shocked Saru could not deny her mother's accusations that she killed her brother. Since then it becomes a habit for her to remain silent over Dhruva's death. Her silence also affects her psyche as she begins to blame herself for his death even though she knew that she had not been at fault. Her parents' disinterest in hearing her side of the story also adds to her silent suffering.

Saru breaks her silence when her mother objects to her studying medicine in Bombay by saying, "What gives her the right to choose?" For the first time Saru breaks her silent endurance and her reply to her mother shows the resentment that she had nourished, "I'm not talking to you. I'm not asking you for anything. I know what your answer will be. No, forever a 'no' to anything I want. You don't want me to have anything, you don't want me to do anything. You don't even want me to live."[19] By asserting herself she succeeds in fulfilling her dream to become a doctor.

However, Saru once again finds herself silently suffering when the man she loved and married becomes a sadist and brutally rapes her. Manu's sexual assault after years of marriage and two children shocks her and she finds herself unable to speak. In spite of being modern, educated, intelligent and financially independent Saru allows herself to be repeatedly raped because of her children sleeping in the next room. She was afraid of the effect it would have on them. Secondly,

Manu's normal attitude in the daytime often deterred her from her resolve to confront him. Traumatised by the experience she even considers seeking professional help but the inhibition of speaking about her personal life to a stranger stops her. Time and again she is troubled by thoughts like:

> I should have spoken about it the very first day. But I didn't. And each time it happens and I don't speak, I put another brick on the wall of silence between us. Maybe one day I will be walled alive within it and die a slow, painful death. Perhaps the process has already begun and what I am is a creature only half alive.[20]

Thus she realises that her inability to speak is gradually destroying her life.

However, only when Saru is away from home and Manu that she realises the damage her silence was causing to herself. She recalls the incident of Dhruva's death, her mother's unreconciled death, her father's indifference and Manu's sadism and all that she had endured in silence. The weight of silence which had taken her peace away and destroyed her self-respect, becomes unbearable. Therefore, after much thinking and soul searching she speaks to Baba. She tells him of her hurt on being accused for Dhruva's death. By speaking about the incident for the first time Saru exorcises her guilt and her grief of being accused by her parents. She voices her hurt and tells him, "And every night he comes and accuses me. Yes, Dhruva. He looks at me as if I killed him. Why are you all against me? Why do you all accuse me for something I never did?"[21] The expression of her thoughts after years of suppressed silence bridges the gap between her and Baba. She is able to relate to him and he encourages her "to let the dead go," and free herself of guilt. Finally, Saru tells her father of the marital rape that had destroyed her peace, confidence and self worth.

Finding her voice, she speaks of all the times she had wanted to confront Manu but failed, and her doubt that she was responsible for his sadism and for deserting her mother. Her father talks her out of blaming herself for Dhruva's death, and helps her bury the past. But he leaves her alone to deal with Manu. The news of Manu's arrival makes her want to run away but Baba helps her realise that she has to face the situation. Alone for sometime she realises that she will have to speak and voice her anger; she will have to confront Manu. Only then can she find peace and her true identity in life. Madhav's words, "It's my life after all," ring in her ears and she decides that she will not endure Manu's beastly behaviour. She realises that she is not responsible for his failure, and she had striven to achieve her success, therefore, she will not allow herself to be forced into silent suppression. Once again her pride in her profession as a doctor is restored and she goes to attend an ailing child. But she tells Baba to ask Manu to wait, as she wanted to talk to him. The end of the novel shows that Saru will no longer remain silent. Her resolve to speak also symbolises that she will no longer let herself be suppressed. With a renewed confidence she is ready to confront Manu and shed the darkness that had terrorised her for so many years.

With her marriage to Jayant, Indu in *Roots and Shadows* sees herself silently accepting Jayant's wishes. Gradually, she slips into the same mould of the silent self-effacing wife, which she had once detested. Jayant's likes and dislikes had begun to completely dominate her life and she had learnt to keep her own views and feelings to herself. Later in retrospect she felt, "That was one thing I had learnt now. One thing my marriage had taught me. The gift of silence."[22] To avoid the clash of views between them, she silently accepts his idea of things. In spite of her unhappiness she accepts his view that a woman should be passive in love, similarly even when she disliked her job, she continued working as Jayant told her "We need the money, don't we? Don't forget we have a long way to go." Thus for a very long time Indu lives her life leaving most of her feelings unexpressed.

But her mounting dissatisfaction and unhappiness compel Indu to break her silence. When she returns to her maternal home for sometime, she is able to view her relationship with Jayant dispassionately. Her meeting with Naren, the responsibility of handling Akka's legacy and her resolve to change things give her the confidence to voice her opinion vociferously. She realises that only by speaking openly will she be able to make a statement and carve out a space and command dignity for herself. And rightly so, as in the end Jayant eventually accepts her decision to quit her job and write a book. Her need to express her love for him, and her decision not to use Akka's money to fulfil her family's personal needs, but to help orphans with it, symbolises the breaking of silence. After breaking her silence she feels, "Now I think he knows me better, my strengths, which I had hidden from him, as well as my weakness. Perhaps, because of this, we have a better chance. There is an ease in our relationship that was not there before."[23]

That Long Silence is the most powerful portrayal of silence in a woman's life. Mohan's belief that, "anger makes a woman 'unwomanly'" teaches Jaya to control her anger. With this begins the process of leaving her thoughts, feelings and needs unexpressed. Jaya is gradually trapped in a vicious cycle that engulfs her. She is made to accept silence which usurps her freedom to speak, her self-confidence and eventually her identity.

Later alone in the Dadar flat, her normal routine disrupted, Jaya realises how awkward and unnatural her silence is. After a lot of soul searching she decides to write about Mohan and herself and thereby break the deafening silence. In the process of writing she realises her own role in imposing the silence. Her fear of breaking the traditional set-up and bringing disharmony in the family and her own lack of self-confidence to pursue her desires, had made her silently accept Mohan's will. In her attempt to please Mohan she had a hair cut 'like Mehra's wife' and had learnt to be docile and silent like the women of Mohan's family. However, it will be unjust to say that, "One ends up by wondering whether Jaya has imposed the long silence on herself not out of a sense of duty or to emulate the ideal Hindu woman of the ages gone by, but in order to camouflage the streaks of ugliness within her."[24] It is no "camouflage" as she resolves to silence because of her fears that a frank admission of her desires may disturb the delicate balance of their relationship. Besides by remaining silent it is

Jaya who suffers the most as she becomes isolated in her own family and her feelings are left unexpressed. She is alienated because of her silence, and she feels, "I had shaped myself so resolutely to his desires all these years, yet what was I left with now? Nothing. Just emptiness and silence."[25]

When Mohan walks out after a fight, she finally resolves to change things. In his absence she realises that to make space for herself she will have to speak:

> Until today, this has been a rhetorical question. I have looked at his face for clues and then given him the answer I know he wants. I have only to do this now and the authority will seep into Mohan once more. But it is no longer possible for me. If I have to plug that 'hole in the heart,' I will have to speak, to listen, I will have to erase the silence between us.[26]

Shashi Deshpande in her novel *The Binding Vine* has tried to dispel the silence in the lives of other women through the character of Urmi. Urmi, the most independent and outspoken heroines of Deshpande, seeks to bring to light the silent suffering of Mira, her dead mother-in-law and Kalpana, a lower middle-class rape victim. The fact that these two women were made to endure the injustice done to them in silence angers Urmi. Mira's untimely death and Kalpana's unconsciousness may have silenced them but Urmi takes the cudgels to bring to light the violence suffered by them. She struggles to publish Mira's poems with the aim to give voice to the silent discourse of the dead woman. In her resolve to let Mira find listeners she even goes against her friend and sister-in-law, Vanaa, who believed that making Mira's life public would be bringing disgrace to her father. But Urmi remains firm the same way she had been in the case of Kalpana. She takes the help of her journalist friend, Malcom, to stop the hospital authorities from shifting Kalpana to a far away hospital. By publicising the case she also tries to bring justice to Kalpana. She breaks away from the general tendency to cover the identity of the rape victim as she tries to break the silence imposed on them by societal norms. By breaking the silence that surrounds Kalpana, Urmi makes the police open

Kalpana's case again and reach the doorsteps of Prabhakar. Urmi represents the new woman who does not believe in passively enduring injustice but strongly voicing her anger.

Though Sumi in *A Matter of Time* remains tight-lipped after her husband Gopal deserts her, her silence is not the resigned silence of hopelessness that an abandoned wife is expected to adopt. Because she understands Gopal, she does not bear any grudges against him. She refuses to be silenced into a life of self-pity and aspires to fulfil the dreams that lay dormant in her. She learns to ride a two-wheeler, looks for an independent house, she takes a teaching job, explores her talents at creative writing, even gets a job in a residential school. Besides, she strives to give a normal life to her daughters and even succeeds in attaining an understanding with them. She tells Aru, "Be happy for me, Aru. This is the first thing in my life I think that I've got for myself. I was sure I wouldn't get it, there's my age, it's against me, and I have no experience at all [...]. And now suddenly I want to do so many things."[27]

Aru who is lauded as the heroine of *A Matter of Time* is shocked at the resigned silence of her grandmother, Kalyani which speaks of the despondency of her life. Initially she even fails to understand her mother's silence at being abandoned. Her feeling that Gopal should not "go scot-free" and her desire to make him pay for what he did to them, shows that she does not agree to Kalyani's resigning to fate nor Sumi's attitude of forgive and forget. As Deshpande writes, "It's the injustice of it that Aru minds, Kalyani's silence that she finds inexplicable."

Her anger takes her to Surekha, a lawyer, with whom she explores the ways to punish Gopal. Her determination not to be hurt the way her mother and grandmother were, makes her aspire to be independent in life. She gives up the idea of getting married and for the time being concentrates on her study of law. Her resentment of the way women are suppressed in the name of tradition makes her join a women's activist group. Through it she hopes to find a platform to voice her feelings and the anger and frustration that she had seen the women of her family silently endure.

Madhu, the central character of *Small Remedies,* has no option but to resign into silence when her husband Som becomes suspicious and questions her fidelity. Her confession of a past sexual encounter committed in a state of shock, destroys his faith in her. In his anger he doubts her integrity and questions her relationship with various men in her life. Full of anguish he is unable to believe anything she says in defence. He traces his way through her life and assumes that all the men she knew were her lovers:

> It's when he adds, in desperation I now think, Tony's name to the list, that I retreat into silence. I will no longer answer him, I will say nothing, I will deny nothing. But my silence makes things worse, it's a bigger barrier between us than my words had been. If my denials could contain untruths, how many more lies did my silences conceal? I sense an enormous grief under his suspicion and his anger, I can feel the weight of his grief, I even share the burden of it with him.[28]

Their relationship is further corroded by the death of their only son, Aditya, in a bomb blast. With the passing away of Aditya the silence in their lives becomes unbreakable.

It is only after a year's separation that Madhu realises that the silence between them will have to be broken as they had to mourn the loss of their son. Then she hopes, "Som and I, we can wash away the darkness and ugliness, not only of Adit's death, but of what happened before, with our own oblations of sesame seeds and water."[29]

Through Leela's life Deshpande has shown the complete breaking of silence. While her other characters initially accede to silence and ponder over the various effects their breaking of the silence will have on their family, Leela expresses her desires and aims to fulfil them. In her struggle to achieve her dreams she shows courage by questioning, subverting and resisting the forces restraining her voice and space.

According to Shashi Deshpande, "Silence has been both the oppressor's infliction and women's strategy. What we want to reach at finally is telling. Like in *That Long Silence*. The breaking of silence."[30]

Shashi Deshpande through her myriad characters has shown how women are trained into silence. Inculcated in the name of social taboos, family harmony, or the ideal of 'sharam', the acceptance of silence confirms their submission. Through their lives Deshpande has shown that silence can often be self-defeating. Their inability to convey their needs or their stubborn silence maintained till death slowly forces them into oblivion. Their refusal to disclose their agony changes nothing for them, as it has no impact on their oppressor. In case of their death another woman replaces them in the lives and hearts of the family members. Their life of self-abnegation is soon forgotten as stifled into silence these women gradually become "echoes and shadows".

Deshpande's heroines too are initiated into the world of silence and submission but becoming a non-entity in their own family disturbs them. The loss of self-respect and dignity in their existing relationships makes them long for an atmosphere congenial for self-expression. Angry and hurt by the injustice that is heaped upon them, they refuse to live a life of passivity and submission that was the lot of their predecessors. These educated women with a modern outlook decide to do something about the problem and not just brood over it. Their analysis of the traditional set-up tells them that breaking the silence requires courage and conviction. It also means risking the certainty of their role and security. But urge to find oneself, to create space for oneself, to grow on one's own—encourages them to break their silence. In breaking their silence they move towards achieving their full growth as individuals.

The protagonists of Deshpande's novels decide to voice their opinion and ensure that it is valued and taken seriously. They realise that by speaking they can create space for themselves and define their being. Thus by voicing their views they are able to define the nature of their relationship with others. Self-expression also helps them fulfil their suppressed desires and retain their individuality and thereby affirm life.

In exploring the thoughts of her protagonists who are caught between the traditional expectations and individual needs, Deshpande employs a number of stylistic devices and techniques. What has become Deshpande's hallmark is the alteration of first person and third person voices. Her choice seems to be affected by the fact that however omnipresent or omniscient the narrator may be, he cannot probe the mind of the characters. Her experiment with the voices gives her the freedom to narrate the story from different perspectives and bring out the innermost thoughts and feelings of the characters.

In *The Dark Holds No Terrors* Deshpande has used double perspective—first person for the protagonist and the third for the narrator in the alternate chapters. Apart from the voices she also alternates the time of action as the narrator reveals the present time while in the next chapter the heroine, Saru through her thoughts goes backwards in time. While talking to Lakshmi Holmstrom, Deshpande herself described her technique as:

> The present is in the third person and the past is in the first. I was doing it throughout in the first. But that's often a perspective I use in my short stories. I wanted to be more objective. So then I tried it in the third. But it wouldn't work at all. Yet I really needed to distance myself from the narrative in the present, otherwise it was going to be far too intense. And then I read an American novel by Lisa Alther where she uses this method. And the minute I came across her novel I thought—let me admit it freely—Oh god, this is how I am going to do my novel.[31]

In the fifth chapter from the end, this past and present interplay comes to an end. After giving the background through Saru's reminiscence, Deshpande takes over as the narrator to show how Saru struggles to amend the wrongs of her life.

Roots and Shadows is narrated in the first person, from

Indu's perspective. Only the prologue states the present time. In the second chapter, Indu takes the readers back in the past when she had returned home after ten years. The novel is an amalgamation of events that take place after Indu's return home and the retrospective thoughts that cross her mind. Through this Deshpande has shown Indu's journey towards self-actualisation. The end of the novel takes the story back to the first chapter and it comes full circle as Indu resolves to break her silence.

Shama Futehally, in her review of *Roots and Shadows,* has rightly pointed Deshpande's narrative technique of going backwards in time as the cause of a number of misinterpretations. Many readers have failed to go back to the prologue to confirm that Indu does assert herself in her personal and professional life. The galaxy of characters that are introduced in the first chapter makes it a struggle for the reader to understand various relationships. It also blocks out the few lines in the prologue that show the result of Indu's self-analysis and assertion. Except in this novel Deshpande's narrative technique has proved to be one of the strengths of her writing. In other novels she has successfully blended past and the present.

Deshpande's belief in Kierkegaard's words that "Life must be lived forwards, but it can only be understood backwards,"[32] which she has quoted in her novel *A Matter of Time*, finds illustration in her works. Her plot moves forward but the flashbacks or introspective return to the past helps her protagonists find their own identity and move towards self-actualisation. It also enables them to critically analyse their lives. It is because of this objective retrospection that Deshpande is lauded for creating balanced characters who are able to accept their own share of blame for the suffering in their lives. This return to the past also gives the readers the background of the characters.

That Long Silence is the most introspective of Deshpande's works as she has made extensive use of interior monologue to show the self-effacing housewife's analysis of her life. Told in the first person voice the novel reveals Jaya's alienation after her Appa's death, her introduction into the traditional role of a wife, her disappointment as a writer, her worries regarding her teenage children and her dissatisfaction in the seventeen years of married life with Mohan.

In *The Binding Vine* Urmi narrates her story in the first person narrative. While telling about her life she weaves the stories of Akka, Mira, Vanna, Shakutai, Sulu and Kalpana. In this novel Deshpande uses little interior monologue and narrates the story of other women as Urmi perceives it.

In the novel *A Matter of Time*, Shashi Deshpande goes back to third person narrative and narrates the story as a detached observer. It is only to depict Gopal's feelings that the novelist brings in 'I', *i.e.* first person, and in a few cases for Sumi and Premi. Otherwise the entire novel is in the third person narrative. Apart from the few reminiscences of Gopal and Kalyani's past life the plot mainly has a linear movement. Deshpande in this novel also uses the idea of the "novelist's crystal ball" to tell us Aru's future—that she will become a lawyer and how she will be able to overcome her despair. "It is only later, nearly a decade after the time when these events are happening, that she will stumble on a secret that will take some of this weight off her. That time is waiting for her in the future and to hitch it to this narrative is not very difficult. A slight sleight of hand will be sufficient."[33]

Ritu Menon in her Afterword, "No Longer Silent," seems to have hurriedly concluded that, "In each of her novels, the past is presented in the first person (usually by the heroine), the present in the third."[34] A careful reading of the texts show that this double perspective of past in the first person narrative and present in the third was used by Deshpande only in *The Dark Holds No Terrors*. In *Roots and Shadows*, *That Long Silence*, *The Binding Vine* and *Small Remedies*, she exclusively uses the first person voice for the past as well as the present. In *A Matter of Time* she has again used both the voices but mainly the third person narrative dominates and the first person is used occasionally.

In *Small Remedies*, her latest novel, Deshpande once again

returns to the first person narrative by making Madhu, the protagonist, tell her own story. With her own recollections of Bai when they were neighbours and by interviewing her, Madhu creates a disjointed picture of Bai's life. Bai's courage to revolt against the social norms makes her compare Bai's life to that of her Aunt Leela's. The story of the struggle of these two women to attain their goals is told by Madhu who in the process also narrates her own life full of trials and tribulations. In the process of narration, Madhu from time to time returns back to the past—her life in Neemgaon with her father, her stay with Leela and Joe, her job at *City Views*, and her family life with Som and their son, Aditya. Deshpande keeps the suspense alive to tell us in the end about the event that destroyed the harmony in Madhu's marital life and led to the death of Aditya.

Most of Deshpande's novels like *The Dark Holds No Terrors*, *Roots and Shadows*, *That Long Silence*, *The Binding Vine* and *Small Remedies* do not progress chronologically, but instead the plot moves back and forth, gradually relating one incident to the other until the entire story is revealed. In *The Binding Vine* and *Small Remedies,* three different stories are interwoven bringing together three women separated by age, status and education. In both the cases the entire story is narrated by the protagonists, who attain wisdom and experience and decide to change their own lives.

Shashi Deshpande's characters are pivotal to her works. She once told Lakshmi Holmstrom, "For me, every novel starts with people. One character, maybe two."[35] For her these characters are real who take their own course. She admits that Indu in *Roots and Shadows* and Hasina in *Small Remedies,* have themselves changed the course of these novels. She once remarked:

> I don't like my characters moving on the path I lay out for them. I don't look at them like puppets whose strings are with me. I feel they too have a life of their own. I want them to go in the direction that they choose. I like following them rather than dragging them with me. Yes, I do have a vague plan about my

> characters. But the truth is, it never works out the way I plan it because they also plan a course for themselves and they prefer their course to mine. I have no choice then but to follow them.[36]

Thus we do not find any wooden characters in her novels. This is mainly due to the freedom that she gives to her characters and her determination not to bring in characters just to serve some need for her. The vast number of characters that she has created show different individual behaviours and a close look at their background reveals the reason for their particular behaviour. As a woman novelist she comes closest in creating most realistic female characters who have their strengths but are also plagued with doubts. Their habit of deep introspection and analysis of life has earned them the tag of "passive characters". But Deshpande has used the action to stir the thoughts of these characters and mingling action with interior monologue she has successfully shown the development in them. Through her skill she has created lifelike characters caught between tradition and individual needs.

However, Deshpande's male characters show little development compared to her heroines. She herself admitted that, "[...] I'm aware of this lack. I've not been able to put myself in the position of a man as well as I can enter a female consciousness, even when it is very different from mine. Especially in *Roots and Shadows* I knew that the husband's character was weak. I'm better now. In *That Long Silence*, there are a number of male characters—some have come out very well."[37] Her writings do show an improvement in her later novels. Gopal, Som, Tony and Joe are some of the characters who come close to real life. Deshpande's awareness of her limitation has made her strive to overcome it as best as she can. She admits, "So maybe I want to reach a stage where I can write about human beings and not about women to men [...]. For I don't believe in having a propagandist or sexist purpose to my writing. If it presents such perspective, it's only a coincidence. It's just the way I feel. Maybe it is a strong point of view to hold."[38]

Deshpande's emphasis on the characters has enabled her to

write novels which have a strong psychological dimension. With the help of interior monologue, flashbacks into the past, dreams and often doodling, she brings out the fear, frustration, anguish and yearning that lie in the innermost recesses of her characters' mind. Saru sees a recurrent dream of Dhruva and herself at the same place where Dhruva died, but in the dream it is she who is drowning. This dream of Saru's, which leaves her restless, depicts her feeling of guilt that she was responsible for Dhruva's death. The fact that she sees herself drowning and Dhruva going away from her, shows her desperate need to get rid of the blame and guilt by being the victim and sufferer.

In *The Binding Vine* Urmi dreams of the absence of her dead daughter, Anu. Her feeling that she had lost her, left her behind in a strange house and her desperation to get back to her child is an illustration of her guilt of not being there with her when she died. Her dream speaks of the emptiness and loss of a mother.

In *A Matter of Time*, after deserting his wife and family, Gopal is haunted by his dreams. But his dream of his father depicts his alienation and desperation to find his roots.

Doodling or aimlessly drawing something while the mind is lost in other thoughts is also a common feature in characters like Saru and Sumi. It is a means through which the writer shows their disturbed psyche and their inability to concentrate in the activities around them.

Shashi Deshpande has adorned her works with innumerable metaphors and similes, which help to illustrate her point. There are a few metaphors that are recurring in her works. A.N. Dwivedi in his article "The Hub of the Wheel: Recurring Metaphors in Shashi Deshpande's Novels," points out darkness and light, death and silence as metaphors that appear again and again in her works.[39] Darkness and light hold importance in the novel, *The Dark Holds No Terrors*, where darkness in case of Dhruva signifies the fear of the unknown in a child. However, in case of Saru it implies the physical and sexual assault that she undergoes in the darkness of the night. Even in her short story, "It Was Dark" the teenage rape victim repeatedly says, "it was dark [...]." Her mother decides to pull away the curtains of the room to end the darkness in her child's life. The light that rushes through the window metaphorically ends the terror and trauma for the girl as she recognises her mother for the first time.

Death, too, is a recurring metaphor in all her novels. In *The Dark Holds No Terrors*, Saru's life changes after Dhruva's death and she calls her life after him as A.D. (After Dhruva). Secondly, her mother's death is the end of another phase in Saru's life, as she gathers courage to return home. Similarly, Indu returns home when Akka is on her deathbed. But the time that she spends there and the money that she inherits, changes her life. Naren's death too ends a phase in Indu's life as she returns home a self-realised person. Jaya recalls her Appa's death as the event that ended her happy childhood. The novel is strewn with the deaths of Kamat, Kusum, Saptagiri-Ajji, Makaranda mama, Mohan's mother and sister, Vimala and Jaya's third child. Though these cannot be marked as incidents that end a phase in Jaya's life but they hold importance because of the way they affect her. *The Binding Vine* begins with Anu's death and marks the beginning of a new quest in Urmi's life. Mira's and Sulu's deaths signify women's submission to silence and suffering. Baiaji's, Ajju's and Papa's deaths are all incidents that affect Urmi's life. In *A Matter of Time* Manorama's death brings Shripati back to the Big House but it dooms Kalyani's marriage. His death with Sumi in an accident ends Kalyani's chance of reconciliation with him. For Aru it is the end of her adolescence as she takes over the responsibility of the family. The death of Aditya in *Small Remedies* acts as the haunting background of the novel. It completely changes the life of his parents, especially Madhu, who is inconsolable. Apart from this her father's death when she was fifteen and the deaths of Joe and Leela, who were her guardians affect the life of Madhu. The knowledge of the painter's suicide becomes the cause of destruction of Madhu's happy world.

Thus death in Deshpande's works is a landmark with which she ends a phase in the life of her central characters. In retrospect through the deaths of their loved ones her protagonists categorise the beginning and the end of different phases of their lives. It also implies change in the life of these characters.

'Silence' as discussed in the beginning of her chapter, is a recurring metaphor, which appears in all her novels. According to A.N. Dwivedi it denotes, "lack of communication, frigidity of feeling, and want of understanding and compassion."

In her works Deshpande has used innumerable similes taken from various scriptures and the day-to-day life of women. In *A Matter of Time* she uses "as painful as the process of childbirth" to compare Kalyani's pain in talking about her hours of desertion on the railway platform amongst strangers. Another fine example of simile is Jaya's comparison of her and Mohan's disgrace to that of squatting village women. The eagerness of these women to just cover their faces if seen by someone and ignore the fact that their bottoms were exposed reminds her of their condition as they went into temporary hiding ignoring the fact that the truth will come out one day.

In Shashi Deshpande's novels the house where the protagonists spend their childhood has immense significance. She herself told Lakshmi Holmstrom:

> And then there is the locale. In the case of *Roots and Shadows*, there was Indu and there was the house. It was only when they came together that there was a novel. For me it's essential—almost as essential as it is for movie director—to have the shape of the house clear. [...] If I have that clear, then the rest of it can happen. Because it is there that it is going to happen.[40]

In all the six novels the return of the protagonists to their natal home symbolises the beginning of their quest for identity. Ritu Menon in her Afterword to *A Matter of Time* writes, "The ancestral house, even more than the town or the city, is central to Deshpande's novels, because it is this that the women return. Saru in *The Dark Holds No Terrors*, Jaya in *That Long Silence*, and Sumi in *A Matter of Time* make a womblike retreat to the natal home, and it is always here that past and present meet and some kind of reckoning takes place."[41] Besides, the house links the characters with the past and rekindles old memories. In the novel *Roots and Shadows* the house holds tremendous importance as it symbolises the old traditional values which Akka stood for. The demolition of the house further symbolises the break from such traditions. In *A Matter of Time* the Big House represents the life of its inhabitants. The life of a lonely recluse lived by Shripati is represented by his secluded room upstairs. In a way the house in this novel is also personified as a member of the family as after Shripati's death, "[...] the house is woken up by a cry [...] there is a strange sound, as if the house has exhaled its breath and shaken itself before settling down into a different rhythm of breathing."[42]

One of the important characteristics of Deshpande's works is her use of allusions taken from myths, folklores and legends. Although she writes in English, the rhythm and the metaphors used are wholly Indian. There are innumerable references from the *Ramayana*, *Mahabharata*, *Upanishads*, *Puranas* and *Vedas*. Sita, Savitri, Gandhari, Draupadi, Yudhistira, Krishna, Arjuna, Duryodhana all find reference in her works. Regarding her use of myths she once told Lakshmi Holmstrom:

> I think a number of us do that in India all the time; we relate a great deal of our personal lives, our daily lives, to the myths. We find parallels as matter of course. And we do this with all the myths, any myth that seems appropriate, whether they were originally about men or women. In that sense it is part of a language, a grammar that one knows and understands, rather than a conscious literary device.[43]

Deshpande's characters too relate their life and situations with the various myths and legends. It helps the novelist illustrate the thoughts and feelings of the characters. For example, Saru while waiting at her father's doorsteps thinks of Sudama waiting at the gates of Krishna's palace. In spite of her financial prosperity and the external appearance of a happy family life, the image of Sudama that comes to her mind reveals her inner turmoil. Like Sudama she also goes to her father hoping to get some help. In *That Long Silence* while silently following Mohan to Dadar flat Jaya thinks of "Sita following her husband into exile, Savitri dogging Death to reclaim her husband, Draupadi stoically sharing her husband's travails [...]."[44]

Besides stray references she also quotes from the *Upanishads*, or *Vedas* or *the Dhammpada*. Most novels begin with an epigraph taken from one of the Hindu scriptures that highlight the theme of the novel. Deshpande has also used references from Kalidasa's *Abhigyanam Shakuntalam* and *Kumarsambhavan* and Bharat Muni's *Natyashastra*. These allusions highlight her rich cultural legacy, which she had inherited from her father, Sri Ranga. In this regard Vimala Rao remarks:

> Deshpande does not use myth and legend as embellishment or for local colour or ethnic appliqué-work. Myths, legends and folklores are deeply engrained in the Indian psyche—especially those which are found in the epics and the puranas. They are so much a part of our psychic make-up that it is in terms of these myths and legends that we try to order our inner world and cognise our experiences.[45]

Another great source from which Shashi Deshpande derives allusions is the Bible and the works of modern philosophers like Kafka, Kierkegaard and Camus. Kierkegaard's line, "Life must be lived forwards, but it can only be understood backwards"[46] forms the key to her heroines' self-realisation. Secondly, Indian saints like Tukaram, Meerabai, Jayadeva and Purandharadasa are mentioned in the same flow of thoughts as Hedge, Gandhi, Indira and Rajiv.

Through the interior monologue Deshpande shows the awareness of her modern educated protagonists. In their chain of thought names like Van Gogh, Raja Ravi Verma, Shivaji and Jeeja Bai or even Bhimsen Joshi appear. But it is the world of literature that brings in the maximum number of names in the minds of her characters. Emma and Mr. Knightley, Raskolnikov and Sonia, Shelly and Harriet, Mr. Rochester and Jane, Bertha Mason and Grace Poole, Fanny Price and Aunt

Bertram, Hamlet, David Copperfield, Man Friday are to name a few. T.S. Eliot, Oscar Wilde, Graham Greene, the Brontë sisters, Virginia Woolf along with Betty Friedan and Erica Jong are the writers her characters read and quote. This illustrates that her characters are intellectually awakened and well-read. It also shows her own ability to utilise her wide knowledge which enriches her works and creates a better understanding for her readers.

Deriving inspiration from her husband's profession she mentions medical terms like the Tower of Babel syndrome, syphilis, ovarian tumour with metastases or leucorrhea, menorrlagea, dysmenorrhea etc. Even movies like Pather Panchali, Devdas, Sholay and film star Raj Kapoor are mentioned to illustrate the thoughts and feelings of the characters.

Shashi Deshpande's love for detail has made her give vivid descriptions not only of the thoughts and feelings but the surroundings, the house and even physical appearance of people. Her description of the morning activities at Saru's natal house becomes a realistic experience for the reader too.

> In the mornings, she listened to the sounds as if she had never heard them before, with a feeling of being swaddled in some kind of a soft cocoon. The hiss of Primus. The clink and clatter of the cups, saucers and spoons. The clang of the bucket and the slap of wet clothes against the stone. Soft swishes as Madhav swept the house. The low hum of devotional songs from the radio. Rarely, a conversation between Baba and Madhav, Madhav's singsong tones interspersed at regular intervals by Baba's 'hum hum.'[47]

However, it is the way Deshpande brings out the feelings of her characters, not by any melodramatic scenes but by the flow of thoughts, that proves her to be a writer of depth. Her description of Madhu's thoughts after Aditya's disappearance brings out the anguish of a bereaved mother.

> I start going out every day, I begin looking for him. And one day I am rewarded, I see him. He's a part of a

> crowd waiting at the traffic light to cross the road. Even as I move towards him, the lights change, the throng races across. I run after them, narrowly escaping collision with a taxi—the lights have changed again, the traffic comes roaring down the road, the taxi driver mouths curses at me. I am uncaring of everything but Adit. I must get to him, I must catch him. But he's disappeared.[48]

Shashi Deshpande in her works presents a vast canvas that envelops people from different ages, castes and stratas of Indian society. The novel *A Matter of Time* spans almost a hundred years to tell the story of four generations of women in a family. Although her characters are mainly Maharashtrian Brahmins, other characters like Manu, Jayant, Mohan, Gopal represent other castes. In *Small Remedies* she has drawn characters from different communities as there is Ghulam Saab, Hamidbhai, Hasina, Joe, Tony, Paula, Dalvi etc. Although her central characters are middle-class Brahmins, she also includes in her novels women from lower strata of society. The picture of Indian women that she draws would be incomplete without Jeeja, Nayana, Manda, Shakutai and Sulu.

In her novels the place of action is mostly Maharashtra and at times Karnataka. The novels depict the culture and ethos of the middle-class Maharashtrian Brahmin family as we find references to Ganapati festival, 'Sankranti kumkum haldi', 'bhajia', 'bhakries' and nine-yard sarees. Words like Appa, Atya, Kaka, Ajji, Ajju which are used for various relatives are Marathi names for relatives. The reason for Deshpande's limited world of middle-class Maharashtrian Brahmins can be traced to her own background. She spent a number of years in Bombay and the fact that her mother and her husband both are Maharashtrian has given her the first hand experience of the middle-class Maharashtrian Brahmin traditions. She may be criticised for her limited periphery but what cannot be denied that this lends authenticity to her works.

Shashi Deshpande's works have an autobiographical strain as like most writers she makes creative use of her experiences and memories. She once stated in an interview to Romita Choudhury that *That Long Silence* was her most autobiographical works because of certain incidents and thoughts. She further adds:

> Yes certain things are autobiographical—a character, an idea. There's a certain intensity about them. Take, for example, Saru's feeling of not being a wanted daughter in *The Dark Holds No Terrors*. Some of that has come from my own life. Then there's Jaya's feeling that she has had to suppress the intellectual part of herself [...]. The struggle not to reveal oneself in one's writing as in *That Long Silence* is partly autobiographical.[49]

Through her works Shashi Deshpande has explored various themes related to woman like—son preference, child abuse, limitation of scope, denial of self-expression, deep inequality, sexual and emotional violence, low self-esteem, economic dependence, alienation and suppression of personality. But what is pivotal to all her writings is the modern educated middle-class woman's struggle to find a balance between the traditional beliefs and individual needs. Although her language is said to be transparent and not drawing attention to itself, with a rare subtlety it creates a background of traditional atmosphere and the woman's uneasiness in it. Thus having found her 'voice' which she considers most important for an artist, Deshpande tells realistic tales of woman's struggle to keep her roots and at the same time attain individuality.

REFERENCES

1. Elizabeth, Robins, a speech in WWSL, 1907, quoted in *That Long Silence* by Shashi Deshpande. New Delhi: Penguin Books, 1989, Epigraph.
2. Parikh, Indira S. and K. Garg, Pulin. *Indian Women: An Inner Dialogue*. New Delhi: Sage Publications, 1989, 34.
3. Roy, Anuradha. *Patterns of Feminist Consciousness in Indian Women Writers*. New Delhi: Prestige Books, 1999, 88.
4. Atrey, Mukta and Kirpal, Vinay. *Shashi Deshpande: A Feminist Study of Her Fiction*. New Delhi: D.K. Publishers, 1988, 83.
5. Deshpande, Shashi. *The Dark Holds No Terrors*. New Delhi: Penguin Books, 1990, 107.

6. Deshpande, Shashi. *That Long Silence*. New Delhi: Penguin Books, 1989, 39.
7. ——. *Silence* 51.
8. ——. *Silence* 26.
9. ——. *Silence* 29.
10. ——. *Silence* 36.
11. ——. *A Matter of Time*. New Delhi: Penguin Books, 1996, 74.
12. ——. *Matter of Time* 144.
13. ——. *No Terrors* 149.
14. ——. *Roots and Shadows*. New Delhi: Orient Longman, 1996, 36.
15. ——. *The Binding Vine,* New Delhi: Penguin Books, 1998, 200.
16. ——. *Binding Vine* 80.
17. ——. *No Terrors* 158-59.
18. ——. *Small Remedies*. New Delhi: Penguin Books, 2000, 154.
19. ——. *No Terrors* 142.
20. ——. *No Terrors* 96.
21. ——. *No Terrors* 181.
22. ——. *Roots and Shadows* 33.
23. ——. *Roots and Shadows* 14.
24. Seshadri, Veena. "Rev. of *That Long Silence* by Shashi Deshpande," *Literature Alive* 1.4 (1988): 95.
25. Deshpande, Shashi, *Silence* 144.
26. ——. *Silence* 192.
27. ——. *Time* 230-31.
28. ——. *Small Remedies* 256.
29. ——. *Small Remedies* 323.
30. ——. Interview with Romita Choudhury, *World Literature Written in English* 1025, 34.2 (1995): 20.
31. ——. Interview with Lakshmi Holmstrom, "Shashi Deshpande Talks to Lakshmi Holmstrom," *The Fiction of Shashi Deshpande*, Ed. R.S. Pathak. New Delhi: Creative Books, 1998, 245.
32. ——. *Time* 98.

33. ——. *Time* 185.

34. Menon, Ritu. "No Longer Silence," Nov. 1998, 22 July 2000 http://ch8m.com/shashi.htm.

35. Deshpande, Shashi. Interview with Lakshmi Holmstrom, 243.

36. ——. Interview with Shobha Warrier, "You Cannot Dismiss My Writing." April 2000, 8 Sept. 2000. http://www.rediff.co.in/theredifbooks/inter.htm.

37. ——. Interview with M.D. Riti, "There's No Looking Back," *The Fiction of Shashi Deshpande*, Ed. R.S. Pathak (New Delhi: Creative Books, 1998) 237.

38. ——. Interview with M.D. Riti, 237.

39. Dwivedi, A.N. Ed. *Papers on Indian Writings in English*, Vol. 2. New Delhi: Atlantic Publishers and Distributors (P) Ltd., 2002, 196.

40. Deshpande, Shashi. Interview with Lakshmi Holmstrom, 243.

41. Menon.

42. Deshpande, Shashi. *Time* 236.

43. ——. Interview with Lakshmi Holmstrom, 246.

44. Deshpande, *Silence* 11.

45. Ramarao, Vimala. "Myth and Folklore in Shashi Deshpande." *The Fiction of Shashi Deshpande*, Ed. R.S. Pathak, New Delhi: Creative Books, 1998, 208-09.

46. Deshpande, Shashi. *Time* 98.

47. ——. *No Terrors* 95.

48. ——. *Small Remedies* 303.

49. ——. Interview with Romita Choudhary, *World Literature Written in English* 1025, 34.2 (1995): 19.

Patterns of Feminism and *That Long Silence*

SANTWANA HALDAR

14

'Tis not a year or two shows us a man:
They are all but stomachs, and we all but food;
They eat us hungerly, and when they are full,
They belch us.

(Emilia to Desdemona, *Othello,* Act III, sc. iv)

Over the centuries literature has been used as a public forum in which gender based discriminations in the society and the torture inflicted on the women in general are expressed. Women themselves have been given the scope to raise the discourse (as the angry outburst of Emilia in *Othello*), though those outbursts were only scattered signals of discontentment and were ignored as social and psychic reality. It was by the end of the eighteenth century that some theoretical attempts were made to shape the demands for women's rights—Mary Wollstonecraft's *A Vindication of the Rights of Women* (1792), for example,—and the representations of sexual identity as well as its social articulation were thought necessary. Those feminist demands paved the way for feminism that emerged as one of the most powerful social, political and cultural movements. Virginia Woolf's *A Room of One's Own* (1929) and numerous other essays attracted the sympathizers' attention; but a more radical approach was launched by Simone de Beauvoir's *The Second Sex* (1949). Since then the feminist movement spread all-over the world and left a major impact on literary studies, demanding reformulation of literary theories. The movement that appeared monolithic at the beginning, soon flourished as a field of different discourses entailing different formulations of feminism. Some critics like to interpret the differences as 'differences within,'[1] though the differences arising out of the groupings of questions and strategies within the field of feminism may not be ignored. Particularly, the problematic connections among issues of development, feminism, subaltern studies and cultural criticism demand new fields of discourse such as feminist deconstruction and post-colonial feminism.[2]

The last two decades of the twentieth century witnessed a variety of theories associated with feminism as well as the emergence of women novelists with distinct approaches to the theme commonly called 'feministic.' The women novelists all-over the world have been greatly influenced by the contradictions in the theories and the feminist issues raised in their novels focus on their respective evaluations of those issues. Margaret Laurence's *The Diviners,* Margaret Atwood's *Bodily Harm,* Mary McCarthy's *The Groves of Academme,* Kamala Markandaya's *Possession,* Anita Desai's *Fire on the Mountain* are some instances. Women in Margaret Laurence's writings (like Morag in *The Diviners*), for example, are portrayed as strong, active, sexually assertive and professionally successful. The writer is perhaps guided by the idea that she should provide role models of the new woman who will encourage other women to follow the way of self-emancipation. Margaret Laurence is accepted as a revolutionary activist by a group of feminist critics who believe that the readers will be influenced to change themselves after reading her novels, and these critics take her type for the standard feminist writer and find fault with those who do not reveal such revolutionary activism. Such tendency develops a sort of 'prescriptive criticism' which is strongly denounced by Margaret Atwood.[3] Shashi Deshpande, a significant woman novelist in Indian English, is also criticized by the feminist critics for what they call her lack of dynamic quality as well as her acceptance of conventional morality.[4] Deshpande's own reluctance to get attached to the term 'feminism' also requires clarification.[5] She says:

> It is a curious fact that serious writing by women is invariably regarded as feminist writing—A woman who writes of women's experiences often brings in some

> aspects of those experiences that have angered her, roused her strong feelings. I don't see why this has to be labeled feminist fiction. A (male) critic once said about a novel of mine, "She can be quite brilliant when she is not raising her banners of protest." What banners of protest was my thought! Any woman who writes fiction shows the world as it looks to a woman—to apply the tag of feminist is one way, I have realized, of dismissing the serious concerns of the novel by labeling them, by calling the work propagandist.[6]

She further says :

> When a man writes of the particular problems a man is facing, he is writing male propaganda. Nobody says that; why is it said only about women writers?[7]

Almost a similar view is expressed by other writers too, among whom there are Gita Hariharan and Shama Futehally. Talking about her novel *The Thousand Faces of the Night* (1992), which was criticized by some for its lack of feminist revolution, Hariharan comments that she was not trying to make any sort of a blueprint for action.[8] Shashi Deshpande also makes no blueprint for action, though she holds that it is not theory but activism which matters for her.[9] The novel *That Long Silence* offers an interesting study of Deshpande's stand as a woman novelist who is seriously concerned with women's problems in India. The protagonist Jaya being a writer, the study gets an extra dimension; for a woman writer's problems in exposing reality as well as the expectation of the male-dominated society in regard to a woman writer are focussed in the novel. The present article seeks to analyze *That Long Silence* from five perspectives in order to clarify Deshpande's approach to the problematic nature of feminism in the Indian context. These perspectives are (1) Feminism and Family, (2) Feminism, Myth and Intertextuality, (3) Feminism and the concept of 'Other,' (4) Feminism and Subaltern Studies, and finally, (5) Ethical Choice, Existentialism and Feminism.

Feminism and Family

Since its primary stage feminism has been raising its voice

against the institution of family that determines a woman's primary identity in a bourgeois society. A woman's identity is traditionally constructed according to the role conferred on her in familial terms—daughter, wife, mother. The family offers her shelter, food and safety and she gets so much habituated to that sheltered existence that she becomes tied to the norms prescribed by the family and is rendered incapable of free thinking. It is within the family that a girl child experiences her feelings of rejection or discrimination on the basis of gender, and she is moulded as a woman as per the demands of the family and the society. In the middle-class and lower-middle-class families of the Indian society, gender based discriminations are the most apparent: the girls are required to perform hard domestic labour of which the boys are exempted; and the girls are sent to schools and colleges so that they may be married off, frequently without their consent and with dowry as per demand. Shashi Deshpande is well aware of these facts and *That Long Silence* records her close study of the gender based discriminations made in the family and their impact on the young girls.

The protagonist Jaya was not however treated with difference for being a girl, thanks to her father who earnestly believed that Jaya would be victorious in life. (The word 'Jaya' means victory, he said.) Jaya was therefore admitted to a convent school along with her brothers and was brought up in a healthy atmosphere. But Jaya noticed the discrimination with which girls are usually treated in a family. She received the rude shock of her life when she found that there was no place of the women in a family tree prepared by her Ramukaka. A family is identified only by its male members; neither the daughters nor the daughters-in-law are mentioned in the family tree. And surprisingly, this practice was never questioned even by the female members of the family. Whenever Jaya would go to her grandmother's house, she found her cousin sisters Veena and Sujata quarrelling about whose term it was to clear up. Clearing up after meal—picking up the plates, clearing the mess on the floor with hands and smearing it with cow dung water—was strictly the duty of the women, and in her paternal grandmother's house Jaya saw her aunts and cousin sisters performing that duty almost religiously. After her marriage Jaya found the same practice in her in-law's house where the women's area of work was demarcated. Though Jaya did not have to be burdened with the odd jobs before her marriage, the scenario was changed after her father's untimely death; her free will was no more valued in the family. She recalls ..ow she was almost forced to marry Mohan: "After Appa's death, the *kakas* had never led Dada forget his role as the man of the house. And so Dada had cleverly maneuvered me into a position from which not marrying Mohan would have been childish, irresponsible and childish to Dada" (93). And once Jaya was married, she entered into the female world, getting her used to the role of a woman sharply defined by Mohan's family, and surprisingly, without any sense of remorse. "They had been a revelation to me, the women in his (Mohan's) family, so definite in their roles, so well-trained in their duties, so skillful in the right areas, so indifferent to everything else" (83). Jaya even felt that her mother should have taught her the 'duties' of a woman. She did not however take much time to pick up the qualities so that her life might revolve around the needs and desires of Mohan. She began to do all the household jobs with vigour and began to take care for her family with passion. When something was wrong—a bottom missing or a meal cooked badly—she felt guilty; and when she was praised for her performance in the new role, she would become ridiculously pleased. After the initial stage of infatuation was over, Jaya felt that she became so much dedicated to her family not because of her love for Mohan, but for a secured shelter ["Love? No, I knew nothing of it. I knew only my need of Mohan and his need of me." (153)]. Jaya repeatedly recalls her Vanitamami who said that a husband is a sheltering tree.

Through Jaya's self-analysis Deshpande exposes the fact that the Indian women have to sacrifice their freedom (and also humanity) for remaining safe, and yet, their life is hardly safe in the family. Jaya started learning this crude fact when allegations of business malpractice were brought against Mohan and they had to take shelter in her small Dadar flat, leaving the well-furnished Churchgate apartment. Mohan was afraid of being sacked and even proposed that Jaya could think of making money through some jobs though he had not allowed her to do so earlier. Jaya was further crestfallen when Mohan told her angrily that he had misappropriated money for Jaya and the children, and thus she was also involved in the scam despite all her attempts to remain indifferent. Finally, Jaya has to face the humiliation of being left alone in the Dadar flat when Mohan left her angrily without telling anything. Her son Rahul was reported missing and she understands that being a mother does not ensure one's hold on the son or the daughter. Jaya hardly understands her daughter Rati who was snob and selfish from the very beginning. Thus the structure of the family she has been sticking to at the cost of sacrificing her individuality as well as ethical sense (she remained blind to the corruption of her husband), appears to crumble. When Mohan told her that he had allowed her to have her way in most things, Jaya did not retort even if she had her answer ready:

> The job I wanted to take, the baby I had wanted to adopt, the anti-price campaign I'd wanted to take part in....But, even as I listed these to myself, it came to me that perhaps it had nothing to do with Mohan... perhaps I had not really cared enough about these things myself. Instead I said, and my voice sounded sullen even to me, 'I've done everything you wanted me to. (120)

Jaya had done everything Mohan wanted her to do, and did not take her own desires seriously only to keep the family life peaceful. She learnt how to maintain peace in the family through her sacrifices; she even stopped writing on real life experiences only to keep Mohan in good humour and to keep the structure of the patriarchal family in good form. Her prize-winning story that dealt with man-woman relationship could not make her husband happy. He accused her of exposing their conjugal relationship and remained blind to the artistic qualities of the story. He wanted her to write for a woman's magazine instead, choosing for her subject matter the make-believe world of the women. And she started writing for the column 'Seeta' and became popular, much to Mohan's satisfaction. Yet she failed to retain the familial safety she hankered after:

> If someone had asked me—what do you want?—I'd have given them an answer at once. Just to live. To know that at the end of the day my family and I are under a roof, safe, enclosed, in a secured world. If it is dark outside, what does it matter? I can close the door and windows, switch on the lights and the darkness will recede. But now I knew that I could never shut out the darkness; the darkness had invaded me. (182)

When circumstances compelled Jaya to face the reality, she did not protest against 'family.' Some critics find fault with what they call Deshpande's conservative attitude. For, when everything seems to be all right (Rahul comes back and Mohan sends a telegram indicating that he is relieved of the charges), Jaya decides to take up her role as the wife and the mother again. The only change in her role is likely to be in her decision to break the silence. She says:

> Mohan will be back. 'All well' his telegram says. Does he mean by this that we will go back to being 'as we were'? Does it mean that, now that Mohan has sorted out his problem, and no longer fears prosecution, joblessness and disgrace, we can go back to our original positions? Does it mean that he will come back and give me a carefully edited version of what has happened—as he has done so often till now—and then ask me, 'What do you say, Jaya'?
>
> Until today, this has been a rhetorical question. I have looked at his face for clues and then given him the answer I know he wants. I have only to do this now and authority will seep into Mohan once more.
>
> But it is no longer possible for me. If I have to plug that 'hole in the heart,' I will have to speak, to listen, I will have to erase the silence between us....
>
> We do not change overnight. It's possible that we may not change even over long periods of time. But we can

> always hope. Without that, life would be impossible. And if there is anything I know now it is this: life has always to be made possible. (192-93)

The concluding passage of the novel makes the novelist's stand clear. Instead of revolting against 'family,' she even accepts it as an integral part of life. She suggests some changes in the age-old concepts in regard to women's role in the family. Jaya's broodings highlight the idea that the women are required to take active roles in constructing ideal families. Safety cannot be guaranteed as such when the women remain passive. A weak and afraid woman can hardly be safe. Jaya's two grandmothers and to some extent her mother also, were entitled to dominate their respective families. They were, however, lacking in self-knowledge and their ideas were moulded by the traditional patriarchal pattern. But no one can deny their hold on the members of their family. This power of the women has to be assimilated with selflessness, strong ethical sense and faith in women's potentiality, and only then the women's position may remain secure. Deshpande's woman protagonist is allotted the task of reconstructing the family on the basis of renewed ideas. She is concerned not only with women's rights, but also with women's duty as a member of the family. And herein lies Deshpande's distinctness as a woman novelist dealing with women's problems.

Feminism, Myth and Intertextuality

Feminist discourse is closely related to myths. Fictional women have been appearing in myths, representing the patriarchal values attached to the gender. Writing about myths Simone de Beauvoir said:

> It is always difficult to describe a myth; it cannot be grasped or encompassed; it haunts the human consciousness without ever appearing before it in fixed form. The myth is so various, so contradictory, that at first its unity is not discerned.[10]

Some feminist critics modified the archetypal theory of myth developed by Northrop Frye while some others were influenced by the semiotic theory of myth conceptualized by Ronald

Barthes. In between these two theories there may be innumerable personal intellectual trajectories. The existing myths often demarcate the activities of the women on the basis of the physical differences between man and woman. The social behaviour of certain insect groups such as ants and bees are also extensively studied to provide 'scientific' proofs in support of the view that in human society too, the 'women' are naturally prepared for some specific works which are done by the queen bees and the slave bees. The child bearing capacity of the women is also interpreted as their special work and it is argued that the women being 'naturally' fit for bearing issues, it will be 'unnatural' to expect any intellectual capacity from them. To quote from *Biological Women: The Convenient Myth:*

> It would no doubt be a great boon to the human race, men might say if women could do the marvelous things men have done, like vote, own property, and get a proper education. But such was not just nature's design when she gave females a head almost too small for intellect but just big enough for love. If women had been meant to vote, they would not have been born with uterus.[11]

Thus, according to different sets of myths, which were thought universal, women were supposed to be incapable of any intellectual capacity and were denied right to property simply because they were not entitled to protect it.

These myths are full of self contradictions as they attribute contradictory qualities to women in general: women are supposed to enjoy their suffering, while any living animal is never seen enjoying suffering; in the myth of motherhood the mother is supposed to be an all-powerful being in regard to her child, and yet she is condemned for giving too much or too little attention to her child. Paula Caplan defines such myths and points out the ideology behind them in her celebrated book, *The Myth of Women's Masochism.* The feminists not only expose those myths and the ideology behind them, but also reconstruct some age-old myths. Kim Chernin's *Reinventing Eve* and Estelle Lauter's *Women as Mythmakers* are well known examples of reconstructing myths. The Biblical myth shows Eve as a great sinner who provoked Adam to eat the fruit of the forbidden tree and caused the fall of mankind. But the feminists have reconstructed the myth and Eve is rendered as an adventurous soul who ventured to know the unknown even at the cost of punishment. To quote Chermin, the "modern woman who is in search of herself will not let herself be tricked into believing Eve is a whore, a great sinner."[12] Chermin suggests that Eve's activity (her persuading Adam to eat the apple) does not tally with the concept of passivity accorded to women in Biblical myth. Thanks to her association with apple, Eve is linked to Gaea, the Greek earth mother, to Idun, the goddess of apple land in Norse mythology and to the Celtic queen of the dead in Avalon, who gave out apples for eternal life (Chermin: xviii). The feminine passivity in the Biblical myth is thus reconstructed, the figure of Eve having been associated with life-giving powers. Estelle Lauter's study of the images of women scattered in poetry and visual art also aims at reappropriation of well known myths. As she says:

> My question presupposed that myths change in relationship to history; that creative individuals play a role in changing them; and most important, that myths are still significant phenomena in our lives.[13]

A thorough study of *That Long Silence* reveals Deshpande's approach to myths while dealing with the experiences of modern Indian women. She takes up myths as belonging to a symbolic system. To identify the experiences of the women—the experiences which are complex by nature and are critical when rendered—Deshpande uses myths, reinterpreting, modifying, and sometimes using the old myths for revealing new ideas. It will be an interesting study to juxtapose her use of myths with the reconstruction of myths by the radical feminists.

The theorists have noted that the use of myth as proverb presents an unalterable hierarchy of the world without explanation. One such proverb is repeatedly used in *That Long Silence* through Jaya's remembrances of her Vanita mami: 'husband is a sheltering tree,' Vanitamami reminded Jaya whenever she had the occasion. And this proverb with its metaphorical significance presents the gender-based classification in Indian society: a husband who gives shelter is automatically given a superior status which is universally accepted. Through Jaya's experiences this proverb is proved wrong. After a lot of suffering Jaya comes to the realization that hardly does a husband give security and shelter. She says, "Mohan's wife, Rahul's and Rati's mother—I can crawl into that hole, I had thought, a warm and safe hole; but here I was now prodded out of it by cruel, sharp staves" (173). When the idea contained in the proverb 'husband is a sheltering tree' is proved wrong, the hierarchy that it offered is also nullified. After some years of marriage Jaya developed a passive attitude and liked to interpret their conjugal relationship as that of a pair of bullocks yoked together. But this myth (along with the idea it reveals) is also rejected by her at the end:

> Two bullocks yoked together—that was how I saw the two of us the day we came here, Mohan and I. Now I reject that image. It is wrong. If I think of us in that way, I condemn myself to a lifetime of disbelief in ourselves. I've always thought—there is only one life, no chance of a reprieve, no second chances. But in this life there are so many crossroads, so many choices. (191-92)

Jaya also experiences the contradiction in the mother image made popular in every sector of the society:

> It seemed amazing that I knew so little, almost nothing, about my son. Whatever had given me the damn fool idea that once I became a mother I would know my children through and through, instinctively? Yes, this was what they had told me: you become a mother, and everything follows naturally and inevitably—love, wisdom, understanding and nobility. But now I feel as helpless to deal with this despairing boy as I had with the floppy-headed, vulnerable infant I had brought back from the hospital.... We had been like two clumsy amateurs, novices playing the roles of mother and child. And now, fifteen years later, we were back at the same point. And there was Rati, Rati mocking at me, jeering

> at me from behind the cardboard cut-out figure of my daughter I had propped up—a girl, grave, serious, independent, understanding....
>
> A mother? Despairingly I relinquished my halo. No, I had been unfit to be trusted with the entire responsibility of another human being. (173)

Through Jaya's experiences the myth of women's masochism is also rejected. Describing the painful story of her mother-in-law's life Jaya reflects on Mohan's comment on his mother's suffering. Like other male members Mohan also shared the preconceived notion that the women are biologically tough, and so his mother's silent suffering was nothing but an expression of her inner strength, according to him. Jaya opposed the notion:

> He saw strength in the woman sitting silently in front of the fire, but I saw despair. I saw a despair so great that it would not voice itself. I saw a struggle so bitter that silence was the only weapon. Silence and surrender. (36)

Like the feminist theorists Deshpande also believes that myths do not evolve out of nature of things, that the myths function only within a specific historical moment. And hence, myths are required to be changed in the changing scenario of history. In the male-dominated societies, myths were grounded in male experiences, and the belief in myths was validated by men; and the women were somehow compelled to believe in those myths. By bringing the ideological premises of the male myths to the readers' attention, Deshpande joins the feminist programme of uncovering the ideas contained in myths that had been treated as facts.[14]

Deshpande has used the Indian myths profusely in order to highlight the change in Jaya's sensibilities. The protagonist is attributed different roles—the roles of Seeta, Gandhari and Maitreyee in particular,—which reveal her search for self identity. When her prize winning story failed to receive her husband's approval—he expressed his great shock at the revelation of reality in her story which, according to him, exposed their personal life—Jaya stopped revealing the facts of man-woman relationship and started writing light humorous pieces on the travails of the middle class housewives in a column entitled 'Seeta.' The central woman character Seeta in the Indian epic *Ramayana* has long been treated as a mythical figure that stands for tolerance infinite. Seeta was true to her husband Rama, despite the humiliation and the suffering inflicted on her all through her life, and as such she is treated as a typical Indian woman who is loved by all. Choosing the column of 'Seeta,' Jaya sought to identify herself as a spokesperson for the typical Indian women who accept everything silently without raising their eyebrows. This column received good responses from all and Mohan too, was happy. And Jaya felt secured as she could maintain peace in the family. Dissecting her creative self, Jaya later acknowledges that her contribution to 'Seeta' column was simply an endeavour to evade reality and to take shelter in a make-believe world. As she says:

> Seeta had been the means through which I had shut the door firmly on all these women who had invaded my being, screaming for attention; women I had known I could not write about, because they might, it was just possible, resemble Mohan's mother or aunt or my mother or aunt. (149)

The well-known myth of Seeta is thus used by the author to define the role of a woman writer adopted by her protagonist. According to Deshpande's analysis, as reflected in the novel, the mythical figure Seeta did not enjoy her suffering; nor was she specially moulded for tolerating continuous torture. She was simply afraid effacing the reality and became a victim of male whims. The age-old interpretation of the myth of Seeta was merely a male creation intended to project the image of Seeta as an ideal one. Jaya's inability to encounter facts of life as a writer—her fear to disturb the comfort of a cosy family life—is camouflaged by the choice of the title 'Seeta' for her column. Jaya's playing the role of Seeta serves a double purpose. At home the role of Seeta is appreciated by her husband and she feels secure. For her writer's career the role helps her find a corner in a woman's magazine and she becomes popular among sentimental readers much to her husband's satisfaction. This role was all-pervasive. Once she took up the role, she had to continue. It was a part of the role that she accepted Mohan as her 'profession,' her 'career,' and her 'means of livelihood.' His desires and approval were the most important things for her life, as it was for Seeta in the ancient days. In the modern context, Jaya had to cut her hair and to follow the advice of the fashion magazines in order to be a saddhi (the follower of one's husband).

However, Jaya learns how to face reality after she has undergone ruthless self-analysis. *That Long Silence* records the process through which Jaya transcends her old self and acquires necessary courage to encounter facts of life. And this time, too, Deshpande uses the myth of Maitreyee (taken from the *Upanishads)* who rejected the wealth of her husband Yajnavalkya on the ground that wealth would not lead to the ultimate reality. Driven by rude shocks of life—the shock of Mohan's being accused and the apprehension of his loss of job as well as Mohan's accusations that he did all these for Jaya and the family—Jaya turned to self-analysis and found that she had been lacking in moral courage necessary for making a choice of her own and therefore, took up a passive role.

> The truth is that it was Mohan who had a clear idea of what he wanted, the kind of life he wanted to lead, the kind of home he would live in, and I went along with him. But I cannot blame Mohan, for even if he had asked me—what do you want?—I would have found it hard to give him a reply. Maitreyee comes to my mind now, Maitreyee who so definitely rejected her philosopher husband Yajnavalkya's offer of half his property. 'Will this property give me immortality?' she asked him. 'No,' he said, and she immediately rejected the property. To know what you want... I have been denied that. (25)

Jaya further says that in answer to Maitreyee's query, Yajnavalkya told her that her life would be like anyone else's if she took his wealth. The idea of immortality still appeared crazy to Jaya. But when her self-scrutiny was completed, Jaya becomes full of courage and is ready to take up the role of

Maitreyee. Taking up this new role required an end of silence. The mythical figure Maitreyee is known for her capacity of arguing with her husband. After a series of conversation between Maitreyee and her philosopher husband, the former got what she aspired for. Jaya, too, decides to break the silence between Mohan and her and wants to make her own choice, as she is no more hankering after a secured life. As she says, "We've been like that, all of us, bound by fear. Yes, I have been scared, scared of breaking through that thin veneer of a happy family" (191). Thus the novel may be described as Jaya's progress from a passive role to an active one. Putting aside the role of Seeta and Gandhari (in the *Mahabarata,* Gandhari bandaged her eyes after she became the wife of blind Dhritarastra, and also remained blind to the moral flaws of her husband and sons), Jaya comes up prepared for the role of Maitreyee. Deshpande is to be credited for utilizing the resources of Indian myths for projecting her protagonist's 'pilgrim's progress'. Hindu mythology has a sizeable stock of archetypal women who are different from one another. There is 'Sati' whose life starts and ends with one man (her husband); there is also Draupadi who had five legal husbands. There is no scarcity of obedient wives, ready to sacrifice themselves for their husbands; there are also all powerful goddesses like 'Shakti,' the primal source of energy, who compel the arrogant men to kneel down before them. Deshpande utilizes these mythical figures successfully.

That Long Silence is a serious novel that deals with the problems of good and evil, and of sin and retribution. Jaya, the protagonist, might not be directly involved in malpractice, but she cannot deny the responsibility of ignoring the immoral ways adopted by her husband. She acknowledges her responsibility after the completion of the process of self-realization. In order to highlight the protagonist's conflicts on the way to self-realization, Deshpande takes up the concept of Intertextuality which has been central to any structuralist or semiotic description of literary significance. For her, Intertextuality functions as an important frame of reference that helps to interpret the text. Thus, when Mohan argues in favour of the malpractice he was accused of, and asks a rhetorical question to Jaya, "What do you think, Jaya? What do you say?," Jaya goes back to Dostoevsky's world in *Crime and Punishment*. Unable to answer Mohan, she recalls the scene of Sonia talking to Raskolnikov:

> I racked my brains to think of an answer. And all that occurred to me was Sonia telling Raskolnikov—Confess your sins. Kneel down, kiss the earth and ask for forgiveness. But, I thought, he might well retort then—Kneel down yourself. Have you forgotten that it is for you I did this? For you and the children.... The children can plead ignorance and get off, but I will have to take on the burden of being a partner in the crime, an ally, an accessory before the fact. Kneel down yourself.... Yes, I will have to join him. (31)

Intertextuality rests on the idea that all texts are variations on previous models. Deshpande's references to previous texts in order to clarify the ideas contained in her text are attempts to enter an old text from a modern protagonist's critical direction. She goes back to *Ramayana* when she feels that Jaya's enlarged consciousness needs a comparison with the classical Indian concept of sin and retribution:

> There was a simple word I had to take into account; retribution. How Ajji had frightened us children with her dire pronouncements—
>
> "Tell lies now and you'll be a lizard in your next life, steal things and you'll be a dog, cheat people and you'll be a snake." Now I knew better. We did not have to wait for another life for our punishment. It was all reserved for us right here and now. An act and retribution—they followed each other naturally and inevitably. Dasarath killed an innocent young boy whose parents died crying out for their son. And years later, Dasarath died too, calling out for his son, 'Rama Rama'. (127-28)

Dasarath was not directly involved in crime, for he killed the innocent boy by mistake; yet, he was to be punished. Jaya feels that she, too, is destined to be punished even if she is not directly involved in crime. She cannot be spared on the plea that she was blind to Mohan's activities. Intertextuality is thus successfully used to restore a woman to her rightful place; she is above all a human being and must therefore try to acquire human qualities before projecting herself as someone's wife or mother. Adrienne Rich's words may be quoted in this context:

> Re-vision—the act of looking back, of seeing with fresh eyes of entering an old text from a new critical direction—is for women more than a chapter in cultural history: it is an act of survival. Until we can understand the assumptions in which we are drenched we cannot know ourselves.[15]

Jaya attempts to place her in the background of India's cultural history and so she places her 'sin' of overlooking Mohan's moral lapses by the side of Dasarath's sin and retribution.

Deshpande's interpretation of the tale about the crow and the sparrow gives a unique touch to her novel. Fairy tales usually present direct images of women who are either fearful, evil forces or powerless figures, subordinate to men. The feminists find in these tales a patriarchal moral code which is meant for women under patriarchy. The magic charm of such tales attracts the child readers/listeners and the patriarchal moral code is injected in their simple minds. Feminists have rewritten many such tales—for example, the tales of Cinderella and Red Riding Hood—replacing the passive female characters with assertive, self-willed ones. The tale of the crow and the sparrow is not however recreated; it is provided with an explanation that comes very close to the feminist definition of fairy tale. *A Feminist Dictionary* defines the fairy tale as a "harmful cross-cultural educative story told to unsuspecting children that shows women as passive, opportunistic or cruel."[16] The bed-time story remembered by Jaya in *That Long Silence* is about a wise sparrow who built her nest of wax in which no outsider was allowed to enter even at the time of calamities. The foolish crow in the story had his nest made of dung which was washed away during rain. Shivering and sodden in the cold, the crow knocked on the door of the sparrow's house and requested her to let him in. The sparrow kept him waiting in the rain outside for a long time saying that she was feeding her babies and was busy with other jobs. At last when she opened the door to let him in, the crow was almost dying of cold. As the crow entered, the sparrow pointed to the hot pan where she had been preparing chapattis, and asked him to get warm on it. Moved by the sparrow's apparent sympathy, the foolish, gullible crow hopped on the stove and was burnt to death. Jaya wonders how such an ugly, sadistic story could be told to children. Particularly, its effect on the girl children is terrifying, she says:

> They (the little girls) will store this story in their subconscious, their unconscious or whatever, and eventually they will become that damnably, insufferably priggish sparrow looking after their homes, their babies ...and to hell with the rest of the world. Stay at home, look after your babies, keep out the rest of the world, and you're safe. (17)

This observation tallies with Marcia R. Liberman's comment that such tales are "training manuals for girls" which aim at preparing women for the traditional roles.[17] Deshpande lays bare such tricks of motivating the girl children towards a selfish and cruel, but secure life in the society. The girl children are taught how to devote themselves totally to their family in order to remain secure. Deshpande wants them to develop human qualities so that they might assert themselves as individuals and not behave as robots. She has used the myths, existing tales and previous literary works for highlighting her views.

The Concept of 'Other'

The construction of the 'Other' is felt necessary for a continued definition of the self. In *Margins of Philosophy* Jacques Derrida says, "Philosophy has always insisted upon this: thinking its other. It's other: that which limits it and from which it derives its essence, its definition, its production".[18] The formation of 'Other' supplements to the subjective self-consciousness. To satisfy its hunger for complete self-knowledge, the self seeks to supplement its self image through filling in the absences or missing parts of personality with the construction of an 'Other' against which it can articulate its identity. In her essay, 'The Laugh of the Medusa' (which is a sort of feminist manifesto), Helene Cixous says that, "There is hidden and always ready in women the source, the locus for the other".[19] The 'Other' refers to 'hysterical' woman and it is suggested that whiie challenging patriarchy one reaches on the verge of madness/hysteria. An obvious reference is *The Mad Woman in the Attic* by Sandra M. Gilbert and Susan Gubar who reconstructed the story *of Jane Eyre,* and argued that Bertha Mason is Jane's "truest and darkest double" (360). The voice of Bertha symbolizes, according to Gilbert and Gubar, a call of madness and challenge from within and thus Jane's struggle is rendered as internal. There are other critics who like to call Bertha the racial 'Other.' All these critics who put forward the concept of 'Other' unanimously agree that Bertha, Jane's alter-ego, must be exorcised so that Jane may progress towards maturity. To quote Foucault in this context, "the sane man could read in the mad man, as in a mirror, the imminent movement of his downfall."[20]

To complete the process of Jaya's self-analysis and acquisition of self-knowledge, an 'Other' is introduced in *That Long Silence* in the form of the character Kusum against whom Jaya identifies herself. Kusum was the niece of Jaya's aunt (Vanitamami) who being childless, took up Kusum as her daughter. Kusum was denied beauty, charm and wealth and became an easy prey to male antagonism. She was married and after giving birth to three daughters she developed insanity and was rejected by her husband. At this stage Jaya arranged for Kusum's treatment in the Dadar flat (which belonged to Jaya and to which she came to stay along with her husband after he had been accused of misappropriation of money) much to Mohan's annoyance. Jaya could not however cure Kusum of her insanity; she insisted on going back to her 'home' where she was despised by all. After she went to her 'home,' she was reported to have thrown herself into a well and found dead. Jaya says:

> 'Ignore her,' Dada said when she (Kusum) was being her silly, tiresome self; but I couldn't. I could feel her anguish, her fears, her despair. They seeped into me drop by drop, until I felt myself burdened with them. The day I heard she was sick, I felt relief. It was like hearing of someone's death. Your own life, your living, becomes a vital truth you're suddenly conscious of. And so with Kusum's madness I became aware of my own blessed sanity. Thank God, Kusum, you're nuts, I had thought; because you're that, I know I'm balanced, normal and sane. Suddenly it occurs to me—as long as Kusum was there, I had known clearly who I was; it had been Kusum who had shown me out to be who I was. I was not-Kusum. Now, with Kusum dead...? (24)

To establish her as a knowing consciousness, Jaya has to be aware of the 'Other' from which she is distinct. Jean-Paul-Sartre's three-part model of the Self offered in *Being and Nothingness* may be recalled in this context. The three parts of the self, according to Sartre, are Being-for-itself, Being-for-Others, and Being-in-the-World. Sartre holds that as Being-for-itself, the self is constituted by its past, present and future. The self has to grasp the past experiences along with the fluid uncertainty of the present moment as well as the unrealized potentials that lie far in the future. Thus it combines both the concrete and the abstract, the known and the knowable unknown.[21] As Being-for-Others, the subject self constructs an image of itself as an object, as it is observed by others. The self's apprehension of the Other's perception of itself is likely to be partial. The Being-in-the-World derives from the self's consciousness of the world as the sum of the possibilities—the possibilities which are not found in the Being-for-itself which alone incorporates the subject self's action, will and idea. In order to satisfy its hunger for complete self-knowledge, the self (Being-for-itself) seeks to fill the absences, the missing pieces, by constructing an ideal 'Other' against which it can articulate its identity and see its own mirror image confirming the subjective view already projected into the consciousness. The feminist critics are much enthusiastic about the concept of other and of alter-ego and they use the concept while deconstructing the female characters in literary works and myths. The modern novelists also use the concept of 'Other' consciously in their works. It is interesting to note that Deshpande has not just referred to Kusum as Jaya's alter-ego for once, but makes an extended use of the concept.

After Mohan has left the Dadar flat angrily, Jaya sits on the sofa, dumbfounded and stiff-kneed, for a long time. She goes back to her past, being forgetful of the present time and when he comes to consciousness she fears that she may be crazy like Kusum. To quote Jaya:

> Kusum—as if the thought of her had been an Open Sesame, I found myself engulfed by the ghost of Kusum, welcoming me to the category of unwanted wives, deserted wives, claiming me joyfully at last as a companion. I could not escape her anymore: there was nowhere I could go, nowhere else she could go either. Here we were at last—Jaya and Kusum. How hatefully they had clubbed our names together when we went to live in Ambegaon after Appa's death. Jaya and Kusum....
>
> Vanitamami too had constantly clubbed our names together and I had pretended not to here. I will go to Bombay, I had decided then, I won't stay here and be one half of the 'Jaya and Kusum' entity. But Kusum had been immensely present. She had been waiting all these years for me. And so here we were, both of us rejected by our husbands, our families, failures at everything. But Kusum was nuts. Thank God, Kusum, you're nuts, I had thought complacently; because you're nuts, I know I'm not, I know I'm sane. (125-26)

Jaya remembers the doctor's words that the mad persons never think that they are mad, and there is only a little difference between a mad person and a sane one. As Kusum thought that she was not mad she told that she needed no treatment. In despair, Jaya compares her present condition to Kusum's when she was mad and finds that her condition is more pitiable than Kusum's. For, Kusum at least took the decision of killing her while Jaya is unable to take such a decision. As Jaya says:

> In her madness, sycophantic, dependent, frightened, clinging Kusum had escaped. In her madness, she had been able to get away from the burden of pleasing others; only in her madness had she been able to be gloriously, unashamedly herself. But we hadn't let her stay there, in that world where the cry of 'Run, Kusum, Chandumama is coming' couldn't penetrate. And so she had thrown herself into a well.
>
> Yes, now that I thought of it, it was quite clear that it could not be 'poor Kusum' at all. Had not he taken the biggest decision of all, the only decision that mattered in life—whether to live or to die? It could not be 'poor Kusum'; it was 'poor Jaya'. (126-27)

Jaya soon comes to her senses and realizes her distinctness from Kusum. Unlike Kusum she is intelligent and capable of self-knowledge. She can know others' minds too, at least Mohan's. As Jaya's despair is gone and she gets a grip on her mind, she becomes sure that Mohan's convictions will bring him back. But this image does not fill her mind with joy, as she can no more treat Mohan as she had done earlier, without questioning his way of life and always satisfying him with her answers. She is a changed person now, as she has acquired moral courage to face the reality and is able to discriminate between right and wrong. She is now ready to accept her responsibility in Mohan's corruption, and this stand makes her different from Kusum:

> Nobody had bothered to tell me what to do when a marriage was over. Kusum...yes, there was Kusum who had opted for madness and death. Opted? No, I was wrong, she had not opted for anything, she had been pushed into it. We'd all helped to push her into that well. No, Kusum was of no use to me, her death was as futile as her life: it provided me with no clues. (138)

At the final stage of her self-realization Jaya is thus deviated from her alter-ego. She now establishes her as the 'Other' of Kusum who was full of negative qualities. Jaya is going to choose the role of Maitreyee, and it will be possible only after she has shaken off all the qualities which were incarnated in Kusum.

Feminism and Subaltern Studies

Post-colonial literature is generally characterized by a tendency to include the hitherto voiceless classes. Feminism, in particular, joins hands with the subaltern studies, confronting thereby the multidimensional manifestations of historically rooted injustices. The suffering of the women belonging to the oppressed classes demands, naturally, a more careful treatment when placed in the wider context of feminist studies. *That Long Silence* offers a detailed analysis of the life of the working class women in India through the protagonist's sympathetic understanding. Jaya says, "It was Jeeja (the maid) and her like I needed; it was these women who saved me from the hell of drudgery. Any little freedom I had depended on them" (52).

Jaya's acute self-analysis makes it clear to her that these unfortunate women are often pitied by the fortunate ones, "the happy women with husbands in good jobs, men who did not drink and beat their wives," and yet none of them likes to change their lot; for, the unfortunate ones are required to keep their "kitchen selves gleamed with brass and stainless steel vessels". One is reminded of Blake's lines: "Pity would be no more/if we did not make somebody poor" ('The Human Abstract'). Exploitation of the poor by the affluent is given an extra dimension when the characters are women. It is curious to note that Jeeja is treated not just as a suffering woman, but as a stoic figure having 'single mindedness'. Jaya even envies her for these qualities which, she feels, she does not possess. As she says:

> Jeeja was basically a realist. She badly needed the money she earned, she knew her value as a good worker, she knew it was her reputation for reliability that enabled her to earn more than the other servants did. She was that rare thing among them—a pure professional, and proud of it. I envied her single mindedness. She knew what her purpose in life was—it was to go on living.

> Enduring was part of it and so she endured all that she had to. (51)

Here is a unique attempt to treat the usually neglected odd jobs done by women for meager wages as professions, and to compare their jobs with those of the higher class and established people in the society.

Jeeja's character is sketched with bold strokes. When her husband was alive, he would beat her regularly, but she never complained. There was again, no anger behind her silence. Once she explained to Jaya that she had actually no valid cause to be angry with anybody. Her parents had not married her to a drunkard. Only after he had lost his job during a strike he started drinking, and that was not his fault. Jeeja also explained her husband's second marriage according to her logic. How could she blame him for marrying again when she failed to give him children? This was her simple logic. She took her fate as inevitable and tolerated it calmly. After her husband's second wife had died, she took it up as her duty to bring up her two children. The son, Rajaram, stepped into his father's shoes; he would drink and beat up his wife Tara regularly so that she and her three children had become Jeeja's responsibility. Jeeja arranged for Tara a 'batatawada business'. She went to the market once a week to buy the potatoes, onions, garlic, etc., and it was the duty of Tara's daughter Manda to bring kerosene, peel the boiled potatoes, etc., and to serve the customers. She could not run that business, as there was no customer because of mill strike. As Manda reports in a matter of fact way, "Nobody has money for 'batatawadas'. Baba beats up Ai because she has no money to give him, and she gives him any money, Ajji scolds her"(53). Jaya reflects:

> Where was it I had read an account of how baby girls were done to death a century back? They were, I had read in horror, buried alive, crushed to death in the room they were born in; and immediately after that, a fire was lit on the spot to purify the place, they said. Perhaps it was to ensure death.
>
> All those agonies... for days I had been unable to get it

> out of my mind, but now I wondered whether it was not more merciful, that swift ending of the agony once and for all, than this prolonging of it for years after years. (53)

The feminist approach and the subaltern studies are thus mixed up to produce, broadly speaking, the colonial female subject produced by history. Mahasweta Devi's writings—take, for example, 'Pterodactyl, Pritha, and Puran Sahay,' in *Imaginary Maps,* translated by Gayatri Chakravorty Spivak—may be cited in this context. Through the central figure, Puran Sahay, Mahasweta exposes the subaltern state functionaries to whom the so-called Enlightenment principles of democracy are counter intuitive. Deshpande, however, keeps clear of politics and sketches a realistic picture of Indian society focussing on the life-system of different classes of women—both culturally and financially different classes—and also on the differences among the individuals in each class. Thus Jeeja is quite different from Tara who has none of Jeeja's "reticence or stoicism". Projecting three generations of women—Jeeja, Tara and Manda—in a working class Indian family, Deshpande explores her favourite theme of a woman set on her way of self-realization through her interaction with other women belonging to different layers of living.

Ethical Choice, Existentialism and Feminism

It may not be wrong to observe that *That Long Silence* reveals the progress of its protagonist from a state of split personality to that of unified sensibility. The protagonist Jaya undergoes ruthless self-criticism in order to achieve self-knowledge, though she had doubt at the beginning in regard to the possibility of knowing oneself. To quote her:

> Trying to find oneself—what a cliche that has become. As if such a thing is possible. As if there is such a thing as one self, intact and whole, waiting to be discovered. On the contrary, there are so many, each self attached like a Siamese twin to a self of another person.... (69)

Jaya denied the possibility of a 'whole' self, because she still did not have the experience of making a free choice of her own. A free choice of an individual is existential by nature and it comes out of a 'whole' self, one that is ready to take full responsibility of the choice made. Jaya's marriage was not her choice; it was thrust on her and so she did not take any responsibility of the married life. That is why she could think of telling Mohan "I wasn't laughing at you, I was laughing at everything—marriage, us, this whole absurd exercise we call life"(122). Jaya's married life seemed absurd because she did not share the life with her husband. She only lived the life chosen by her husband. However, Jaya believed in change as a natural process. She said:

> Things can never be as they were. It's astonishing how we comment on change, as if change is something remarkable. On the contrary, not to change is unnatural, against nature. Biology recognizes this fact; it is stasis that is aberration. (47)

Jaya spoke of outer change, the change that is inevitable on each object and on every human being with the passage of time. She had no idea that she would soon be changed internally, that her fearful and docile nature which had never allowed her to make a choice of her own would be replaced with a free and fearless soul. She developed the habit of shrinking from reality as she was lacking in necessary courage.

The novel displays at least two incidents which reveal Jaya's fear to face reality. These are her literary career in a women's journal and her relation to Kamat. After her prize-winning story, written on the real experience of man-woman relationship, was disapproved by Mohan, Jaya ceased writing about facts of life lest Mohan be disappointed and angry, and after a period of time she started writing humorous stories on silly matters for a women's magazine. She knew that she was writing about unreal matters, and she could not yet gather courage to face reality; she was in fact afraid of losing the cosy comfort of family life. Her own words bring out the falsity in her writing:

> That column, yes, it had made me known. My profile silhouetted in stark black that accompanied each article

> frightened me each time I saw it. It was like seeing someone masquerading as myself, or as if I was masquerading as the woman who wrote that column. The woman who wrote this had no doubts anything, only strong convictions. (119)

Against her convictions Jaya posed to share the view that women writers are supposed to be exhibitionists. She was afraid to disturb the society (and also her husband) that does not like exposure of an intimate relationship (including sexual life) from a woman writer. She knew that she deviated from truth and was writing about unreal matters and yet she continued till she was rudely shaken by the charge of corruption brought against Mohan and by Mohan's accusation that he had done everything for Jaya and the children.

Again, Jaya had a sort of mysterious relation to her elderly neighbour Kamat who could read her mind accurately and could assess her properly. Jaya would run to him whenever she encountered a serious problem, be it her father's death or her failure to get her stories published. Kamat was her true friend who always told the truth about her writings. He told that a woman's story is supposed to express anger and gave her a warning: "Beware of this 'women are the victims' theory of yours. It will drag you down into a soft, squishy bog of self pity. Take yourself seriously, woman. Don't skulk behind a false name"(148). Jaya was attracted towards Kamat who would bring back her lost faith, but never dared to analyse her feelings towards him. After her father's death she rushed to Kamat: "There were no more words and suddenly I had realized I was crying and she was holding me...it had been warm and comforting...but it was not Appa... and it was not Kamat either, the man to whom I'd been telling all these things. It had frightened me to find myself with this stranger. I had made a quick flurried movement as if to get away from him, but it had been he who had released me first"(156). This was Jaya's first experience of love which she did not acknowledge. She, yet, came to him as she "needed" him for getting back her strength. Kamat once told her, 'Your name is like your face,' and passed his fingers lightly on her face. Jaya did not have the courage to face the reality that he loved her. The description of her last meeting with him reveals the latent conflict in her mind:

> His eyes had looked steadily, almost dispassionately at me. And my body had responded to that look, that voice, that touch. I had almost felt his body on mine, I had almost been able to smell and taste his lips. The body's response is so much simpler, so much more direct; is it possible that it is therefore more likely to be right? (157)

Jaya, yet, moved away from him, resisting her 'overwhelming urge to respond to him' with her body. She learnt that Kamat had died after that meeting, but she did not blame herself for her inhuman behaviour towards him until Mukta created the occasion for her, disclosing her (Mukta's) deep emotion for him. Mukta accused Jaya of leaving a dying person alone:

> 'He was frightened of dying, Jaya, he was afraid of being alone. You could have been with him, you could have stayed by his side, but you didn't, you just walked away; he could have been lying there for days, he could have just rotted there if he hadn't given me the keys, if I had not gone there that day. He was a very lonely man, Jaya, didn't you ever think of that? He was terribly lonely, specially after his son went away.'
>
> (Jaya says) I knew it now. 'Jaya,' he had said, and I had run away. He tried to reach out to me in his loneliness and it had frightened me. I'm Mohan's wife, I had thought, I'm only Mohan's wife, and I had run away. (186)

Jaya now shares the suffering with Mukta, and realizes that her attempt to accept one fragment of herself (Mohan's wife) as the only reality was lying to herself. She suppressed her other selves and fell a prey to split personality. And this was due to her fear that Mohan would not approve of any sort of attachment to Kamat. She now accepts the burden of the sin of leaving Kamat alone in his death bed. So long Jaya was lying to herself, she was in what Jean-Paul-Sartre says 'bad faith,'[22] and was unable to make a free choice. Only after she acknowledges her real feelings towards Kamat, and her sin of leaving him alone in his death bed, her fearless acceptance of the responsibility of sin makes the process of self-realization complete.

Towards the end of the novel Jaya finds in her soul the unexpected resource that supplies her with moral courage and enables her to make a choice of her own. She remembers the Sanskrit words in her father's diary—*Yathecchasi tatha kuru*—meaning 'Do as you desire,' the words that were taken from the *Bhagavad Gita*. These are the words that Lord Sri Krishna told Arjuna and asked him to make his own choice. Sri Krishna gave knowledge to Arjuna all about the indestructible souls and desireless action, and made it clear that the course of action was not to be dictated, but to be chosen by the individual. An action is always to be chosen; otherwise it cannot be action proper. Surprisingly, the existentialist thinkers express quite a similar view in regard to proper action. To quote Kierkegaard:

> The real action is not the external act, but an internal decision in which the individual puts an end to the mere possibility and identifies himself with the content of his thought in order to exist in it.[23]

To take an internal decision an individual is required to be true to himself/herself and must acquire moral courage to face the result of the decision. Such a decision is integrated to the 'whole' self of the individual, and there is no chance of holding back. After a rigorous process of self-realization Jaya is prepared to make such a choice. She chooses to break the silence between Mohan and her. With much faith in her power she decides to take up the role of Maitreyee who argued with her philosopher husband, and thereby she rejects the role of Seeta who followed her husband's decision without a question, and also the role of Gandhari who remained blind to her husband's faults. This decision is not easy to take: it suggests an end to the life of comfort and peace with which Jaya has been accustomed to. She has by now developed moral courage and has taken the joint responsibility of family life. *That Long*

Silence is thus a unique novel by a woman writer who projects her woman protagonist as an individual who lives up to the standard of what Kierkegaard calls 'ethical reality'.[24]

NOTES AND REFERENCES

1. Elizabeth Meese, for example, took up Barbara Johnson's words 'differences within' while exploring the recent trends of feminism. *The Difference Within: Feminism and Critical Theory* (Amsterdam; John Benjamin; 1989). To quote Barbara Johnson, "To say, for instance, that the difference between man and woman is an illusion created by the repression of differences within each may to some extent be true." *A World of Difference*. Baltimore: Johns Hopkins: 1987, 8.
2. Gayatri Chakravorty Spivak, a noted critic of the modern time, associates individualistic feminism with Western imperialism. Feminism is also closely related to Subaltern studies and post-colonialism. The noted Bengali writer Mahasweta Devi writes about the tribes in India—the destruction of their lifestyle in the name of development, their anger and despair—, but she is more famous as a feminist. All these instances support the view that feminism is no more monolithic.
3. The typical women figures in the writings of most of the Western feminists are found always protesting, and never compromising, and such characters are usually accepted as the epitome of feminism. Commenting on this trend of some Canadian critics who find fault with the women characters of McLennan, Callaghan and Davies, Margaret Atwood says, "A feminist criticism is emerging...in which a novelist was criticized for not having made her heroine's life different, even though that life was more typical of the average woman's life in this society than the reviewer's 'liberated' version would have been. Perhaps, Women's Lib. Reviewers will start demanding that heroines resolve their difficulties with husband, kids, or themselves by stomping out to join a consciousness rising group, which will be no more satisfactory from the point of view of literature than the legendary Socialist Realist romance with one's tractor." 'Paradoxes and Dilemmas: On Being a Woman Writer.' *Second Words*. Toronto: McClelland & Stewart, 1982, 192. This ironic remark by Atwood expresses her disgust with prescriptive criticism.

4. Critics find conventional morality in Deshpande's women. These women are "unfairly abused, misused and ill-used... (they) believe in conformity and compromise for the sake of retention of domestic harmony rather than revolt which might result in the disruption of familial concord." G.S. Balaram Gupta, 'Indian English Women Short Story Writers: An Overview,' *Vikram Journal of English Studies,* Vol. 1, 39. Laeeq Futehally observes that Deshpande writes about the middle class Indian women and their feelings, "not as their champion but as their articulator"[*Ibid*].
5. Shashi Deshpande does not like to be treated as a 'feminist' writer, and wonders why a serious woman writer dealing with women's problems should always be called a feminist writer. She says in an interview, "The Women in my books are people who come to realize what it is to be a woman in the process of their own lives and the situations they face not through books and theories. I think feminism is an entirely personalized perception. It is when you start questioning preconceived notions about your roles. I don't think there is anything 'inherent' in a woman apart from the fact that she can conceive. All other things are equally important for them as they are for the men" [Shashi Deshpande interviewed by Malini Nair, 'The Message is Incidental,' *Times of India,* No. 25, Nov. 1989.] In another interview, taken recently, Deshpande answers to the question: "You have expressed your dislike of being labeled a woman writer. Yet, your protagonists have always been women and the point of view has also been that of several women. How do you explain the contradiction?" Deshpande says, "There is absolutely no contradiction here. Why does the fact of my protagonists being women have to give me the title of being a woman writer? So many men have male protagonists. Are they labeled male writers? A writer is a writer first and foremost. Gender is one of the many things that go into the writing. Different themes, people, situations and ideas ignite our imagination. But once we begin to write we are simply and solely writers, trying to say something, finding the best way of saying these things, struggling with language, form, etc. Secondly and most importantly, the term "woman writer" is, we must admit a pejorative connotation. It brings in nuances of being limited, secondary, concerned with rather insignificant themes. This is what to deny when I want to deny when I reject the label." 'Beginning Anew,'

Shashi Deshpande interviewed by Shoma A. Chatterji, *The Sunday Statesman Magazine*, Nov. 7, 2004.

6. Deshpande, Shashi. 'The Dilemma of a Woman Writer,' *The Literary Criterion,* Vol. 20, No. 4, 1985.
7. *Ibid.*, 33.
8. Talking about her novel *The Thousand Faces of the Night* (1992), Gita Hariharan is reported to have said, "Some feminist readers asked me for instance, 'where is the feminist revolution?' And my answer of course was that I was not trying to make any sort of blueprint for action." Quoted by Joel Kuortti in the essay, '"Why I do not call myself a feminist: Problematic Identity of Feminism in Indian Context' *The Atlantic Literary Review*. New Delhi, Vol. 1, No. 2, 114.
9. Shashi Deshpande is reported to have said, "It's not theory. It's not Simone de Beauvoir; it's not Germaine Greer, or anything. Some people will read these, but what changes is activism." *Ibid.* 113.
10. *The Second Sex* (1949), trs. H.M. Parshley. Harmondsworth: Penguin, 175.
11. Hubbard, Ruth, *et. al.* Eds. *Biological Women: The Convenient Myth.* Cambridge, Ma.: Schenkman, 1982, 5.
12. Chermin, Kim. *Reinventing Eve: Modern Woman in Search of Herself.* New York: Time Books, 1987, 176.
13. *Women as Mythmakers: Poetry and Visual Art by Twentieth Century Women.* Bloomington: Indiana University: 1984, vii.
14. Feminist writers have also highlighted the common duties of the housewives which are usually neglected by the male. To quote Paula Caplan, "There is nothing essentially more masochistic about a housewife running herself ragged waiting on her husband hand and foot, than there is about a business driving himself to a heart attack to further pad an already solid bank account. The only difference lies in the social value attributed to each activity." *The Myth of Women's Masochism.* New York: E.P. Dutton, 1985, 2. Deshpande also reflects on the sufferings of women who are to wait for others in the family for the entire day, and hardly have time for themselves.
15. Humm, Maggie, *Feminist Criticism: Women as Contemporary Critics.* London: The Harvest Press; 1986, 181.

16. Cheris, Kramarse and Treichler, A. Paula. *A Feminist Dictionary*. London: Padora Press, 1985, 149.
17. Ruthven, K.K. *Feminist Literary Studies: An Introduction*. Cambridge: Cambridge UP, 1984, 80.
18. *Margins of Philosophy*, Trs. Alan Bass. Chicago: University of Chicago Press X.
19. *Critical Theory Since 1965*. Ed. Adams Hazard & Leroy Searle. Tallahassee: Florida State UP, 1992, 313.
20. *Madness and Civilization: A History of Insanity in the Age of Reason*, Trs. Richard and Howard: New York: Vintage Books, 1973, 248.
21. *Being and Nothingness*. Trs. H.E. Barnes. New York: Washington Square Press, 1966, 172.
22. According to Jean Paul Sartre, man is condemned to be free; but this freedom being unbearable, man escapes freedom of choice and seeks comfort of excuses. This state of pretending that one is not free to choose for oneself is called 'bad faith.' Sartre described 'bad faith' as lying to oneself: "To be sure, the one who practices bad faith is hiding a displeasing truth or presenting as truth a pleasing untruth. Bad faith, then, has in appearance the structure of falsehood." *Ibid*. 49.
23. *Concluding Unscientific Postscript*. Trs. David F. Swenson; Princeton: Princeton University Press, 1960/i, 302.
24. According to Kierkegaard, the ethical requirement is imposed upon each individual, and when it judges, it judges each individual by himself...It can be realized only by the individual subject, who alone can know what it is that moves within him. This ethical reality is the only reality...which can be known only through being thought; for it is the individual's own reality." *Ibid*. 284.

Splintered Self Journeying Toward Integration: *A Matter of Time*

15

ASHA SHARMA

The novel *A Matter of Time* focusses on the predicament of a male character, Gopal. On the surface it projects the world of middle-class educated women who are caught in the net of problems which arise from the conflict between their view of life and the conventional values of society. Gopal's walking out on his family initiates the narrative of the novel and a major part of it deals with the attempts of the other characters to find out the cause of his desertion. His desertion of his family for no obvious reason expresses his mental conflicts and his fragmented personality. His desertion becomes the immediate cause of the mental turmoil which his wife, his mother-in-law and his eldest daughter, Aru, experience. In a way this act of desertion stands for his sincere effort to discover meaning in life and integrate his fragmented self. The novelist's concern with the human predicament becomes more pronounced as Gopal, the protagonist, touches the philosophical dimensions of life and death in his yearnings.

The Big House, where Sumi goes to live with her parents after Gopal walks out on her, has both thematic and symbolic function in the novel. The Big House with "A festoon of cobwebs, hanging in a canopy over the huge front door..."[1](3) suggests the criss-cross of emotions and neglect of Kalyani by her husband, Shripati. The past of Kalyani and Shripati is suggested by the bougainvillea that "has become a monster parasite"(4) and threatens to kill the plant it grows on. Shripati, who has lived his life on Kalyani's wealth and property, bears comparison to the parasitic bougainvillea. The fragmented personalities of the characters associated with the Big House are suggested also by the plan of the house:

> Inside, the house seems to echo the schizophrenic character of its exterior. A long passage running along the length of the house bisects it with an almost mathematical accuracy, marking out clearly the two parts of its divided personality. (5)

The walls of the house which remain damp long after the monsoon become covered with huge mass of creeping insects which present an ugly and horrifying sight. The house assumes the dimension of a living character "... as if it were holding its breath, waiting for something" (5). The isolated room built on the first floor of the house again suggests the divided personality of the house. The novelist describes it as "... an excrescence perched on the top of the house, detracting from its main quality of integrity" (5). During the day there is no sound in the garden but at night "... there are ominous rustlings, sounds of unknown creatures of the night" (7). The entire description symbolically suggests whisperings of the unconscious mind coming into conflict with the conscious thoughts and feelings of the characters and causing split in their inner personalities.

Gopal, the protagonist of the novel, is different from the male characters in Deshpande's other novels. He is free from male chauvinism. He is a teacher at the university but he resigns his job when he is assaulted by his students for his orthodox views published in an article. He becomes frightened and resigns his job as he has already lost his respect as a teacher. His simplicity of heart is revealed by the fact that he does not attempt to find pretexts for giving up his wife and daughters. In fact, it is an act of giving up the life of a householder. He has nothing against his wife, Sumi, and his daughters. After giving up the life of a householder he goes to live in the house of an old student of his but does not try to conceal the information about his changed dwelling-place. He is an idealist. As a student he believed that "...there was a truth that lay at the end of the road, waiting to be revealed to him." (98, 99) But he soon realizes that it was a vain hope. He wonders at Kierkegaard's statement that past alone can help one to understand life. He fails to understand what kind of understanding of life a knowledge of the past yields.

Gopal's productivity to idealism shows that he cannot compromise with the pragmatic aspects of life. The potential to break himself free from worldly ties has always been there in him. He was twenty-six when he decided to marry Sumi but told her that "'...at any time if either of us wanted to be free, the other would let go. We are not going to be tied together.... No handcuffs....'" (221). When he walks out on his family Sumi does not ask him any question. He tries to justify to himself his desertion of his family on the ground that he had lost faith in the kind of life he was leading. Meaninglessness of his life impelled him to forsake the life of a householder and set out in search of some lasting purpose. Since his arrival at his student's house, he keeps dreaming of a man whom he believes to be his father. His father died when he was only eight years old. Split in Gopal's self can be seen through his ambivalent attitude to his long dead father. He has no memory of the appearance and manners of his father, yet he feels certain that the man who appears in his dream, is his father. Gopal's reaction to his dream reflects the split in his personality. He recalls that as an adolescent he looked upon his father as guilty of moral aberration in marrying his brother's widow. He compared the guilt of his father to that of Claudius in *Hamlet*. He imagined that his father sinned against his brother by secretly loving the latter's wife. Burdened with the guilt of parents, his mind, like Hamlet's is torn asunder:

> But that was how it was for me—my father was never a father to me—not after I knew their story. He was my mother's guilty partner, he was Sudha's uncle, her stepfather, he was my mother's husband... (43)

But now he experiences a change in his attitude toward his long dead father. He feels that his relationship with his dead father has become peaceful and harmonious. This ambivalent attitude to his father is characteristic of the schism in his personality.

Gopal's sense of loneliness and the fear associated with it lie at the root of his neurosis. His mental state shows that he is a victim of psychoneurosis as his thoughts and actions are interpretable in terms of conflict between ego and id. His ego is intact and he is aware of his distressing thoughts and emotions. The beginning of his distress dates back to his adolescent years. Sudha's school certificate reveals to him that she is his stepsister. Gopal feels shocked at the concealment of this fact. It is an act of "betrayal that cut away at the foundations of my life" (52). He feels alienated from Sudha and as his parents have already died he feels utterly lonely. His consciousness of his own mortality fills him with fear and a sense of utter loneliness. His detachment from others suddenly comes to an end the day he is charmed by Sumi's looks and her innocent laughter. However, as he recalls his love for Sumi and his married life he thinks like a man disillusioned of the snares of the world. Ruminating on his past Gopal realizes that he has always been a victim of the fear of loneliness. He again became aware of his fear when Sudha came to live with him and Sumi after her illness. Her husband's sudden death left her empty and isolated from others. She changed from a confident and cheerful woman to a peevish and complaining person. Gopal realized that "... she was frightened of this world of loneliness she suddenly found herself in" (51). In his present state, he is painfully aware of the human predicament of intense loneliness. His sister Sudha cultivated family ties and relationships with love and care but these could not alleviate her fear and loneliness in moments of her need:

> ... it's just deceiving ourselves when we say we are not alone. It is the desperation of a drowning person that makes us cling to other humans. All human ties are only a masquerade. Some day, some time, the pretence fails us and we have to face the truth. Like Sudha did. And I. (52)

Gopal's attempt to analyse and understand the motive that drove him to withdraw from his wife and his daughters reveals his acute awareness of the absurdity of worldly life. As he thinks of the frigidity of his passion for Sumi, he remembers that "It was my body that told me the truth once again, my body that could lie beside Sumi night after night, quiescent, feeling nothing" (69). He fails to discover some lasting purpose in marriage, although he admits that it was his body that told him the truth of his feelings for Sumi when he decided to marry her. After his marriage with Sumi he became engrossed with her and their children. He looked after his children "tending them, caressing them—with joy and passion" (68). In the night, Sumi was seldom awakened from her sleep by her hungry and crying babies. It was Gopal who attended to the needs of his children and was "filled with an emotion I had never known until then" (68). It was the time when the life of the body delighted him. As he recalls these past events of his life he wonders why saints despise the life of the body while the fact is that existence becomes possible through our bodies only. However, even in the early period of his married life, Gopal was vaguely aware that a woman and her child belonged together whereas a man was always alone:

> Even when Sumi was impatient, when she showed a flash of temper as she often did for being deprived of her sleep, they were together in that magic circle. Woman and child. And I was outside. A man is always an outsider. (68)

He believes that it is this sense of belongingness that gives the woman the purpose of her life since the beginning of her pregnancy, whereas a man has to search for it and find justification for living. He admits to Premi, Sumi's sister, that he had become tired of the life he was living. His sudden awareness of the Yaksha's question to Yudhishtira about "the greatest wonder in the world" (133) and Yudhishtira's reply to that gave him a jolt. He realized that Yudhishtira was right when he said that the greatest miracle of the world was people's unmindfulness of their own mortality though they saw many others suffering in life and dying everyday. The day he became conscious of his own mortality he was filled with fear and a sense of utter loneliness. It became impossible for him to go on living a worldly life:

> ... It happened to me. I stopped believing. The miracle failed for me and there was nothing left. You've got to

> be the Buddha for that emptiness to be filled with compassion for the world. For me there was just emptiness. (134)

His life became devoid of meaning to him. He realized that living with a person of his mental frame was not healthy and proper for Sumi and their children.

In the light of his philosophical leanings Gopal's walking out on his family raises the issue of the nature of his desertion. In a conversation with Ramesh, Sudha's son, Sumi estimates Gopal's act of desertion as *sanyas* which is the fourth stage in a person's life according to the Indian system of righteously living this life. A *sanyas* is impelled by a desire to know the truth and is firm in his conviction. His mind is not rocked by doubts and conflicting emotions. The epigraph to the first part of the novel is a quote from *Brhadaranyaka Upanishad.* It announces the sage Yajnavalkya's decision to renounce his worldly life and go in search of spiritual truth. It reads as follows: "'Maitreyi,' said Yajnavalkya, 'verily I am about to go forth from this state (of householder)'"(1). Apparently, the situation bears a parallel to Gopal's act of renouncing his family. But whereas Yajnavalkya was impelled by a desire to know the truth, Gopal walked out on his family because he was frightened of his mortality and loneliness. Gopal's act of desertion can be understood as the result of his existentialist anguish which his sense of alienation and his awareness of the absurdity of life breed in him. As such, his act of desertion cannot be accepted as *sanyas* or renunciation.[2] The *Bhagavadgita* lays down that a man of renunciation "remains the same in pain and pleasure."[3] Moreover, the Hindu scriptures hold that a man can take to *sanyas* only after discharging his worldly duties. Gopal gives up his family without fulfilling his obligations toward his wife and daughters. He does not have the mental state of a man of renunciation as he is torn by conflicting thoughts and emotions. The undue pressure of the conflicting thoughts and emotions traps him in a situation from which he is unable to extricate himself. He lacks the purpose that may hold together his fragmented personality. He views marriage as an act which demands "a lifetime of commitment" (69) but runs away from his commitment to his wife and daughters.

He recalls his first love making to Sumi after their marriage and also his awareness that her body made him oblivious to his dream of freedom and everything else. At a party thrown by Devaki in the hope of reuniting Sumi and Gopal, he ruminates about Sumi and compares himself to king Dushyanta who recalled his marriage with Shakuntala when the lost ring was brought to him. He is aware of his "very complex relationship with the past" (100). He knows that in the act of resisting or recreating one's past one always tries to reshape it to one's desires. For this reason Gopal thinks that the "idea of 'oneself' is, actually, what we want ourselves to be" (100).

Sumi's sudden death in a road accident, in which her father also dies, leads Gopal to a new understanding of life. He keeps his emotions in control as long as he is surrounded by others, but mourns for Sumi in private. As he contemplates on life and death he admits to himself that Sumi has become free from the burdens of existence. But it is a freedom that she has achieved "at the cost of her body, of life itself" (237). He wonders if it can be called freedom, for "We live through our bodies, we relate to the world, to others, through our bodies. Without the body there is nothing left; ..." (237). But the next moment he grows aware of Sumi's presence.

But he fails to understand the mystery of life and death and gives up the effort in despair. As soon as he stops thinking, realization dawns on him that life in terms of time exists in his consciousness though. Its gross physical forms come to an end:

> ...Suddenly there comes to him a moment as when the body is fighting fever, all sensation heightened, sharpened to a fine point of acuity. He has a feeling of stepping out of his body, out of this plane of existence, of seeing time, past, present and future, existing simultaneously with him. (248)

The novelist, however, comments that Gopal fails to understand the significance of this vision. The novelist's comment becomes significant as Gopal is yet torn within himself. Although he realizes that he is the only anchor for his daughters now, he has yet to "make peace with himself" (245). He tells Kalyani and Aru that he is going to immerse some of Sumi's ashes in the river Alaknanda and promises to Kalyani that he will be back as soon as he can. To him, the "unsullied purity" (245) of Alaknanda is like Sumi himself. In his emotional return to Sumi and his daughters, Gopal finds deliverance from the bondage of life and overcomes the fragmentation of his mind:

> If it is indeed true that we are bound to our destinies, that there is no point struggling against them, even then this remains—that we do not submit passively or cravenly, but with dignity and strength. Surely, this, to some extent, frees us from our bonds? (246)

Sumi is a woman who suffers silently and does not reveal to others the broken bits of her personality. She does not indulge in self-deprecation and holds a good opinion of herself. Getting on with life is important to her. She does not even ask Gopal why, without any apparent reason, he walked out on her. She holds her emotions in control. She does not show any distress or anger when her daughters speak of their father. Yet, despite her show of normality she "has a quality about her—a kind of blankness"(10-11). Her "apparent stoicism" (15) fails to conceal her hope that Gopal may come back to them. She is overcome by a sense of alienation but wants to stay alone. She stays alone, against her mother's wish, in her grandfather's room so that she may become accustomed to her loneliness. She does not want to discuss the issue of Gopal's desertion and is indifferent to sympathy. She wishes that she could reveal her hurt to her daughters and tell them that the reason of Gopal's desertion lies in his being. She recalls the incident when during a discussion on the meaning of the word "*Sa-hriday*" (23) Gopal had told her that it had no equivalent word in English. It expressed "an impossible concept" (24) in the sense of oneness between two hearts. He abruptly drew her close and pointed out that their two hearts did not beat in unison. In the beginning Sumi was fascinated by "these unexpected quirks" (24) in Gopal but soon she lost interest in them. She realizes now that they were hints of his moving away from her. Gopal's personality and his idea of destiny indicate the possibility that he could give up his family. He believes that "Destiny is just us, and therefore inescapable, because we can never escape ourselves" (26). But it does not explain the situation in which Sumi and her daughters are caught. Their predicament is the result of Gopal's actions. Sumi, who does not ask Gopal any explanation for his act of desertion, wishes to ask him one question but she does not. She wants to tell him that he is also the product of his age which is characterised by craving for material possessions. In view of this, how he could renounce his family:

> What is it, Gopal...that makes a man in this age of acquisition and possession walk out on his family and all that he owns?...it was you who said that we are shaped by the age we live in, by the society we are part of. How then can you, in this age, a part of this society, turn your back on everything in your life? (27)

Sumi's decision to vacate her house and move to her parents' home arouses her from the inertia she falls into after Gopal's departure. But the decision to vacate the house puts her in "a frenzy of movement" (28). This sudden change in Sumi, from low spirits to wild excitement, suggests the precarious balance of her mind:

> But now, in the silence of the night, ... the house rushes forward to claim her with memories. She has a strange sense of seeing all of them, even her own self, moving about the house, as if they have come together for one last time, reenacting scenes from the past for her benefit. (30)

Sumi's state of mind, at this point in the novel, is close to the state of traumatic neurosis in which a person assimilates "...retrospectively an unexpected experience by...getting in front of it again... "[4] Sumi feels that she is an outsider in her parents' home. She has "... the air of being lost, of having no place in her childhood home" (33). Although she does not show her distress, her exaggerated and stylized manners suggest it. The memory of her parents' life frightens her on account of her daughters. Her parents, Kalyani and Shripati, have not spoken to each other for decades. Gopal's desertion of Sumi is a parallel to Shripati's desertion of Kalyani. She does not like that Aru is becoming conscious of "the queer relationship between her grandparents" (60). It serves as a constant reminder of what Gopal has done to Sumi and her daughters. Haunted by the fear and pathos of situation, which has become a part of her consciousness, she worries about the future of her daughters as she thinks: "And will this, what is happening to me now, become part of my daughters too? Will I burden them with my past and my mother's as well?" (75). Whenever Sumi enters her father's room she is reminded of her childhood. She grows aware of her father's ambition for her. She wanted to realize his unfulfilled ambition by making Sumi "a distinguished lawyer" (72) and a judge. But Sumi married Gopal and put an end to her father's ambition.

The incident of the road accident in which both Aru and Sumi are injured, focusses on Sumi's fears and her fragmented self. Her sense of alienation makes her vulnerable to fears and she becomes a victim of disruptive thinking. She feels that all people in this world are strangers to one another. Her visions, in which she sees "...the fan coming down on her body, crushing it...her body hanging from the fan, the ghostly shape slowly spinning...." (190) breed in her a sense of horror and make her conscious of some impending disaster. Writing of a play, tilted 'The Gardener's Son,' for the school function provides Sumi an opportunity to rediscover her creative potential. The success of the play gives her joy and satisfaction and helps her establish a smooth relationship with her students. She thinks that "If we are to construct a world, why not shape one with the hopelessness left out, why not end with the hope of happiness..." (158). This rediscovery of her creativity begins the process of integration of her fragmented self. She views her mother also in a different light. She contrasts the present Kalyani with the Kalyani of her own memory whom she recalls as a woman striking herself in agony when she lost her son and Shripati deserted her. Kalyani has survived her misery and the agony of desertion. She has formed a "complex net of relationships...with so many people" (185). Looking at her, Sumi recalls to her mind "...the spider she had seen one morning, scuttling from point to point, drawing silken threads out of itself, weaving in the process a web with a beautiful design" (185). She comes to an understanding of Gopal's desertion even. Going back to her parent's house reminded her of the tragic fate of her mother. It appeared to her that her desertion by Gopal was a repetition of Kalyani's desertion by Shripati. She was frightened to think that a similar fate might befall her daughters. But as she gains control over herself, she realizes "...my life is not like my mother's. Our life, yours and mine, was complete" (222). Her confidence revives as she gets a job in school at Devgiri. She feels that now she can live on her own. She tells Aru that she has been idle all her life but now she wants to be active and busy. But her happiness does not last long; the next day she dies in a road accident. However, a moment before her death she has a glimpse of that duality of life which "...ends all fragmentation and knits the world together..." (238). While driving her scooter, with her aged father on the rear seat, she turns round to look at him and discovers "a kind of brooding tenderness on his face" (232-233). It is a moment of enlightenment for her. Suddenly, she grows aware that despite his apparent cruelty his father has a kind and human heart and that this entire creation is composed of both good and evil. In the act of accepting the one, one naturally accepts the other.

Kalyani's desertion by her husband lies at the root of her fragmented personality, though the role of her childhood experiences and her forced marriage with Shripati cannot be overlooked. Kalyani is an apparently week and fumbling person who conceals great fortitude. She proves to be the anchor of the family in times of distress. The cause of estrangement between Kalyani and Shripati is the loss of their four-year old mentally retarded son at the Bombay railway station. When going to Bangalore on her usual visit to her parents' home, she lost her son, Madhav. She waited on the platform while Shripati went to check out the reservations. On his return Shripati discovered that he had lost his son. Leaving

Kalyani and her children on the platform, Shripati rushed out in search of the lost boy. Searching for his lost son, "he went about the city like a mad man" (140). Since that day he has not spoken to Kalyani. In fact, the relationship between Kalyani and Shripati was marked by a "hopelessness...that doomed it from the start" (143). Kalyani's parents Vithalrao and Manorama did not have a son. She exploited Shripati's indebtedness to her and made him marry Kalyani. It was a contrivance to gain security by keeping the property in the family. Manorama never forgave Kalyani for her desertion by Shripati. She felt disgraced by Kalyani's coming back home as a rejected wife. Her cruel treatment of Kalyani created a breach between Vithalrao and her. When Vithalrao suffered a stroke and became a suffering invalid, she blamed Kalyani for his sufferings. In contrast to her, Kalyani looked after her father with sympathy and gentle care.

In her last days, Manorama "was not only tyrannical" (153) to Kalyani, she even suspected that she wanted to kill her. The novelist brings out the fragmentation in Kalyani through Aru's consciousness who fails to "...connect the two women, the Kalyani left stranded by her husband in public and this Kalyani who seems to have exercised all her ghosts" (153).

Kalyani's reaction to Sumi's desertion by Gopal brings back to her mind her own sufferings and she cries out abruptly "no, my God, not again" (12). Again, her strange reaction to Aru's fainting reveals that she has not been able to free herself completely from her past. Her sudden realization that Aru is Shripati's granddaughter stupefies her. The incident reveals a terrified Kalyani who is different from her usual self. She indulges in self-flagellation when she meets Gopal after his walking out on Sumi. She pleads with him that he should not let that happen to Sumi what happened to her years ago. In an effort to know the reason of Gopal's desertion of Sumi, she asks him whether Sumi has done something wrong or lack of money is the source of his trouble. Kalyani's behaviour reveals her anxiety about the future of her daughter and grand-daughters; but it also focusses on her shattered self as she often reverts to her tortured past. She is obsessively conscious of her sense of guilt. Her occasional narration of the history of her family is her defence against the terrors of the past. She glorifies her ancestors, including her father, in her narration. This glorification is a projection of her suppressed desire for happiness which she was deprived of.

Deaths of Sumi and Shripati petrify Kalyani. She sits by the dead body of her daughter and does not move even when the dead are taken away for their cremation. In the night, when everyone is asleep "... the house is woken up by a cry. It is a cry of pain, like that of a woman in labour" (236). None but Goda knows that the cry was uttered by Kalyani who suddenly woke up and called Shripati by the name she used to call him in her childhood. It is "...by going back to her childhood, to her earlier relationship with him...." (236) that she mourns Shripati. Her sudden, though brief, reversal of childhood, in the act of mourning the death of her husband, again reflects the fragmented state of her self. But her sense of responsibility toward her granddaughters revives her courage to stand firmly against the onslaughts of existence. When Gopal tells her of his intention that he wants to immerse a part of Sumi's ashes in the Alaknanda, she encourages him to go. She is aware that he cannot be at peace with himself without satisfying his urge for self-knowledge. In response to Gopal's assurance that he will come back soon, she replies that she knows it and assures him in turn that she is there to take care of the girls. The death of her husband frees her from the burdens of her painful and incompatible marriage and she becomes her own self again. Shripati's will leaves the house to Kalyani who is daughter of Vithalrao and Manorama. His will does not mention her as his wife. It bequeaths her not only the house but "restored something she had lost" (245).

Though Aru is not a sharply fragmented person, she shows signs of ambivalence in her relationship with Kalyani, Gopal and Shripati. Kalyani's abrupt reaction to the shocking news of Gopal's desertion of his family, overwhelms Aru with a "sense of unreality" (12). She loses contact with the "people around her and their distress" (12). As she thinks of the disgrace that Gopal's desertion has brought on them, she is filled with fear. Sumi's stoic indifference to Gopal's walking out on the family annoys her. She is acutely conscious of having lost her father and her home. Contemplation on the unusual and estranged relationship between her grandparents carries her mind to her father's desertion of the family. She feels that Gopal's act of giving up his family is not an isolated occurrence "but connected somehow to the curious story of her grandparents" (39).

Aru makes her first visit to her father in the hope of learning from him the reason of his desertion and persuading him to come back home. Her effort to elicit something from Gopal fails utterly. Aru had trusted her "special relationship" (56) with her father and had imagined that he would reveal to her the reason of his walking out on the family. She is hurt at the discovery of her changed relationship with her father. Aru's frustration is brought out by her desire to seek legal help against Gopal. She is surprised at Sumi's indifferent attitude to Gopal's desertion of them and tells her that she should claim maintenance from him and not let him go without punishment. Her revolt against Gopal expresses her anxiety and frustration as well as her attempt "to reclaim ... a situation" (61) of which Gopal was a part. Her ambivalent attitude to Gopal is revealed by the fact that she wants to reclaim him and yet she hates him for what he has done to the entire family. The thought of her father fills her with anger and she visualizes her mother "... as a victim ... in fact, she has begun to see a victim in every woman, a betrayer in every man" (144). Her disrupted thinking makes her view marriage as a hollow and meaningless thing. She feels disillusioned of marriage as she thinks of Sumi's desertion by Gopal and of Kalyani's sufferings in marriage. Immature and frustrated as she is, she does not understand the importance of love in life. She does not know that "... without that kind of a companionship some part of us withers ..." (169). Her view of children also reflects her aversion to marriage. She considers babies as " ...Nature's trap, the fly-paper to catch women and pin them down to the nurturing role. Nature needs them to take on for her purposes" (142). In fact, Gopal's desertion of the family lies at the root of her disrupted thinking. She feels that it has led to the disintegration of the family which has been split into "Five units that don't add up to a whole" (184).

Aru begins to unite her scattered self through the influence of Surekha, an advocate, whom she frequently visits with the intention of filing a legal suit against Gopal. Surekha admires Gopal for his honesty as he confesses to her that he was frightened when some students attacked him. Surekha makes Aru understand the futility of taking legal action against him. A life account of Yamunabai, Manorama's teacher, gives Aru the idea that human beings are mere instruments in the cosmic plan. Yamunabai's magic formula was "Nimittamatram bhava Savyasachi—be thou only the instrument, Arjuna. The end is not in us, it is outside us, it is quite separate from us. We are only the instruments" (188). Aru's changed relationship with her grandmother reveals the development of her inner personality. When the shock of the deaths of Sumi and Shripati makes Kalyani faint, it is Aru who rushes to help her and console her with the words "... 'Amma, I'm here, I'm your daughter, Amma, I'm your son ... '" (133). Though for a while, Aru bursts into a violent fit of crying when Gopal is about to go on his quest for peace, she gains control on her emotions and lets him go.

WORKS CITED

1. Shashi Deshpande, *A Matter of Time.* New Delhi: Penguin Books India, 1996. All textual quotations, given parenthetically, are from this edition.
2. Concerning this R.S. Pathak opines, "A careful examination of the whole issue, however, will significantly reveal that Gopal's way of life and thinking do not have a close similarity with the Indian ideal of *Sanyasa.*" "*A Matter of Time*: Of Human Bonds and Bondages." *The Fiction of Shashi Deshpande* Ed. R.S. Pathak New Delhi: Creative Books, 1998, 165.
3. *The Bhagwadgita,* trans., S. Radhakrishnan. Bombay: Blackie & Son (India) Ltd., 1976, 105.
4. Charles Rycroft, *A Critical Dictionary of Psychoanalysis.* Harmondsworth, Middlesex, England: Penguin Books, 1979, 171.

Theme and Structure in Shashi Deshpande's *Moving On*

16

V.R. BADIGER

Shashi Deshpande's novel *Moving On* (2004) is her typical novel. After going through the first hundred boring pages or so, one finds out that she repeats her old pattern once again into this realistic novel within a network of 'family stories' (what she calls) within the same family (perhaps her own family) she wrote about in her other novels but with different names of characters. A student of Deshpande's novels is not at all surprised by what she has written in this—'the usual stuff', he or she will say—'the woman protagonist at the centre, love and quarrel between husband and wife...there is death somewhere, the fear of death and fear of living etc.'

At the centre, as usual, again there is a Brahmin family—the family of Baba and Vasu—the parents of Manjari Ahuja, the daughter-widow who, at present, lives in the ancestral house at Bangalore. She, being old and aged, intends to live a mentally and physically good life by conducting yoga classes to the neighbouring children. Her prime worry in the present time is that she is afraid that her house that is in the name of Sachi, her daughter, is going to be sold unexpectedly. Her aged mind is full of irrational fears, anxieties, fantasies and nightmares. Selling of her house is one of her irrational fears. If the house is sold by her she will be out—a derelict on the footpath or on her way to some kind of living in an *ashram*. She is afraid of her own existence, the old age and disease and possibly the end of her life. Even in her old age she is bit possessive as any other old women. Her problem is to cope with the younger generation represented by Raja, Abhishek, and Sachi, her much loved-hated daughter, 'the bad fairy' (*MO*, 325). Abhishek is a software engineer-tenant who dreams of going to U.S. and make a lot of money. Abhishek lives a 'computer' life and loves to speak 'computer language' to her. Also there is an episode of her 'fantasy' of theft and rape by the intruder in the house, followed by anonymous 'phone calls' regarding the selling of her house, and compulsion to sell the house only to the unnamed party. She, having had her injuries, struggles hard to express what has happened to the police. It is a sort of house-break in as it happens in big cities. Raja arranges for police inquiry Venkat, one of her relatives, who is a DIG but nothing happens. The incident is brushed aside simply as a casual case.

The novel as such is divided into two main parts – Part 1 and Part 2. The Part 1 has the quotation from Erica Jong's *Inventing Memory*: "All the stories that have ever been told are the stories of the families—from Adam and Eve onward" (*MO*, 2). The Part 2 has the quotation from Italo Calvino's *If on a Winter's Night a Traveller*: The ultimate meaning to which all stories refer has two faces: the continuity of life, the inevitability of death. By these quotations she implies that her novel tells such stories of family of Adams and Eves who live, love and die. For Shashi Deshpande, a novel is not an intricately and elaborately told long and complex single narrative but it is an embodiment of several interlinked short stories, episodes and anecdotes about the individual characters within a fictitious family.

The main story is of two generations—generation gaps—'a sort of digging into the history of one's own family but the stories of the individuals are casual but not very interesting or thrilling. One good thing is that the stories are held together by the central consciousness of Manjari, the narrator. There are flashbacks into the past by narrator's recalling memories of the past or reading the excerpts from the diaries of Baba, her doctor-father and stories left behind by Mai, her writer-mother. The ultimate message of the novel is that we continue to live in spite of all sorts of troubles—including the imminent fact of reality, i.e. Death. Life never ends with death; it moves on and beyond death. Parents, children and grandchildren continue to live in future with their parents in them. The novelist lays her finger on the right on her lifetime preoccupation as theme, i.e. the existential theme—'the essential aloneness of the individual.' Is there a way out from life other than death? No. One must live. So one continues to live. There are several deaths in the thematic pattern—Mai's death, Baba's death, Malu's death, Ajji's death, Shyam's death etc.

The structure of the novel is spiral. It is of the old-fashion, i.e. all stories remain as memories in the mind of the narrator, Manjari Ahuja. Does Shashi Deshpande take this family-name from *Kayamat*? She unravels the layers one by one—her own story, story of her parents, Baba and Mai, their youth, their college days, their love affair before marriage, their initial married life and later 'battles' etc., her own birth, childhood girlhood, her youth, affair with Shyam, her estrangement and alienation from her family members, her own living with daughter Sachi, Abhishek and Raja, her estrangement between herself and her daughter etc. So, Manjari is the central consciousness of the novel. She, after the death of her parents (one after other—first Mai dies and later Baba) discovers her Baba's diaries (to be read or not?) and Mai's stories. Mai is the alter ego of the novelist. One feels that Shashi Deshpande writes about herself as a writer in the character of Vasu (Mai) and attempts to reassess herself from her daughter's point of view. She herself chooses to be a doctor and her husband is also a doctor who dies in her early-married life. Consequently she transforms into a widow. Sachi is her daughter in whose name the house is registered. In the novel there are four exerts from Baba's diary on different dates—"1 January 1997, 10 March 1997, 27 April 1997 and the last 1 October 1997." It is clearly mentioned that he dies on '30 March 1998' (*MO*, 316). These excerpts help the readers to look into Baba's past as narrated by him. The first may be misread as a part of Manjari's own narrative as there is no bifurcating mark. One does not understand where his writing stops and Manjari's authorial narration starts. The second Baba's writing is better than the first one. There is dullness in the first that is placed by mistake in the very beginning of the novel. The third one reveals his own liking for Charles Dickens's novel *Bleak House* especially the subject of conjugal infidelity between husband and wife.

The novelist goes deep into the past on Mai's side of the story, revealing her brothers—Luxman and Bharat. Of the two, Luxman is revealed to be a civilian-criminal and his Mangal who gets him killed by hiring gangsters. Manjari also narrates the married life of Bharat and Medha and Malu's adoption of Malu as their daughter as they were childless and Malu's separation and estrangement from them and transformation of Malu as '*Amachi Tai*'. Her mother's attitudes towards her brother are also reviewed and explained how he caused fissure in their love-hate relationship between Manjari's parents.

Themes are old—the same themes—the fear of rape and death what one finds in her first novel *The Dark Holds No Terrors*. The episode is revised of her own story in the earliest collection *The Intrusion and Other Stories*. Are the family stories interesting? No. There lies the demerit of the novel. As it is said in her recent interview arranged at Bangalore—"She is writing about her experience of life as it is." She does it with different names. To justify her existential theme she quotes lines from *Isa Upanishad*: "'Purnam adah, purnam idah, purnat porunam, udachyate/Purnasya purnam aadaya purnam evavasisyate.'...this is God! We created God to embody the idea of a self that is complete in it. This is the harmony that the astronomers of old dreamt of. To achieve this wholeness is the final stage of evolution, it is *nirvana*. But, for us who are only a part of that wholeness, it is unattainable....we look for that...It never happens" (*MO*, 336). *Nirvana* is not possible for ordinary men and women like Baba and Mai. Galileo's *Eppur si muove* ('Still it moves') are quoted (*MO*, 16) to support Isa Upanishadic lines on secular plane—What is *poorna*? What is *apoorna*? The realization of love by the completely understood male (husband) and female (wife).

On a secular plane, the theme of love and death are polarized. Mai and Baba do not lead to a sort of complete understanding and experience of the wholeness of love although they try. The wholeness of conjugal love but it is an ideal. In opposition to love, sex is treated as a hard fact of life of the body, so every one's love or understanding of love of husband/ wife is incomplete. So is Vasu's of Baba and Baba's of Vasu. In course of time they develop estrangement after some years of married life with illusions of love and fulfilment of 'body.' Love, in *Moving On*, is a sort of incomplete experience of oneness or else it is sort of thing that leads to suffering. Shashi Deshpande writes her own experience of marital love as she remembers and recreates in her portrayals of Baba and Mai. On the contrary, it is good that she holds Manjari's love affair with Shyam. Manjari's love affair with Shyam is intense and goes beyond the choice of her parents—an inter-caste marriage—a Brahmin girl is married to a Gujarati. One can contrast Mai and Manjari as two different women who have two different experiences of erotic love with different attitudes towards man and sex. Her married life with Shyam is, of course, also shortened by her husband's untimely death; but she, unlike her mother on who is Baba's passion is forced. She asserts her passion and fulfils her body's craving for Shyam in her marriage. The novelist would have enlarged Manjari's character still more. Baba and Mai remain dominant characters.

The theme of victimization of single woman is repeated from her earlier novels—especially women who are young and old. The triangular affair of love and the 'invisible' other man is always there. So is in this novel, Baba suspects that Mai has relationship with her leader-writer and Manjari reveals of her reality and fantasy of rape and also of Raja's endearments, teasing, and chastising. As a single woman living in a big house, she faces the problem of living among men who are found to be dangerous—Raja, Raman Kumar Joy, Abhishek. Anand, her son, and the one who uses to give threatening phone calls. She may be contrasted with Sachi, her daughter who represents a 'new woman' who seeks compromise with habits of 'bad men'.

The language of the narrative is that of a typical modern Kannada housewife. Manjari addresses her relatives with initials—RK, BK, Jiji, Mai. In some places, the novelist uses a housewife's language, that too language that is spoken by idle housewives during evening 'gossip' time. Her Indian English is full of colloquialisms and strange expressions that are unacceptable to one who is used to Standard English. It is shadowed by her 'translating consciousness'—from L1 to L2.

There is no experimentation of fictional language as one finds in Arundhati Roy's *The God of Small Things*: but no critic has right to dictate a novelist to use a particular kind of language but he can point out obscurities and ambiguities created by unskilled handling of language of the novel. The obscurities and ambiguities certainly affect the style of the narrative as a whole. By reading her acknowledgments one comes to know that Shashi Deshpande's husband 'gave her all medical knowledge'. In her interview she made clear that he reads the novel first and "declines to comment."[1] How is it possible for her to grow into a better novelist when she has doctor-husband as her silent critic? She should better choose an outsider-expert like Amurjee for her careful reading of the text before publishing it.

In *Moving On* Shashi Deshpande ultimately deals with 'unbearable problem of living' of a lone woman in old age—it is final question—a preoccupation since the publication of her first novel *The Dark Holds No Terrors*—the main facts of life—birth, copulation and death are frequently questioned; but answers are not found. Thus her vision of life is—Life is mysterious and has no meaning to one's own existence; but human being whether a man or woman (Baba or Vasu) attempts to make meaningful by the choice of work. Work brings meaning to one's own existence—it is one's assertion of existence. Of her later novels, *Small Remedies* (2000) is the best wherein the theme and structure are knit very well tightly together in harmony, in a commanding prose style. Both individual characters and stories have depth and dimension of past—the past of a nation. The stories of *Small Remedies* are more interestingly relevant because of inter-religious marriages. The stories of *Moving On* are less interesting because those are of inter-caste marriages within a fictitious family. So the harmony within the family and between the families is steadily decreased. All her philosophical, social and psychological themes are finally culminated into one dominant theme of unending continuity of life in this not so remarkable novel.

NOTE

1. In her interview at Taj Krishna Hotel, Bangalore, on the occasion of launching her novel.

Contributors

Bhaskar Roy Barman. South Bank of Girls Bodhjung Dighi, Itakhola Road, Banamalipur Post Box 51, Agartala, West Tripura.

Liza Das. Assistant Professor, Indian Institute of Technology, Guwahati, Assam.

Mallikarjun Patil. Department of English, Gulbarga University, Gulbarga, Karnataka.

Raja Sekhar Patteti. Associate Professor, Deptt. of English, Nagarjuna University, Nagarjuna Nagar, Andhra Pradesh.

Pedro Carmona Rodríguez. University of La Laguna, Department of English and German Languages, Facultad de Filologia, E 38071. Campus de Guajara, Spain, S/C de Tenerife, Canary Islands, SPAIN.

Jaydeep Rishi. Lecturer, Department of English, S.R.L. Mahavidyalaya, Nadia, West Bengal.

R.S. Jain. Reader and Head, P.G. Department of English, C.T. Bora College, Pune, Maharashtra.

Nandini Sahu. Reader in English (Editorial Unit), School of Humanities, Indira Gandhi National Open University, New Delhi.

Manisha Sharma. 827, Elizabeth Avenue, Salem, VA 24153, USA.

Shubha Tiwari. Senior Lecturer, Department of English, A.P.S. University, Rewa, Madhya Pradesh.

R.K. Mishra. Reader in English, D.A.V. College, Titilagarh, Orissa.

Urvashi, Sinha. 3/72, Premnagar, Dayalbagh, Agra, Uttar Pradesh.

Gur Pyari Jandial. 3/72, Premnagar, Dayalbagh, Agra, Uttar Pradesh.

Santwana Haldar. F.M. Auto College, Balasore, Orissa.

Asha Sharma. H. No. 13, Urban Estate, Sector-6, Bahadurgarh.

V.R. Badiger. Department of English, Gulbarga University, Gulbarga, Karnataka.